James Wilson Hyde

The Royal Mail

Its Curiosities and Romance

James Wilson Hyde

The Royal Mail
Its Curiosities and Romance

ISBN/EAN: 9783744769884

Printed in Europe, USA, Canada, Australia, Japan

Cover: Foto ©ninafisch / pixelio.de

More available books at **www.hansebooks.com**

THE ROYAL MAIL

ITS CURIOSITIES AND ROMANCE

BY

JAMES WILSON HYDE
SUPERINTENDENT IN THE GENERAL POST-OFFICE,
EDINBURGH

SECOND EDITION

WILLIAM BLACKWOOD AND SONS
EDINBURGH AND LONDON
MDCCCLXXXV

All Rights reserved

NOTE.—It is of melancholy interest that Mr Fawcett's death occurred within a month from the date on which he accepted the following Dedication, and before the issue of the Work.

TO

THE RIGHT HONOURABLE

HENRY FAWCETT, M.P.

HER MAJESTY'S POSTMASTER-GENERAL,

THE FOLLOWING PAGES ARE, BY PERMISSION,

RESPECTFULLY DEDICATED.

PREFACE TO SECOND EDITION.

THE favour with which 'The Royal Mail' has been received by the public, as evinced by the rapid sale of the first issue, has induced the Author to arrange for the publication of a second edition. This edition has been revised and slightly enlarged; the new matter consisting of two additional illustrations, contributions to the chapters on "Mail Packets," "How Letters are Lost," and "Singular Coincidences," and a fresh chapter on the subject of Postmasters.

The Author ventures to hope that the generous appreciation which has been accorded to the first edition may be extended to the work in its revised form.

EDINBURGH, *June* 1885.

INTRODUCTION.

OF all institutions of modern times, there is, perhaps, none so pre-eminently a people's institution as is the Post-office. Not only does it carry letters and newspapers everywhere, both within and without the kingdom, but it is the transmitter of messages by telegraph, a vast banker for the savings of the working classes, an insurer of lives, a carrier of parcels, and a distributor of various kinds of Government licences. Its services are claimed exclusively or mainly by no one class; the rich, the poor, the educated, and the illiterate, and, indeed, the young as well as the old,—all have dealings with the Post-office. Yet it may seem strange that an institution which is familiar by its operations to all classes alike, should be so little known by its internal management and organisation. A few persons, no doubt, have been privileged to see the interior working of some important Post-office, but it is the bare truth to say that *the people* know nothing of what goes on within the doors of that ubiquitous establishment. When it is remembered that the metropolitan offices of London, Edinburgh, and Dublin have to maintain touch with every petty office and every one of their servants scattered throughout England, Scotland, and Ireland; that discipline has to be exercised everywhere; that a system of accounting must necessarily be maintained, reaching to the remotest corners; and that the whole threads have to be gathered up and made answerable to the great head, which is London,—some vague idea may be formed of what must come within the view of whoever pretends to a knowledge of Post-office work. But intimately connected with that which was the original work of the Post-office, and is still the main work—the conveyance of letters—there is the subject of circulation, the simple yet complex scheme under which letters flow from each individual centre to every other part of the country. Circulation as a system is the outcome of planning, devising, and scheming by many heads during a long series of years—its object, of course, being to bring letters to their destinations in the shortest possible time. So intricate and delicate is the fabric, that by interference an unskilled hand could not fail to produce an effect upon the structure analogous to that which would certainly follow any rude treatment applied to a house built of cards.

These various subjects, especially when they have become settled into the routine state, might be considered as affording a poor soil for the growth of anything of interest—that is, of curious interest—apart from that which duty calls upon a man to find in his proper work. Yet the Post-office is not without its veins of humour, though the metal to be extracted may perhaps be scanty as compared with the vast extent of the mine from which it has to be taken.

The compiler of the following pages has held an appointment in the Post-office for a period of twenty-five years—the best, perhaps, of his life; and during that term it has been his practice to note and collect facts connected with the Department whenever they appeared of a curious, interesting, or amusing character. While making use of such notes in connection with this work, he has had recourse to the Post-office Annual Reports, to old official documents, to books on various subjects, and to newspapers, all of which have been laid under contribution to furnish material for these pages.

The work is in no sense a historical work: it deals with the lighter features of a plain, matter-of-fact department; and though some of the incidents mentioned may be deemed of trivial account, they will be found, it is thought, to have at least a curious or amusing side.

The author desires to mention that he has received valuable help from several of his brother officers, who have supplied him with facts or anecdotes; and to these, as well as to gentlemen who have lent him books or given him access to files of old newspapers, he expresses his grateful acknowledgments. He also tenders his sincere and respectful thanks to the Postmaster-General for permission granted to make extracts from official papers.

The Post-office renders an unpretending yet most important service to commerce and to society; and it will be a source of deep gratification to the author if what he has written should inspire in the reader a new and unexpected interest in "the hundred-handed giant who keeps up the intercourse between the different parts of the country, and wafts a sigh from Indus to the Pole."

NOTE.—The Author will be glad to be furnished with any curious facts or anecdotes relating to the Post-office, either from his brother officers or the public, for use in the event of further editions being called for.

CONTENTS.

CHAP.		PAGE
I.	OLD ROADS,	1
II.	POSTBOYS,	14
III.	STAGE AND MAIL COACHES,	29
IV.	FOOT-POSTS,	76
V.	MAIL-PACKETS,	85
VI.	SHIPWRECKED MAILS,	100
VII.	AMOUNT OF WORK,	103
VIII.	GROWTH OF CERTAIN POST-OFFICES,	118
IX.	CLAIMS FOR POST-OFFICE SERVICE,	128
X.	THE TRAVELLING POST-OFFICE,	145
XI.	SORTERS AND CIRCULATION,	155
XII.	PIGEON-POST,	168
XIII.	ABUSE OF THE FRANKING PRIVILEGE, AND OTHER PETTY FRAUDS,	175

CONTENTS.

XIV. STRANGE ADDRESSES,	190
XV. POST-OFFICE ROBBERIES,	210
XVI. TELEGRAPHIC BLUNDERS,	249
XVII. HOW LETTERS ARE LOST,	255
XVIII. ODD COMPLAINTS,	304
XIX. CURIOUS LETTERS ADDRESSED TO THE POST-OFFICE,	313
XX. SINGULAR COINCIDENCES,	336
XXI. SAVINGS-BANK CURIOSITIES,	345
XXII. REPLIES TO MEDICAL INQUIRIES,	353
XXIII. VARIOUS,	355
XXIV. ABOUT POSTMASTERS,	376
XXV. RED TAPE,	387

ILLUSTRATIONS.

MAIL-COACH ACCIDENT AT ELVANFOOT, . .	*Frontispiece*
HOLYHEAD AND CHESTER MAILS SNOWED UP NEAR DUNSTABLE — 26TH DEC. 1836. (*From an old Print,*)	*To face p.* 52
THE DEVONPORT MAIL-COACH FORCING ITS WAY THROUGH A SNOWDRIFT NEAR AMESBURY — 27TH DEC. 1836. (*From an old Print,*)	,, ,, . 54
POST-BOY JACK, ...	*Page* 96
TRAVELLING POST-OFFICE, ...	,, 146
DELIVERING ARM, SHOWING HOW THE POUCH IS SUSPENDED, ...	,, 152
STRANGE ADDRESSES, ...	,, 197-209
LETTER-BOX TAKEN POSSESSION OF BY TOMTITS,	,, 265
THE MULREADY ENVELOPE, . . .	,, 366

THE ROYAL MAIL.

CHAPTER I.

OLD ROADS.

THE present generation, who are accustomed to see the streets of our cities paved with wood or stone, or otherwise so laid out as to provide a hard and even surface suited to the locomotion of wheeled vehicles, or who by business or pleasure have been led to journey over the principal highways intersecting the kingdom in every direction, can form no idea of the state of the roads in this country during the earlier years of the Post-office —or even in times comparatively recent—unless their reading has led them to the perusal of accounts written by travellers of the periods we now refer to. The highways of the present day, radiating from London and the other large centres of industry, and extending their arms to every corner of the land, are wellnigh perfect in their kind, and present a picture of careful and efficient maintenance. Whether we look, for example, at the great north road leading from London, the Carlisle to Glasgow road, or the Highland road passing through Dunkeld, we find the roads have certain features in common: a broad hard roadway for vehicles; a neatly kept footpath where required; limits strictly defined by trim hedges, stone walls, or palings; and means provided for carrying off surface-water. The picture will, of course, vary as the traveller proceeds, flat country alternating with undulating country, and wood or moorland with cultivated fields; but the chief characteristics remain the same, constituting the roads as worthy of the age we live in.

How the people managed to get from place to place before the Post-office had a history, or indeed for long after the birth of that institution, it is hard to conceive. Then, the roads were little better than tracks worn out of the surface of the virgin land,— proceeding in some cases in a manner approaching to a right line, over hills, down valleys, through forests and the like; in others following the natural features of the country, but giving evidence that they had never been systematically made, being rather the outcome of a mere habit of travel, just as sheep-tracks are produced on a mountain-side. Such roads in winter weather, or in rainy seasons, became terrible to the traveller: yet the only repairs that were vouchsafed consisted in filling up some of the larger holes with rude stones; and when this method of keeping up repairs no longer availed, another track was formed by bringing under foot a fresh strip of the adjoining land (generally unenclosed), and thus creating a wholly new road in place of the old one. Smiles in his 'Lives of the Engineers' thus describes certain of the English roads: "In some of the older settled districts of England, the old roads are still to be traced in the hollow ways or lanes, which are met with, in some places, eight and ten feet deep. Horse-tracks in summer and rivulets in winter, the earth became gradually worn into these deep furrows, many of which, in Wilts, Somerset, and Devon, represent the tracks of roads as old as, if not older than, the Conquest." And again: "Similar roads existed until recently in the immediate neighbourhood of Birmingham, long the centre of considerable traffic. The sandy soil was sawn through, as it were, by generation after generation of human feet, and by pack-horses, helped by the rains, until in some places the tracks were as much as from twelve to fourteen yards deep." In the year 1690, Chancellor Cowper, who was then a barrister on circuit, thus wrote to his wife: "The Sussex ways are bad and ruinous beyond imagination. I vow 'tis melancholy consideration that mankind will inhabit such a heap of dirt for a poor livelihood. The country is a sink of about fourteen miles broad, which receives all the water that falls from two long ranges of hills on both sides of it, and not being furnished with convenient draining, is kept moist and soft by the water till the middle of a dry summer, which is only able to make it tolerable to ride for a short time."

In Scotland, about the same time, the roads were no better. The first four miles out of Edinburgh, on the road towards London, were described in the Privy Council Record of 1680 to have been in so wretched a state that passengers were in danger of their lives, "either by their coaches overturning, their horse falling, their carts breaking, their loads casting and horse stumbling, the poor people with the burdens on their backs sorely grieved and discouraged; moreover, strangers do often exclaim thereat." Nor does there appear to have been any considerable improvement in the state of the roads in the northern kingdom for long afterwards, as we find that in 1750, according to Lang's 'Historical Summary of the Post-office in Scotland,' "the channel of the river Gala, which ran for some distance parallel with the road, was, when not flooded, the track chosen as the most level and the easiest to travel in." The common carrier from Edinburgh to Selkirk, a distance of thirty-eight miles, required a fortnight for the journey, going and returning; and the stage-coach from Edinburgh to Glasgow took a day and a half for the journey. A Yorkshire squire, Thomas Kirke, who travelled in Scotland in 1679, gave a better account of the roads; but his opinion may have been merely relative, for travelling showmen to this day prefer the roads in the south of Scotland to those in the north of England, on account of their greater hardness; and this derives, no doubt, from the more adamantine material used in the repair of the Scotch roads. This traveller wrote: "The highways in Scotland are tolerably good, which is the greatest comfort a traveller meets with amongst them. The Scotch gentry generally travel from one friend's house to another; so seldom require a change-house (inn). Their way is to hire a horse and a man for twopence a mile; they ride on the horse thirty or forty miles a-day, and the man who is his guide foots it beside him, and carries his luggage to boot." Another visitor to Scotland in 1702, named Morer, thus describes the roads: " The truth is, the roads will hardly allow these conveniences " (meaning stage-coaches, which did not as yet exist in Scotland), " which is the reason that the gentry, men and women, choose rather to use their horses. However, their great men often travel with coach-and-six, but with so little caution, that, besides their other attendance, they have a lusty running-footman on each side of the coach, to manage and keep it up in rough places."[1] It might be supposed that the roads leading from Windsor, where one of the royal residences was, would have been kept in a tolerable state, so as to secure the sovereign some comfort in travelling. But their condition seems to have been no better than that of roads elsewhere. An account of a journey made in 1703 by Prince George of Denmark, the husband of Queen Anne, from Windsor to Petworth, runs as follows:—

"The length of way was only forty miles, but fourteen hours were consumed in traversing it; while almost every mile was signalised by the overturn of a carriage, or its temporary swamping in the mire. Even the royal chariot would have fared

[1] In the north of Scotland a similar account was given of the roads there about the year 1730. The writer of 'Letters from a Gentleman in the North of Scotland' stated that "the Highlands are but little known even to the inhabitants of the low country of Scotland, for they have ever dreaded the difficulties and dangers of travelling among the mountains; and when some extraordinary occasion has obliged any one of them to such a progress, he has, generally speaking, made his testament before he set out, as though he were entering upon a long and dangerous sea-voyage, wherein it was very doubtful if he should ever return."

no better than the rest had it not been for the relays of peasants who poised and kept it erect by strength of arm, and shouldered it forward the last nine miles, in which tedious operation six good hours were consumed."

Yet later still, and in close proximity to London, a royal party had a most unsatisfactory journey, owing to the miserable state of the roads. It happened that in 1727 George II. and Queen Caroline were proceeding from the palace at Kew to that at St James's, when they had to spend a whole night upon the way; and between Hammersmith and Fulham they were overturned, the royal occupants of the coach being landed in a quagmire. A year or two after this, Lord Hervey wrote that "the road between this place [Kensington] and London is grown so infamously bad, that we live here in the same solitude as we would do if cast on a rock in the middle of the ocean; and all the Londoners tell us that there is between them and us an impassable gulf of mud."

No part of the country could boast of a satisfactory condition of the roads, these being everywhere in the same neglected and wretched state, and travellers who had the misfortune to use them have recorded their ideas on the subject in no gentle terms. Arthur Young, who travelled much in the middle of last century, thus alludes to a road in Essex: "Of all the cursed roads that ever disgraced this kingdom in the very ages of barbarism, none ever equalled that from Billericay to the King's Head at Tilbury. It is for near twelve miles so narrow that a mouse cannot pass by any carriage. I saw a fellow creep under his waggon to assist me to lift, if possible, my chaise over a hedge. To add to all the infamous circumstances which concur to plague a traveller, I must not forget the eternally meeting with chalk-waggons, themselves frequently stuck fast, till a collection of them are in the same situation, and twenty or thirty horses may be tacked to each to draw them out one by one." In a somewhat similar way he describes the road from Bury to Sudbury in Suffolk. Here, he says, "I was forced to move as slow in it as in any unmended lane in Wales. For ponds of liquid dirt, and a scattering of loose flints just sufficient to lame every horse that moves near them, with the addition of cutting vile grips across the road under the pretence of letting the water off, but without effect, altogether render at least twelve out of these sixteen miles as infamous a turnpike as ever was beheld." In one of his journeys, Young proceeded to the north by the great north road, thence making branch trips to the various agricultural districts. Of many of these roads he gives a sorry account. Thus: "To Wakefield, indifferent; through the town of Wakefield so bad that it ought to be indicted. To Castle Howard, infamous; I was near being swallowed up in a slough. From Newton to Stokesley in Cleveland, execrably bad. You are obliged to cross the moors they call Black Hambledon, over which the road runs in narrow hollows that admit a south-country chaise with such difficulty, that I reckon this part of the journey made at the hazard of my neck. The going down into Cleveland is beyond all description terrible; for you go through such steep, rough, narrow, rocky precipices, that I would sincerely advise any friend to go a hundred miles to escape it. The name of this path is very judicious, *Scarthneck* —that is, *Scare-Nick*, or frighten the devil.

"From Richmond to Darlington, part of the great north road; execrably broke into holes like an old pavement, sufficient to dislocate one's bones."

"To Morpeth; a pavement a mile or two out of Newcastle; all the rest *vile*.

"To Carlisle; cut up by innumerable little paltry one-horse carts."

One more instance from the pen of Young and we leave him. In the course of one of his journeys, he makes his way into Wales, where he finds his *bête noire* in the roads, and freely expresses himself thereupon in his usual forcible style: "But, my dear sir, what am I to say of the roads in this country? the turnpikes, as they have the assurance to call them, and the hardiness to make one pay for? From Chepstow to the half-way house between Newport and Cardiff they continue mere rocky lanes, full of hugeous stones as big as one's horse, and abominable holes. The first six miles from Newport they were so detestable, and without either direction-posts or milestones, that I could not well persuade myself I was on the turnpike, but had mistook the road, and therefore asked every one I met, who answered me to my astonishment, 'Ya-as.' Whatever business carries you into this country, avoid it, at least till they have good roads; if they were good, travelling would be very pleasant."

The necessity for a better class of road cannot but have forced itself upon the Government of the country from time to time, if not for the benefit of travellers and to encourage trade, at any rate to secure a rapid movement of troops in times of disturbance or rebellion; yet we find the state of streets in the metropolis, and roads in the country, as in 1750, thus described in Blackie's 'Comprehensive History of England': "When the only public approaches to Parliament were King Street and Union Street, these were so wretchedly paved, that when the King went in state to the House, the ruts had to be filled up with bundles of fagots to allow the royal coach a safe transit. While the art of street-paving was thus so imperfect, that of road-making was equally defective, so that the country visitor to the metropolis, and its dangers of coach-driving, had generally a sufficient preparative for the worst during his journey to town. This may easily be understood from the fact that, so late as 1754, few turnpikes were to be seen, after leaving the vicinity of London, for 200 miles together, although it had been made felony to pull them down. These roads, indeed, were merely the produce of compulsory pauper labour, contributed by the different parishes; and, like all such work, it was performed in a very perfunctory manner."

The same authority gives a further picture of the state of the highways some twenty years later, when apparently little improvement had taken place in their condition: "Notwithstanding the numerous Acts of Parliament, of which no less than 452 were emitted between the years 1760 and 1764, for the improvement of the principal highways, they still continued narrow, darkened with trees, and intersected with ruts and miry swamps, through which the progress of a waggon was a work of difficulty and danger. One of these—the turnpike road from

Preston to Wigan—is thus described by an angry tourist in 1770, and the picture seems to have been too generally realised over the whole kingdom: "To look over a map, and perceive that it is a principal one, not only to some towns, but even whole counties, one would naturally conclude it to be at least decent; but let me most seriously caution all travellers who may accidentally purpose to travel this terrible country, to avoid it as they would the devil; for a thousand to one but they break their necks or their limbs by overthrows or breakings down. They will here meet with ruts, which I actually measured, four feet deep, and floating with mud only from a wet summer; what, therefore, must they be after a winter? The only mending it receives is the tumbling in some loose stones, which serve no other purpose but jolting a carriage in the most intolerable manner. These are not merely opinions, but facts; for I actually passed three carts broken down in these eighteen miles, of execrable memory."

Obvious as it must be to every mind capable of apprehending ordinary matters in the present day, that the opening up of the country by the laying down of good roads would encourage trade, promote social intercourse, knit together the whole kingdom, and render its government the more easy and effective; yet it is a fact that the improvement of the roads in various parts of the country, both in England and Scotland, was stoutly opposed by the people, even in certain places entailing riot and bloodshed. So strong were the prejudices against the improved roads, that the country people would not use them after being made. This bias may perhaps have partaken largely of that unreasoning conservatism which is always prone to pronounce that that which *is* is best, and opposes change on principle—an example of which is afforded by the conduct of the driver of the Marlborough coach, who, when the new Bath road was opened, obstinately refused to travel by it, and stuck to the old waggon-track. "He was an old man," he said; "his grandfather and father had driven the aforesaid way before him, and he would continue in the old track till death." Other grounds of objection were not wanting, having some show of reason; but these, like the others, were useless in stemming the tide of improvement which eventually set in, and brought the roads of the nation into their present admirable state.

CHAPTER II.

POSTBOYS.

" Hark ! 'tis the twanging horn ! . . .
He comes, the herald of a noisy world,
With spatter'd boots, strapp'd waist, and frozen locks,
News from all nations lumbering at his back,
True to his charge the close-pack'd load behind ;
Yet careless what he brings, his one concern
Is to conduct it to the destined inn,
And, having dropp'd the expected bag, pass on.
He whistles as he goes, light-hearted wretch,
Cold and yet cheerful : messenger of grief
Perhaps to thousands, and of joy to some,
To him indifferent whether grief or joy."
—COWPER.

AS described in the preceding chapter, these were the roads over which postboys had to travel with their precious charges during a long series of years, and to their wild and disreputable state must to a great extent be attributed the slow rate at which the post was then wont to travel. When it is considered that these men or boys were exposed to all accidents of weather, stoppages by swollen rivers, delays through the roads being cut up, to their straying from the beaten track during fogs, and to all other chances of the road, including attacks by footpads or highwaymen, their occupation cannot have been a light or agreeable one. It is by no means easy to construct a detailed outline of the duties which postboys had to perform, or to describe under what rules they proceeded from stage to stage; but we have ample evidence of the rate at which they covered the ground, and how their speed varied at different periods, owing, it must have been in some cases, to the lack of supervision.

The following evidence of the speed of a post messenger in the latter half of the sixteenth century is furnished by a letter in the correspondence of Archbishop Parker, the times at which the letter reached the various stages on its journey being endorsed upon it. The letter is as follows, viz. :—

"ARCHBISHOP PARKER to SIR W. CECIL.

"SIR,—According to the Queen's Majesty's pleasure, and your advertisement, you shall receive a form of prayer, which, after you have perused and judged of it, shall be put in print and published immediately," &c. &c.

"From my house at Croydon this 22d July 1566, at 4 of the clock afternoon.—Your honour's alway,
"MATTH. CANT.
"To the Rt. Honble. Sir W. CECIL."

Endorsed by successive postmasters :—
"Received at Waltham Cross, the 23d of July, about 9 at night."
"Received at Ware, the 23d July, at 12 o'clock at night."
"Received at Croxton, the 24th of July, between 7 and 8 of the clock in the morning."
"So that his Grace's letter, leaving Croydon at 4 in the afternoon of July 22d, reached Waltham Cross, a distance of nearly 26 miles, by 9 at night of the 23d, whence, in 3 hours, it seems to have advanced 8 miles to Ware; and within 8 hours more to have reached Croxton, a further distance of 29 miles, having taken nearly 40 hours to travel about 63 miles."

In 1635 a public post between London and Edinburgh was established, the journey being limited to three days. This mail set out as a rule but twice a-week, and sometimes only once a-week. An express messenger conveying news of the death of Charles II., who died on the 6th February 1685, was received in Edinburgh at one o'clock on the morning of the 10th February; and it may also be mentioned here—though the matter hardly reflects upon the speed of postboys, who travel by land and not by water—that in 1688 it required three months to convey the tidings of the abdication of James II. of England and VII. of Scotland to the Orkney Islands.

Down to this period the mails from London to Scotland were carried on horseback with something like tolerable speed, taking previous performances into account, for in 1689 it is noted that parliamentary proceedings of Saturday were in the hands of the Edinburgh public on the ensuing Thursday. This rate of travelling does not appear to have been kept up, for in 1715 the post from London to Edinburgh took six days to perform the journey. When it is considered that nearly a century before, the same distance could be covered in three days, this relapse seems to bespeak a sad want of vitality in the Post-office management of the age. The cause of the slow travelling, which appears to have continued for over forty years, comes out in a memorial of traders to the Convention of Burghs in 1758, wherein dissatisfaction was expressed with the existing arrangements of the post,—the mail for London on reaching Newcastle being there delayed about a day, again detained some time at York, and probably further delayed in the south; so that the double journey to and from London occupied eleven days instead of seven or eight, as the memorial deemed sufficient. To the Post-office mind of the present age, this dilatory method of performing the service of forwarding mails is incomprehensible, and the circumstance reflects discreditably both on the Post-office officials who were cognisant of it, and on the public who submitted to it. It is fair to mention, however, that at this period the mail *from* London *to* Edinburgh covered the ground in eighty-seven hours, or in fully three and a half days; and that as a result of the memorial, the time was reduced to eighty-two hours, and the journey from Edinburgh to London reduced to eighty-five hours. In 1763, the London to Edinburgh mail commenced to be despatched five times a-week, instead of only three times; and at this time, during the winter season, the mail leaving London on Tuesday night was generally not in the hands of the people of Edinburgh until the afternoon of Sunday. We are informed, in Lang's 'Historical Summary of the Post-office in Scotland,' that in 1715 there was not a single horse-post in that country. There must, however, have been some earlier attempts to establish horse-posts in the northern kingdom, for Chambers in his 'Domestic Annals of Scotland,' under the year 1660, refers to the fact of a warrant being granted against interlopers who were carrying letters by foot on the same line on which Mr Mean had set up a horse-post. A traveller in 1688 relates, also, that besides the horse-post from Edinburgh to Berwick, there was a similar post from Edinburgh to Portpatrick in connection with the Irish packet service. Again, Chambers tells us that in 1667 the good people of Aberdeen having had "long experience of the prejudice sustained, not only by the said burgh of Aberdeen, but by the nobility, gentry, and others in the north country, by the miscarrying of missive letters, and by the not timeous delivery and receiving returns of the samen," bestirred themselves to establish a better state of things. It was considered proper that "every man might have their letters delivered and answers returned at certain diets and times;" and it was accordingly arranged, under Post-office sanction, that Lieutenant John Wales should provide a regular horse-service to carry letters to Edinburgh every Wednesday and Friday, returning every Tuesday and Thursday in the afternoon.

In 1715 the first horse-post between Edinburgh and Stirling was established, and in March 1717 a similar post between Edinburgh and Glasgow was set up. This latter post went three times a-week, travelled during the night, and performed the distance between the two places in ten hours—being at the rate of about four miles an hour. Were we to give further instances of the slowness of the horse-posts, we should probably prove tedious, and therefore the proofs adduced on this point must suffice. Though the state of the roads may be held to account for some of the delay, the roads must not be charged with everything. In 1799 a surveyor in the north of Scotland wrote as follows: "It is impossible to obtain any other contractors to ride the mails at 3d. out, or 1½d. per mile each way. On this account we have been so much distressed with mail-riders, that we have sometimes to submit to the mails being conveyed by mules and such species of horses as were a disgrace to any public service." The same surveyor reported in 1805, that it would give rise to great inconvenience if no boys under sixteen years were allowed to be employed in riding the posts—many of them ranging down from that age to fourteen. So, what from the condition of the highways, the sorry quality of the horses, and the youthfulness of the riders, it is not surprising that the writers of letters should inscribe on their missives: "Be this letter delivered with haste—haste—haste! Post haste! Ride, villain, ride,—for thy life—for thy life—for thy life!" unnecessary though that injunction be in the present day.

The postboys were a source of great trouble and vexation to the authorities of the Post-office through the whole course of their connection with the department. A surveyor who held office about the commencement of the eighteenth century, found, on the occasion of a visit to Salisbury, something wrong there, which he reported to headquarters in these terms :—

"At this place [Salisbury] found the postboys to have carried on vile practices in taking bye-letters, delivering them in that city, and taking back the answers — and especially the Andover riders. On a certain day he found on Richard Kent, one of the Andover riders, five bye-letters—all for Salisbury. Upon examination of the fellow, he confessed that he had made it a practice, and persisted to continue in it, saying that he had no wages from his master. The surveyor took the fellow before the magistrate, proved the facts, and as the fellow could not get bail, was committed; but pleading to have no friends nor money, desired a punishment to be whipped, and accordingly he was to the purpose. The surveyor wrote the case to Andover, and ordered that the fellow should be discharged; but no regard was had thereto. But the next day the same rider came post, run about the cittye for letters, and was insolent. The second time the said Richard Kent came post with two gentlemen, made it his business to take up letters; the fellow, instead of returning to Andover, gets two idle fellows and rides away with three horses, which was a return for his masters not obeying instructions, as he ought not have been suffered to ride after the said facts was proved against him."

The same surveyor complained bitterly, with respect to the postboys, "that the gentry doe give much money to the riders, whereby they be very subject to get in liquor, which stops the males." Indeed the temptation of the ale-house was no doubt another factor in the slow journeying of the postboys, as it was the source of much trouble in the days of mail-coaches.

Mr Palmer, through whose initiative and perseverance mail-coaches were subsequently established throughout the country, thus described the post as it existed in 1783:—

"The post, at present, instead of being the swiftest, is almost the slowest, conveyance in the country; and though, from the great improvement in our roads, other carriers have proportionably mended their speed, the post is as slow as ever. It is likewise very unsafe, as the frequent robberies of it testify; and to avoid a loss of this nature, people generally cut bank bills, or bills at sight, in two, and send the bills by different posts. The mails are generally intrusted to some idle boy, without character, mounted on a worn-out hack, and who, so far from being able to defend himself or escape from a robber, is much more likely to be in league with him."

Including stoppages, this mode of travelling was, up to 1783, at the rate of about three to four miles an hour.

We are again indebted to Mr Chambers for the following statement of careless blunders made by postboys in connection with the Edinburgh mails: "As indicating the simplicity of the institution in those days, may be noticed a mistake of February 1720, when, instead of the mail which should have come in yesterday (Sunday), *we had our own mail of Thursday last returned*—the presumption being, that the mail for Edinburgh had been in like manner sent back from some unknown point in the road to London. And this mistake happened once more in December 1728, the bag despatched on a Saturday night being returned *the second Sunday morning after;* 'tis reckoned this mistake happened about half-way on the road." We hardly agree, however, that these mistakes were owing to the simplicity of the institution, but rather to the routine nature of the work ; for it is the fact that blunders equally flagrant have occurred in the Post-office in recent times, even under elaborate checks, which, if rightly applied, would have rendered the mistakes impossible.

Many of the troubles which the Post-office had with its postboys may possibly be ascribed to the low rate of wages paid by the contractors for their services. This matter is referred to by the Solicitor to the Scotch Post-office, who was engaged upon an inquiry into the robbery of the mail on the stage between Dingwall and Tain in the year 1805. The distance between these places is about twenty-five miles, and five hours were occupied in making the journey. One of the postboys concerned stated in his declaration that his whole wages were 5s. a-week; and with reference to this, the solicitor in his report observes as follows: "Of course it may fairly be presumed that no respectable man will be got to perform this duty. Dismission to such a man for committing a fault is no punishment; and the safety of the conveyance of the mail, which the public have a right to require, seems to render some regulation in this respect necessary."

The following account of the violation of the mails by a postboy may perhaps be aptly introduced here :—

In the autumn of 1808, a good deal of anxiety was caused to the authorities of the Post-office in

Scotland, in consequence of reports being made to them that many bankers' letters had been tampered with in course of their transmission by post through certain of the northern counties. To discover who was concerned in the irregularities was rendered the more difficult, owing to the fact that the mail-bags in which the letters had been despatched were reported to have reached their destinations duly sealed. But a thing of this kind could not go on without discovery, and investigation being made, the storm burst over the head of a poor little postboy named William Shearer, a lad of fifteen years of age, who was employed riding the north mail over the stage from Turriff to Banff. From the account we have of the matter, it would seem that in this case, as in many others, it was opportunity that made the thief; for the mail-bags had on some occasions been insecurely sealed, the despatching postmasters having failed to place the wax over the knots of the string—and the postboy was thus able to get to the inside of the bags without cutting the string or breaking the seals, by simply undoing the knots. Here the temptation presented itself; and although some twenty-six letters were found inside his hat when he was searched, it is not unlikely that he commenced by merely peeping into the letters by pulling out their ends, for several bank letters containing notes for considerable sums had been so violated, while the contents were found safe. To cover one delinquency the boy had recourse to others. In order to account for his delay on the road, he opened the bag containing his waybill, borrowed a knife from a shoemaker who kept one of the toll-houses, and altered his hour of despatch from his starting-point. The unfortunate youth also gave way to drink, stopping at the tollhouses, and calling sometimes for rum, sometimes for whisky, the keepers sharing in the refreshments, which were purchased with stolen money. On one occasion the boy opened a parcel intrusted to him, and from a letter inside abstracted a twenty-shilling note. Whether to render himself all the more redoubtable on the road, over a section of which he travelled in the dark, or for some other purpose, is not clear, but with six shillings of the aforesaid sum he bought a sword, and with two shillings a pistol, the balance going in drink. The occupation of riding the mail was not for one so young: yet it was found that full-grown men often gave more trouble than boys; and it may be here remarked that the adventure of Davie Mailsetter in the 'Antiquary' is no great exaggeration of the service of postboys at the period to which it refers. The poor boy Shearer was put upon his trial before the Circuit Court of Justiciary at Aberdeen; and when called upon to plead, confessed his guilt. There was every disposition on the part of the public prosecutor, and of the presiding judge, to let the case go as lightly as possible against the prisoner—doubtless on account of his youth; but the law had to be vindicated, and the sentence passed was that of transportation for a period of seven years. Since then humanity has made progress, and no such punishment would be inflicted in such a case nowadays.

Exposed to all the inclemency of the seasons, both by night and day; having to weather snowstorms and suffer the drenchings of heavy rain; to grope a way through the dense fogs of our climate, and endure the biting frosts of midwinter; or yet to face the masked highwayman on the open heath, or the footpad in the deep and narrow road,—these were the unpleasantnesses and the dangers which beset the couriers of the Post-office in past years, ere the department had grown to its present robust manhood. As to the exposure in wintry weather, it is stated that postboys on reaching the end of their stages were sometimes so benumbed with the cold that they had to be lifted out of their saddles. Of the attacks made upon them by highwaymen some instances are given in another chapter. This we will conclude by recording the fate that befell a postboy who was charged with the conveyance of the mail for London which left Edinburgh on Saturday, the 20th November 1725. This mail, after reaching Berwick in safety and proceeding thence, was never again heard of. A notice issued by the Post-office at the time ran as follows: "A most diligent search has been made; but neither the boy, the horse, nor the packet has yet been heard of. The boy, after passing Goswick, having a part of the sands to ride which divide the Holy Island from the mainland, it is supposed he has missed his way, and rode towards the sea, where he and his horse have both perished." The explanation here suggested is not at all improbable, in view of the fact that November is a month given to fogs, when a rider might readily go astray crossing treacherous sands.

CHAPTER III.

STAGE AND MAIL COACHES.

PRIOR to the middle of the seventeenth century, about which period stage-coaches came into use in England, the only vehicles available to ordinary travellers would seem to have been the carrier's stage-waggon, which, owing to its lumbering build and the deplorable state of the roads, made only from ten to fifteen miles in a long summer's day. The interior of such waggons exhibited none of the refinements of modern means of travel, the only furnishing of the machine being a quantity of straw littered on the floor, on which the passengers could sit or lie during the weary hours of their journey. Though the stage-coaches came into vogue about the middle of the seventeenth century, as already stated, the heavy waggons seem also to have held a place till much later—for in one of these Roderick Random performed part of his journey to London in 1739; and it was doubtless only the meaner class of people who travelled in that way, as the description given by Smollett of his companions does not mirror, certainly, people of fashion. M. Sobrière, a Frenchman, on his way from Dover to London in the reign of Charles II., thus writes of his experience of the waggon: " That I might not take post, or be obliged to use the stage-coach, I went from Dover to London in a waggon. It was drawn by six horses, one before another, and driven by a waggoner, who walked by the side of it. He was clothed in black, and appointed in all things like another St George. He had a brave Montero on his head, and was a merry fellow, fancied he made a figure, and seemed mightily pleased with himself." Unlike travelling in the present day, when one may go 100 miles in a railway carriage without speaking to a fellow-passenger, the journey in the old-fashioned waggon brought all the travellers too close and too long together to admit of individual isolation, for the passengers might be associated for days together as companions, had to take their refreshment together, lived as it were in common, and it was even the custom to elect a chairman at the outset to preside over the company during the journey. But the stage-coach gradually became the established public conveyance of the country, improving in its construction and its rate of progression as the improved state of the roads admitted of and encouraged such improvement. Still, compared with the stage-coaches of the best period, travelling by the earlier stage-coaches was a sorry achievement. Here is an advertisement of stage-coaches of the year 1658 :—

"From the 26th April there will continue to go stage-coaches from the George Inn, without Aldersgate, London, unto the several cities and towns, for the rates and at the times hereafter mentioned and declared :—

"Every Monday, Wednesday, and Friday — To Salisbury, in two days, for xx. s.; to Blandford and Dorchester, in two days and half, for xxx. s.; to Burput, in three days, for xxx. s.; to Exmister, Hunnington, and Exeter, in four days, for xl. s.; to Stamford, in two days, for xx. s.; . . . to York, in four days, for xl. s."

Indeed the charges might have been reckoned by time, the travelling being at the rate of about 10s. a-day. Another advertisement in 1739 thus sets forth the merits of some of the stage-coaches of the period :

"Exeter Flying Stage-coach in three days, and Dorchester and Blandford in two days. Go from the Saracen's Head Inn, in Friday Street, London, every Monday, Wednesday, and Friday; and from the New Inn, in Exeter, every Tuesday and Thursday." Then the advertisement makes known the fact, with regard to another coach, that the stage begins "Flying on Monday next." They were not satisfied in those days with a coach "going," "running," or "proceeding," but they set them "flying" at the rates of speed which may be gathered from these notices. Nearly thirty years later another advertisement set forth that the Taunton Flying Machine, hung on steel springs, sets out from the Saracen's Head Inn, in Friday Street, London, and Taunton, every Monday, Wednesday, and Friday, at three o'clock in the morning, the journey taking two days. There were places inside for six passengers, and the fares were as follows, viz.:—

To Taunton,	£1 16 0
„ Ilminster,	1 14 0
„ Yeovil,	1 8 0
„ Sherborne,	1 6 0
„ Shaftesbury,	1 4 0

Outside passengers, and children in the lap, were half these fares.

To follow out in a historical fashion the development of the coaching period down to the introduction of railways, would be beyond the purpose of this work, nor will the limits of these pages admit of so great an extension of the subject. The earlier modes of travelling, and the difficulties of the roads, are treated of in several histories of England in a general way, and more fully in such books as the 'Lives of the Engineers,' by Smiles; 'Old Coaching Days,' by Stanley Harris; and 'Annals of the Road,' by Captain Malet,'—all of which contain much that is entertaining and interesting. Here it is proposed merely to recall some of the incidents of the coaching days, so far as they relate to the mail-service, between the time when Palmer's mail-coaches were put on the road in 1784, down to the time when they were shouldered off the road by the more powerful iron horse.

The dangers to which the mail-coaches were exposed were chiefly of three kinds,—the danger of being robbed by footpads or highwaymen; that of being upset in the road by running foul of some cart, dray, or waggon, or other object placed in the way; and the peril of being overtaken by snowstorms, and so rendered helpless and cut off from the usual communications.

It was an almost everyday occurrence for the mail-bags to be robbed on the night journeys, when the principal mails were carried. We know of these things now through notices which were issued by the Post-office at the time, of which copies are still in existence. Here are the terms of a notice issued to the mail-guards in March 1802:—

"Three Irishmen are in custody for highway robbery. One of them has confessed, and declares that their purpose in going out was to rob the mail-coach. Their first step was to watch an opportunity and fire at the guard, which it is supposed might have been easily obtained, as they are so frequently off their guard. They had pistols found on them. It is therefore necessary, in addition to your former instructions, to direct that you are particularly vigilant and watchful, that you keep a quick eye to every person stirring, and that you see your arms are in the best possible condition, and ready for instant duty."

On the 21st December 1805, a bag of letters for Stockport was stolen out of the mail-box while the coach was in Macclesfield. It was a Sunday night about ten o'clock when the robbery took place, and the bag was found empty under a haystack near the town. The following notice of another robbery was issued by the Postmaster-General on the 1st March 1810:—

"Whereas the bags of letters from this office (London), of last night, for the following towns—viz.,

Hatfield,	St Neots,	Spalding,
Welwyn,	Oundle,	Lowth,
Stevenage,	Stilton,	Horncastle,
Baldock,	Wansford,	and
Biggleswade,	Grantham,	Boston,
Kimbolton,	Spilsby,	

—were stolen from the mail-box, about ten o'clock on the same night, supposed at Barnet, by forcibly wrenching off the lock whilst the horses were changing; whoever shall apprehend and convict, or cause to be apprehended and convicted, the person or persons who stole the said bags, shall be entitled to a reward of One Hundred Pounds," &c.

On Monday the 19th November of the same year, the bags of letters from

Melton Mowbray,	Thrapston,
Oakham,	Higham Ferrers,
Uppingham,	and
Kettering,	Wellingborough,

were stolen at Bedford at about nine o'clock in the evening.

Again, in January 1813, a further warning to the guards was issued, showing the necessity for vigilance on the part of these officers, by describing some of the recent robberies which were the occasion for the warning:—

"The guards are desired by Mr Hasker to be particularly attentive to their mail-box. Depredations are committed every night on some stage-coaches by stealing parcels. I shall relate a few, which I trust will make you circumspect. The Bristol mail-coach has been robbed within a week of the bankers' parcel, value £1000 or upwards. The Bristol mail-coach was robbed of money the 3d instant to a large amount. The 'Expedition' coach has been twice robbed in the last week—the last time of all the parcels out of the seats. The 'Telegraph' was robbed last Monday night between Saracen's Head, Aldgate, and Whitechapel Church, of all the parcels out of the dicky. It was broken open while the guard was on it, standing up blowing his horn. The York mail was robbed of parcels out of the seats to a large amount."

The following account of a stage-coach robbery committed on that, at one time, notoriously dangerous ground called Hounslow Heath, is taken from the 'Annals of the Road,' already referred to in this work :—

"In the reign of King George III., a stage-coach, driven by one Williams, and going over Hounslow Heath on the road between Reading and London, was stopped by a highwayman, who, riding up, demanded money of the passengers. A lady gave up her watch, a gent his purse, and away goes the highwayman, followed, however, by Williams (the bold) on one of the leaders, who 'nailed' and brought him back to the coach, on which he was placed and taken to Staines. This occurred on a Tuesday; the hearing before the magistrates took place on Wednesday; on Thursday he was in Newgate; on Friday he was tried, and sentenced to be hung on Monday. Williams then got up a memorial, petitioning for a reprieve;

and on this being presented to his Majesty, the sentence was commuted to transportation for life. The King was so pleased with Williams's daring, that he presented him with a key of Windsor Park gates, to be used by him and his descendants so long as they drove a coach from Reading to London. This royal authority allowed them to pass through the park instead of going by the turnpike road."

Another very interesting account of a mail-coach robbery is given by Mr S. C. Hall in his 'Retrospect of a Long Life,' the object of the outrage being, not apparently plunder for plunder's sake in the ordinary sense, but to recover some legal documents and money paid as rent by a man in the neighbourhood who stood high in local favour, but was understood to have been harshly treated by his landlord. The case occurred in Ireland, and is characteristic of the way in which the Irish people give vent to their feelings when they are stirred by affection or sentiment.

"I was travelling in Ireland (it must have been about the year 1818), between Cork and Skibbereen, when I witnessed a stoppage of the mail to rob it. The road was effectually barricaded by a huge tree, passage was impossible, and a dozen men with blackened faces speedily surrounded the coach. To attempt resistance would have been madness: the guard wisely abstained from any, but surrendered his arms; the priming was removed, and they were returned to him. The object of the gang was limited to acquiring the mail-bags; they were known to contain some writs against a gentleman very popular in the district. These being extracted, the coach pursued its way without further interruption. The whole affair did not occupy five minutes. It was subsequently ascertained, however, that there had been a further purpose. The gentleman had that day paid his rent—all in bank-notes; when the agent desired to mark them, there was neither pen nor ink in the house; the mail-bag contained these notes. Where they eventually found their way was never proved, but it was certain they did not reach the landlord, whose receipt was in the hands of his tenant, duly signed."

Interceptions of the mail for the purpose of preventing the serving of writs by means of the post are not unknown in Ireland at the present time. In August 1883 a post-runner near Mallow was stopped by two men, dressed in women's clothes and with blackened faces, who seized his mail-bag, and made search for registered letters which it was supposed might have contained ejectment notices. None were found, however, and the men returned the other letters to the runner. A similar outrage was committed in the same neighbourhood in 1881.

The following exciting and unpleasant adventure happened to the passengers by the Enniskillen mail-coach on its way to Dublin on the morning of the 4th January 1813. The coach had safely made its journey to a point within two miles of a place called Dunshaughlin, the time being about 3 A.M., when the mail-guard, watchful as his duty required, espied a number of men suspiciously lying on each side of the road in advance of him. The night must have been clear, and probably there was bright moonlight; as otherwise, at that early hour in the month of January, the men lying in wait could not have been observed. There being little doubt that an attack upon the mail was contemplated, the carriage was at once drawn up, and the alarm given. The drowsy or benumbed travellers, thus rudely aroused and brought to a sense of their danger, hastily jumped to the ground, and demanded the spare arms which were carried for use on like emergencies. These were immediately served out to the passengers, who, if not animated by true Irish spirit at so early an hour, to fight for fighting's sake, were at any rate determined to defend their lives and property. At the head of the coach-party in this lonely and trying situation was a clergyman of the County Cavan named King, who, like Father Tom in the play, had not forgotten the accomplishments of his youth, and who was prepared to carry the message of peace and goodwill with the blunderbuss at the ready, this being the weapon with which he had armed himself. The robbers, perceiving that they were to encounter a determined opposition, thought it wise to retreat; and while the guards stood by their charge—the mail-coach—the men were pursued over a field by Mr King, on whom they fired, without, however, doing any damage. The parson, deeming a return necessary, replied with the gaping blunderbuss—and to some purpose, it was thought, for three of the men were within twenty yards of him when he fired. The would-be robbers being now driven off, the passengers had time to realise their fright; and gathering themselves again into the coach, the journey was continued, though it is hardly likely that sleep resumed its sway over the terrified passengers for the remaining hours of that particular night.

These are but a few instances of the robberies against which the guards were constantly warned to be on the alert, and which they were enjoined to prevent. They were provided with a blunderbuss and a brace of pistols, to make a good defence in case of need; and it may be interesting to recall that the charge for the former was ten or twelve shot the size of a pea, and two-thirds of such charge for the latter—the quantity of lead mentioned being sufficient, one would suppose, if well directed, to give a hot welcome to any one attempting the mail.

But the guards were very often not so vigilant as they should have been, the ale-houses having then the attractions which to many they still have: sometimes they fell asleep on their boxes, and in other respects wofully infringed the regulations. The following official notice plainly shows this:—

"I am very sorry to be under the necessity of addressing the mail-guards on such a subject; but though every direction and inspection are given them, and they are fully informed of the punishments that must follow if they do not do their duty, yet, notwithstanding this, and every admonition given in every way that can be devised, four guards that were looked upon as very good ones, have in the course of last week been guilty of such misconduct as obliges their discharge—for the public, who trust their lives and property in the conduct of the office, can never be expected to suffer such neglect to pass unnoticed. The four guards discharged are John ———, for having his mail-box unlocked at Ferrybridge while the mail was therein; Wm. ———, for going to the office at York drunk to fetch his mail, though barely able to stand; W. ———, for bringing the mail on the outside of the mail-box and on the roof, and converting the mail-box to another use;

W. ———, for going from London to Newmarket without firearms."

On another occasion a guard was fined five guineas " for suffering a man to ride on the roof of the mail-coach," and at the same time he was told that if he had not owned the truth he would have been dismissed—this being followed by the quaint observation, looking like a grim official joke, " which he may be now if he had rather than pay the fine to the fund"! One more notice as to the vice of taking drink on the part of the guards, and as showing the impressive and formal manner of carrying out a dismissal in the coaching days. The document is of the year 1803, and runs as follows, viz.:—

"I am very sorry to order in all the guards to witness the dismissal of one old in the service; but so imperious is the duty, that was he my brother he would be dismissed: indeed I do not think there is a guard who hears this but will say, a man who goes into an ale-house, stays to drink (and at Brentford) at the dusk of morning, leaving his mail-box unlocked, deserves to lose his situation; and he is dismissed accordingly. And I am sure I need not stimulate you to avoid fresh misconduct—to read your instructions, and to mind them. I am the more sorry for this, as guards who have been some time in the service are fit for no other duty."

Towards the drivers also of the mail-coaches severe measures were taken when they got drunk; and the penalty sometimes took a peculiar form, as witness the following public act of submission and contrition :—

"Whereas I, John ———, being driver of the mail-coach, on my way from Congleton to Coleshill on Monday, December 25, 1809" (some excuse, perhaps, on account of its being Christmas-day), "did stop at several places on the road to drink, and thereby got intoxicated,—from which misconduct, driving furiously, and being from my coach on its returning, suffered the horses to set off and run through the town of Coleshill, at the risk of overturning the carriage, and thereby endangering the lives of the passengers, and other misfortunes which might otherwise have occurred: for which misdeeds the Postmasters-General were determined to punish me with the utmost rigour, and if it had been prosecuted, would have made me liable to the penalty incurred by the said offence of *imprisonment for six months, and not less than three;* but from my general good character, and having a large family, have generously forgiven me on my showing contrition for the past offence, as a caution to all mail and other coachmen, and making this public acknowledgment."

In another case a mail-coach driver was summoned before a magistrate for intoxication, and impertinence to passengers, and was thereupon mulcted in a penalty of £10, with costs.

The accidents that befell the coaches were sometimes of a really serious character, and were of very frequent occurrence—some of them, or perhaps many of them, being due wholly to carelessness. A person writing in 1822 remarks as follows: "It is really heartrending to hear of the dreadful accidents that befall his Majesty's subjects now on their travels through the country. In my younger days, when I was on the eve of setting out on a journey, my wife was in the habit of giving me her parting blessing, concluding with the words, 'God bless you, my dear; I hope you will not be robbed.' But it is now changed to 'God bless you, my dear; I hope you will not get your neck broke, and that you will bring all your legs safe home again.'" Sometimes the drivers, if it fell in their way to overtake or be overtaken by an opposition coach, would go in for proving who had the best team, and an exciting race would result. Sometimes a horse would fall, and bring the coach to grief; and in the night-time the horses would occasionally tumble over obstacles maliciously placed on the road to bring this about. Whether this was always done to facilitate robbery, or out of sheer wantonness, is not quite clear, but instances of such acts of wickedness were frequent. On the night of the 5th June 1804, some evil-disposed persons placed a gate in the middle of the turnpike road near Welwyn Green, and set up two other gates at the entrance of Welwyn Lane, also across the road, with the view of obstructing the mail-coach and injuring the persons of the passengers. Early on the morning of the 14th April 1806, the mail-coach was obstructed, in coming out of Dumfries, by some evil-disposed persons placing boughs or branches of trees across the turnpike road, by which the lives of the passengers were put in peril and the mail much delayed. A similar outrage was committed on the night of the 27th August 1809, when a large gate was placed in the middle of the road on Ewenny Bridge, near Bridgend, in Glamorganshire. In this instance the horses of the mail-coach took fright, imperilling the lives of all upon the coach; for it is very likely that they narrowly escaped being thrown over the bridge. Again, on the night of the 30th April 1812, some persons placed eleven gates at different points across the road two or three miles out of Lancaster, on the way to Burton-in-Kendal, whereby destruction was nearly brought upon the mail-coach and its human freight. Between North-wich and Warrington, early on the morning of the

19th November 1815, eight or ten gates and a door were placed in the way of the mail-coach, and further on a broad-wheeled cart, with the view of wrecking the mail. On Sunday, the 15th June 1817, the horses of the mail-coach were thrown down near Newmarket, and much injured, by stumbling over a plough and harrow, wickedly placed in their way by some evil-doers. These are but a few of the cases of such malicious acts, with respect to which rewards were offered by the Postmaster-General at the time, for the discovery of the offenders.

But there were other ways in which the mail was placed in jeopardy — namely, by waggoners with teams getting in the middle of the highway, and not clearing out smartly to let the mails go by, or by otherwise so driving their horses as to foul with the mail-coach. And it is curious to observe how such cases were dealt with by the Post-office. The following poster, issued publicly, will explain the matter :—

"CAUTION TO CARTERS.

"Whereas I, Edward Monk, servant to James Smith of Pendlebury, near Manchester, farmer, did, on Tuesday the 24th day of July last, misconduct myself in the driving of my master's cart on the Pendleton road, by not only riding furiously in the cart, but damaging the York and Liverpool mail-coach, and endangering the lives of the passengers—for which the conductor of the mails has directed a prosecution against me; but on condition of this my public submission, and paying the expenses attending it, all proceedings have been discontinued. And I thank the conductor, and the gentlemen whose lives I endangered, for their very great lenity shown me; and I promise not to be guilty of such outrage in future. And I trust this will operate as a caution to all carters or persons who may have the care of carts and other carriages, to behave themselves peaceably and properly on the king's highway. Witness my hand, the 2d Aug. 1804."

Then there was the danger attending the running away of the horses with the coach, of which the following is an instance, the facts being succinctly set forth in a notice of 1810, of which the following is a copy:—

"Whereas Walter Price, the driver of the Chester and Manchester mail-coach, on Thursday night the 22d Nov. 1810, on arriving in Chester, incautiously left his horses without any person at their heads, to give out a passenger's luggage (while the guard was gone to the post-office with the mail-bags), when they ran off with the mail-coach through the city of Chester, taking the road to Holywell, but fortunately without doing any injury; in consequence of which neglect, the driver was, on the Saturday following, brought before the magistrates, and fined in the full penalty of Five pounds, according to the late Act of Parliament." And through the city of Chester, with its narrow streets! It seems a miracle how four runaway horses, with a coach at their heels, could have cleared the town without dire disaster.

Again, it would come to pass that in dark nights the horses would sometimes stumble over a stray donkey or other animal which had taken up its night-quarters in the middle of the road, and there made its bed. Nor were these the only perils of the road, which were always increased when the nights were thick with fog. On the morning of the 30th December 1813, the mail from the South reached Berwick late owing to a fog, the horses being led by the driver, notwithstanding whose care the coach had been overturned twice. The drivers were called upon on occasions to make up their minds in a moment to choose one of two courses, when danger suddenly burst upon them and there was no escape from it. A good instance of such a case happened to the driver of the Edinburgh to Dumfries mail-coach, who proved that he could reason his case quickly and take his resolve. At one of the stages he had changed horses, and was proceeding on his way, the first portion of the road being down a steep hill with an abrupt turn at the foot. He had hardly got his coach fairly set in motion, when to his dismay he perceived that the wheelers, two new horses, had no notion of holding back. The animals became furious, while the passengers became alarmed. It seemed a hopeless task to control the horses under the circumstances, and to attempt to take the turn at the foot of the hill would have assured the upsetting of the coach and all its belongings. At this juncture the passengers observed a strange smile creep over the coachman's face, while he gathered up the reins in the best style of the profession, at the same time lashing his horses into a good gallop. Terror-struck, the passengers saw nothing but destruction before them; yet they had no alternative but to await the issue. Opposite the foot of the hill was a stout gate leading into a field, and this was the goal the driver had in view. Steadying the coach by keeping its course straight, he gave his horses all the momentum they could gather, and shot them direct at the gate. The gate went into splinters, the horses and coach bounded into the field, and were there immediately drawn up, neither horses, coach, nor passengers being seriously hurt by the adventure.

Of all the interruptions to the mail-coach service, none were so serious as those which were occasioned by snowstorms, nor were the dangers attending them of a light nature to the drivers, guards, or passengers. The work achieved by man, either for good or evil, how insignificant does it not seem when contrasted with the phenomena of nature!

In the year 1799 a severe snowstorm occurred in the country, which very much deranged the mail-service, as may be gathered from the following circular issued by the London Post-office on the 27th April of that year:—

"Several mail-coaches being still missing that were obstructed in the snow since the 1st February last, this is to desire you will immediately represent to me an account of all spare patent mail-coaches that are in the stage where you travel over, whether they are regular stationed mail-coaches or extra spare coaches, and the exact place where they are, either in barn, field, yard, or coach-house, and the condition they are in, and if they have seats, rugs, and windows complete." So that here, after a lapse of about three months, the Post-office had not recovered the use of all its mail-coaches, and was beginning to hunt up the missing vehicles.

Another snowstorm occurred in January 1814, evidence of which, from a passenger's point of view, is furnished by Macready in his 'Reminiscences.' He wrote as follows:—

"The snow was falling fast, and had already drifted so high between the Ross Inn and Berwick-on-Tweed that it had been necessary to cut a passage for carriages for some miles. We did not reach Newcastle until nearly two hours after midnight: and fortunate was it for the theatre and ourselves that we had not delayed our journey, for the next day the mails were stopped; nor for more than six weeks was there any conveyance by carriage between Edinburgh and Newcastle. After some weeks a passage was cut through the snow for the guards to carry the mails on horseback, but for a length of time the communications every way were very irregular."

But Christmas of 1836 must bear the palm for snowstorms which have succeeded in deranging the mail-service in England, and it may be well to quote here some accounts of the circumstances written at the time:—

"The guard of the Glasgow mail, which arrived on Sunday morning, said that the roads were in the northern parts heavy with snow, and that at one place the mail was two hours getting over four miles of road. Never before, within recollection, was the London mail stopped for a whole night at a few miles from London; and never before has the intercourse between the southern shires of England and the metropolis been interrupted for two whole days."

"Fourteen mail-coaches were abandoned on the various roads."

"The Brighton mail (from London) reached Crawley, but was compelled to return. The Dover mail also returned, not being able to proceed farther than Gravesend. The Hastings mail was also obliged to return. The Brighton up-mail of Sunday had travelled about eight miles from that town, when it fell into a drift of snow, from which it was impossible to extricate it without further assistance. The guard immediately set off to obtain all necessary aid; but when he returned, no trace whatever could be found either of the coach, coachman, or passengers, three in number. After much difficulty the coach was found, but could not be extricated from the hollow into which it had got. The guard did not reach town until seven o'clock on Tuesday night, having been obliged to travel with the bags on horseback, and in many instances to leave the main road and proceed across fields, in order to avoid the deep drifts of snow."

"The Bath and Bristol mails, due on Tuesday morning, were abandoned eighty miles from London, and the mail-bags brought up in a postchaise-and-four by the two guards, who reached London at six o'clock on Wednesday morning. For seventeen miles of the distance they had to come across fields."

HOLYHEAD AND CHESTER MAILS SNOWED UP NEAR DUNSTABLE—26TH DEC. 1836.
(From an old Print.)

"The Manchester down-mail reached St Albans, and getting off the road into a hollow, was upset. The guard returned to London in a post-chaise and four horses with the bags and passengers."

"About a mile from St Albans, on the London side, a chariot without horses was seen on Tuesday nearly buried in the snow. There were two ladies inside, who made an earnest appeal to the mail-guard, whose coach had got into a drift nearly at the same spot. The ladies said the post-boy had left them to go to St Albans to get fresh cattle, and had been gone two hours. The guard was unable to assist them, and his mail being extracted, he pursued his journey for London, leaving the chariot and ladies in the situation where they were first seen."

"The Devonport mail arrived at half-past eleven o'clock. The guard, who had travelled with it from Ilminster, a distance of 140 miles, states that journey to have been a most trying one to both men and cattle. The storm commenced when they reached Wincanton, and never afterwards ceased. The wind blew fresh, and the snow and sleet in crossing Salisbury Plain were driving into their faces so as almost to blind them. Between Andover and Whitchurch the mail was stuck fast in a snow-drift, and the horses, in attempting to get out, were nearly buried. The coachman got down, and almost disappeared in the drift upon which he alighted. Fortunately, at this juncture, a waggon with four horses came up, and by unyoking these from the waggon and attaching them to the mail, it was got out of the hollow in which it was sunk."

These are some of the reports, written at the time, of the disorganisation of the mail-service in consequence of the snowstorm. Some slight idea of the magnitude of the drifts may be obtained from one or two additional particulars. The mail proceeding from Exeter for London was five times buried in the snow, and had to be dug out. A mail-coach got off the road seven miles from Louth, and went over into a gravel-pit, one of the horses being killed and the guard severely bruised. So deeply was another coach buried on this line of road that it took 300 men, principally sappers and miners, working several hours, to make a passage to the coach and rescue the mails and passengers. Near Chatham the snow lay to a depth of 30 or 40 feet, and the military were turned out to the number of 600 to clear the roads.

On the line of road from Chatham to Dover, a sum of £700 was spent by the road-trustees in opening up the road for the resumption of traffic, an official report stating that for 26 miles the road " was blocked up by an impenetrable mass of snow varying from 3 feet to 18 feet in depth."

THE DEVONPORT MAIL-COACH FORCING ITS WAY THROUGH A SNOWDRIFT NEAR AMESBURY—27TH DEC. 1836.
(*From an old Print.*)

Between Leicester and Northampton cuttings were made, just wide enough for a coach to pass, where the snow was heaped up to a height of 30, 40, and in some places 50 feet. About a stage from Coventry, near a place called Dunchurch, seventeen coaches were reported to be laid up in the snow; and in other parts of the country a similar wholesale derangement or stoppage of road-traffic took place.

On the 9th January 1837, an official report set forth that "the mail-coach road between Louth and Sheffield had on the 6th inst. been closed twelve days in consequence of the snow, and it is stated that it will be a week before the mail can run." An attempt was made to get the mail forward from Lewes to London by post-chaise and four horses; but after proceeding about a mile from the town, the chaise returned, the driver reporting that it was impossible to proceed, as the main road was quite blocked up with snow to a depth of 10 or 12 feet.

These were the good old times; and no doubt to us they have a romance, though to the people who lived in them they had a very practical aspect.

The general instructions to mail-guards in cases of breakdown were as follows:—

"When the coach is so broke down that it cannot proceed as it is on its way to London, if you have not above two passengers, and you can procure a post-chaise without loss of time, get them and the mail forward in that way, with the horses that used to draw the mail-coach, that they may be in their places (till you come to where a coach is stationed); and if you have lost any time, you must endeavour to fetch it up, which may be easily done, as the chaise is lighter than the coach.

"If you cannot get a post-chaise, take off one of the coach-horses, and ride with your bags to the next stage; there take another horse,—and so on till you come to the end of your ground, when you must deliver the bags to the next guard, who must proceed in the same manner. If your mail is so large (as the York, Manchester, and two or three others are at some part of the road) that one horse cannot carry it, you may take two; tie the mail on one horse and ride the other. The person who horses the mail must order his horsekeeper at every stage to furnish you with horses in case of accidents. Change your horses at every post-town, and do all your office-duty the same as if the coach travelled.

"If in travelling from London an accident happens, use all possible expedition in repairing the coach to proceed; and if it cannot be repaired in an hour or two, take the mail forward by horse or chaise—if the latter, the passengers will go with you."

In pursuance of these instructions, many instances of devotion to duty were given by the mail-guards, in labouring to get the mails forward in the midst of the snowstorm of 1836.

On the 26th of December the Birmingham mail-coach, proceeding to London, got rather beyond Aylesbury, where it broke down. Some things having been set right, another effort was made, and some little further way made; but the attempt to go on had to be given up, for the snow was getting deeper at every step. A hurricane was blowing, accompanied with a fall of fine snow, and the horses shook with extreme cold. In these circumstances, Price the mail-guard mounted one of the horses, tied his mail-bags on the back of another, and set out for London. He was joined farther on by two postboys on other horses with the bye-bags, and all three journeyed in company. The road-marks being frequently effaced, they were constantly deviating from their proper course, clearing gates, hedges, and ditches; but having a general knowledge of the lie of the country, and Price being possessed of good nerves, they succeeded in reaching the metropolis. The guard was in a distressing state of exhaustion when he reached his destination. This was only one instance of the way in which the guards acquitted themselves during this memorable storm, and for their great exertions they received the special thanks of the Postmaster-General.

At a place called Cavendish Bridge the mails were arrested by the storm, and the exertions of the coachman and guard were thus referred to by a private gentleman of the neighbourhood, who communicated with the Post-office on the subject: "I take leave to remark that the zeal and industry evinced by the guard and coachman, more especially the former (named Needle), upon the trying occasion to which your communication has reference, was well worthy of imitation, and formed a striking contrast to the reprehensible apathy of two gentlemen who were inside passengers by the mail."

A notable instance of the devotion to duty of a coachman and mail-guard, and one illustrating the dangers and hardships which Post-office servants of that class had to encounter, occurred in the winter of 1831. On Tuesday the 1st February of that year, James M'George, mail-guard, and John Goodfellow, coachman, set out from Dumfries for Edinburgh at seven o'clock in the morning, and after extraordinary exertions reached Moffat,— beyond which, however, they found it impossible to proceed with the coach, owing to the accumulation of snow. They then procured saddle-horses, and with these, accompanied by a postboy, they went on, intending to continue their journey in this way. They had not proceeded beyond Erickstane Hill, a rising ground in close proximity to the well-known natural enclosure called the Deil's Beef-Tub, when it became evident that the horses could not make the journey, and these were sent back in charge of the postboy to Moffat. The guard and coachman, unwilling to give in, continued their journey on foot, having in view to reach a roadside inn at Tweedshaws, some two or three miles farther on. The exact particulars of what thereafter happened will never be known, beyond this, that the mail-bags were afterwards found tied to one of the road-posts set up in like situations to mark the line of road on occasions of snowstorms, and that the two men perished in the drift. The last act performed by them, before being quite overcome by exhaustion and fatigue, was inspired by a sense of duty, their aim being to leave the bags where they would more readily be found by others, should they themselves not live to recover them. Shortly after this the two men appear to have succumbed; for their bodies were found five days afterwards within a hundred yards of the place where they left the bags, and where at the cost of their lives they had rendered their last service to the Post-office and their country.

We who are accustomed to the comforts of railway

travelling, are nevertheless, in regard to accidents, very much like the ostrich; for though we do not purposely close our eyes to danger, we are nevertheless placed in such a position that we are unable, when shut up in a railway carriage, to see what is before us, or about to happen.

Far otherwise was the case in the days of coaching. The passengers, as well as the drivers and guards, were not only exposed to the drenchings from long-continued rain, the terrible exposure to the cold night-air in winter travelling, and the danger of attack from highwaymen, but they ran the risks of all the accidents of the road, many of which they could see to be inevitable before they happened. There were occasions when passengers were frozen to death on the coaches, and others when they fell off benumbed with cold. It is said sometimes that first impressions are often correct; but there are, of course, erroneous first impressions as well. A story is told of a mail-guard in Scotland who had the misfortune to be on a coach which upset, and from which all the outside people were thrown to the ground. The guard came down upon his head on the top of a stiff hedge, and from this temporary situation rolled into a ditch, where for a moment he lay. Coming to himself from a partial stupor, he imagined there was something wrong with the top of his head, and putting up his hand, he felt a flat surface, which to his dawning perception appeared to be a section of his neck, his impression being that his head had been cut off. This was, however, nothing but the crown of his hat, which, being forced down over his head and face, had probably saved him from more serious damage. Broken limbs were accidents of common occurrence; but affairs of much more serious import occasionally took place, of which the following is a notable example:—

On the night of Tuesday the 25th October 1808, the road between Carlisle and Glasgow was the scene of a catastrophe which will serve to illustrate in a striking degree one of the perils of the postal service in the mail-coach era. The place where the event now to be described occurred, lies between Beattock and Elvanfoot (about five miles from the latter place), where the highway crosses the Evan Water, a stream which takes its rise near the sources of the Clyde, but whose waters are carried southward into Dumfriesshire. To be more precise, the situation is between two places called Raecleuch and Howcleuch, on the Carlisle road; and a bridge which now spans the water, in lieu of a former bridge, retains by association, to this day, the name of the "Broken Bridge."

It was at the breaking up of a severe storm of

frost and snow, when the rivers were flooded to such an extent as had never been seen by the oldest people in the neighbourhood. The bridge had been but recently built; and though it was afterwards stated that the materials composing the mortar must have been of bad quality, no doubt would seem to have been entertained as to the security of the bridge. The night was dark, and accompanied by both wind and rain—elements which frequently usher in a state of thaw. The mail-coach having passed the *summit*, was speeding along at a good round pace, the "outsiders" doubtless making themselves as comfortable as circumstances would allow, while the "insides," as we might imagine, had composed themselves into some semblance of sleep, the time being between nine and ten o'clock, when, suddenly and without warning, the whole equipage—horses, coach, driver, guard, and passengers—on reaching the middle of the bridge, went headlong precipitate into the swollen stream through a chasm left by the collapse of the arch. It is by no means easy to realise what the thoughts would be of those concerned in this dreadful experience—pitched into a roaring torrent, in a most lonely place, at a late hour on such a night. The actual results were, however, very serious. The two leading horses were killed outright by the fall, while one of the wheelers was killed by a heavy stone descending upon it from the still impending portions of the wrecked structure. The coach and harness also were utterly destroyed. But, worse still, two outside passengers, one a Mr Lund, a partner in a London house, and the other named Brand, a merchant in Ecclefechan, were killed on the spot, while a lady and three gentlemen who were inside passengers miraculously escaped with their lives, though they were severely bruised. The lady, who had scrambled out of the vehicle, sought refuge on a rock in mid-stream, there remaining prisoner for a time; and by her means a second catastrophe of a similar kind was happily averted. The mail from Carlisle for Glasgow usually exchanged "Good-night" with the south-going coach, when they were running to time, just about the scene of the accident. Fortunately the coach from Carlisle was rather late; but when it did arrive, the lady on the rock, seeing the lights approach, screamed aloud, and thus warned the driver to draw up in time. Succour was now at hand. Something ludicrous generally finds itself in company with whatever is of a tragic nature. The guard of the Carlisle coach was let down to the place where the lady was, by means of the reins taken from the horses. *Hughie* Campbell—that was the guard's name—when deliberating upon the plan of rescue, had some delicacy as to how he should affix the reins to the person of the lady, and called up to those above, "Where will I grip her?" But before he could be otherwise advised, the lady, long enough already on the rock, broke in, "Grip me where you like, but grip me firm," which observation at once removed Hughie's difficulty, and set his scruples at ease. The driver of the wrecked coach, Alexander Cooper, was at first thought to have been carried away; but he was afterwards found caught between two stones in the river. He survived the accident only a few weeks—serious injuries to his back proving fatal. As for the guard, Thomas Kinghorn, he was severely cut about the head, but eventually recovered.

It was usual for the coachman and guard over this wild and exposed road to be strapped to their seats in stormy weather; but on this occasion Kinghorn, as it happened, was not strapped, and to this circumstance he attributed his escape from death. When the mail went down, he was sent flying over the bridge, and alighted clear from the wreck of the coach. The dead passengers and the wounded persons were taken by the other coach into Moffat.

It may be added that the fourth horse was got out of its predicament little the worse for the fall, and continued to run for many a day over the same road; but it was always observed to evince great nervousness and excitement whenever it approached the scene of the accident.

Yet the mail-coach days had charms and attractions for travellers, if they at the same time had their drawbacks: the bustle and excitement of the start, when the horses were loosed and the driver let them have rein, under the eyes of interested and admiring spectators; the exhilarating gallop as a good pace was achieved on the open country-road; the keen relish of the meals, more especially of breakfast, at the neatly kept and hospitable inn; the blithe note of the guard's horn, as a turnpike-gate or the end of a stage was approached; and the hurried changing of horses from time to time as the journey progressed. Ever-varying scene is the characteristic of the occasion: the village with its rustic quiet, and odd characters, who were sure to present themselves as the coach flew by; the fresh and blooming fields; the soft and pastoral downs; the scented hedgerows in May and June; the stretches of road embowered with wood, affording a grateful shade in warm weather; the farmer's children swinging on a gate or overtopping a fence, and cheering lustily with their small voices as the coach swept along. And then, the hours of twilight being past, when

"Day hath put on his jacket, and around
His burning bosom buttoned it with stars,"

E

the eeriness of a night-journey would be experienced. During hard frost the clear ring of the horses' feet would be heard upon the road; the discomfort of fellow-passengers rolling about in their places, overcome by sleep, would be felt; while in the solemn dulness of the darker hours of night the monotony of the situation would be relieved at intervals, in the mineral districts, by miniature mountains of blazing coal, shedding their lurid glare upon the coach as it passed, and showing up the figures of soiled and dusky men employed thereat, thus creating a horrible impression upon the passengers, and seeming to afford an effective representation of Dante's shadowy world.

Or, on occasions of great national triumph—when, for example, some important victory crowned our arms—the coach, decked out with ribbons or green leaves, would be the bearer of the joyful and intoxicating news down into the country,—the driver and guard, as the official representatives of the Crown, being the heroes of the hour.

But it may be of interest to learn what a mail-coach journey was from one who had just completed such a trip, and who, in the freshness of youth, and with the unreserve which can only subsist in correspondence between members of a family or dear friends, immediately commits his impressions to writing. We have a vivid sketch of a journey of this kind from no less a personage than Felix Mendelssohn, the great musical composer. Mendelssohn was at the time a young man of twenty : he had been making a tour in Scotland with his friend Klingemann— the visit being that from which, by the way, Mendelssohn derived inspiration for the composition of his delightful Scotch symphony; and the means by which he quitted the northern kingdom was by mail-coach from Glasgow to Liverpool. The following letter, descriptive of the journey, and dated August 19, 1829, is copied from an interesting work called 'The Mendelssohn Family':—

"We flew away from Glasgow on the top of the mail, ten miles an hour, past steaming meadows and smoking chimneys, to the Cumberland lakes, to Keswick, Kendal, and the prettiest towns and villages. The whole country is like a drawing-room. The rocky walls are papered with bushes, moss, and firs; the trees are carefully wrapped up in ivy; there are no walls or fences, only high hedges, and you see them all the way up flat hill-tops. On all sides carriages full of travellers fly along the roads; the corn stands in sheaves; slopes, hills, precipices, are all covered with thick, warm foliage. Then again our eyes dwelt on the dark-blue English distance— many a noble castle, and so on, until we reached

Ambleside. There the sky turned gloomy again, and we had rain and storm. Sitting on the top of the 'stage,' and madly careering along ravines, past lakes, up-hill, down-hill, wrapped in cloaks, and umbrellas up, we could see nothing but railings, heaps of stones or ditches, and but rarely catch glimpses of hills and lakes. Sometimes our umbrellas scraped against the roofs of the houses, and then, wet through, we would come to a second-rate inn, with a high blazing fire, and English conversation about walking, coals, supper, the weather, and Bonaparte. Yesterday our seats on the coach were accidentally separated, so that I hardly spoke to Klingemann, for changing horses was done in about forty seconds. I sat on the box next by the coachman, who asked me whether I flirted much, and made me talk a good deal, and taught me the slang of horsemanship. Klingemann sat next to two old women, with whom he shared his umbrella. Again manufactories, meadows, parks, provincial towns, here a canal, there a railway, then the sea with ships, six full coaches with towering outsiders following each other; in the evening a thick fog, the stage running madly in the darkness. Through the fog we see lamps gleaming all about the horizon; the smoke of manufactories envelops us on all sides; gentlemen on horseback ride past; one coach-horn blows in B flat, another in D, others follow in the distance, and here we are at Liverpool."

Speed was of the first consideration, and the stoppages at the wayside stages were of very limited duration. At an inn, the travellers would hardly have made a fair start in appeasing their hunger, when the guard would be heard calling upon them to take their seats, which, with mouths full, and still hungry, they would be forced to do, though with a bad grace and a growl—the acknowledged privilege of Englishmen. A story is told of one passenger, however, who was equal to the occasion. Leisurely sipping his tea and eating his toast, this traveller was found by the landlord in the breakfast-room when the other passengers were seated and the coach was on the point of starting. Boniface appealed to him to take his place, or he would be left behind. "But," replied the traveller, "*that* I will not do till I have a spoon to sup my egg." A glance apprised the landlord that not a spoon adorned the table, and rushing out he detained the coach while all the passengers were searched for the missing articles. Then out came the satisfied traveller, who also submitted to be searched, and afterwards mounted the coach; and as the mail drove off he called to the landlord to look inside the teapot, where the artful traveller had placed the dozen spoons, with the double object of cooling the tea for his second cup, and detaining the coach till he drank it.

In the year 1836 the speed of some of the mail-coaches was nearly ten miles an hour, including stoppages, and this was kept up over very long distances. From Edinburgh to London, a distance of 400 miles, the time allowed was forty-five and a half hours; in the opposite direction the time was curtailed to forty-two and a half hours. From London to York, 197 miles, twenty hours were allowed; London to Manchester, 185 miles, nineteen hours; London to Exeter, 176 miles, nineteen hours; London to Holyhead, 259 miles, twenty-seven hours; London to Devonport, 216 miles, twenty-one hours. But in the earlier days of the mail-coach, travelling was much less rapid; for we find that in 1804 the mail-coach from Perth to Edinburgh, a distance by way of Fife of 40 miles, took eight hours for the journey, including stoppages and the transit by ferry across the Forth—that is, at the rate of five miles an hour. The mail-guards rode about twelve hours at a stretch—quite long enough, in all conscience, on a wet or frosty night.

An incident of a romantic nature happened about the year 1780 in connection with the stage-coach (not a mail-coach, however, be it noted) running between Edinburgh and Glasgow at that period. The stage-coach, drawn by four horses, had been on the road for many years, having been established about the year 1758. The time occupied in the journey was twelve hours; nor, down to the period in question, had any acceleration taken place. A young lady of Glasgow, of distinguished beauty, having to travel to Edinburgh, a lover whose suit towards her had not hitherto proved successful, took the remaining tickets for the journey, and so became her sole companion on the way. By assiduous attentions, and all the winsome ways which the tender passion knows to suggest, as well as by earnestness of pursuit, the lover won the lady to his favour, and she soon thereafter became his wife. But the full day did not justify the brightness of the morning: the husband failed to prove himself worthy of his good fortune; "and the lady, in a state worse than widowhood, was, a few years after, the subject of the celebrated Clarinda correspondence of Burns."

In addition to the obvious duties of the mail-guards—to protect the mails and carry out their exchange at the several stations—they were sometimes required to perform special duties unconnected with Post-office work. They were, for example, called upon to keep watch in the early part of the present century upon French prisoners of war who might be breaking their parole, a likely way of escaping being by the mail-coaches. The guards were instructed to question any suspicious foreigner travelling by the coach, and to report the matter to the postmaster at the first town at which they arrived. This was doubtless looked upon as a pleasure rather than as a hardship; for they were reminded that the usual reward was ten guineas each—not a bad price for a Frenchman under the circumstances.

No record of the mail-coach days would be complete without a description of the annual procession of mail-coaches which used to be held in the metropolis on the monarch's birthday. As every corporation or society has its saint's day, or yearly festival, so the Jehus of the Post-office were not without theirs; an occasion on which they showed themselves to advantage, and drew admiring crowds to behold them. The following account of one of these displays is from the 'Annals of the Road,' a work of great interest on subjects connected with coaching generally; and as the description is given with spirit and apparent truthfulness, we cannot do better than give it at length, and in this way bring the present chapter to a close:—

"The great day of the year was the King's birthday, when a goodly procession of four-in-hands started from the great coach manufactory of Mr John Vidler, in the neighbourhood of Millbank, and wended its way to St Martin's-le-Grand. Splendid in fresh paint and varnish, gold lettering and Royal arms, they were the perfection of neatness and practical utility in build, horsed to perfection, and *leathered* to match. They were driven by coachmen who, as well as the guards behind, were arrayed in spick-and-span new scarlet and gold. No delicate bouquets, but mighty nosegays of the size of a cabbage, adorned the breasts of these portly mail coachmen and guards, while bunches of cabbage-roses decorated the heads of the proud steeds. In the cramped interior of the vehicles were closely packed buxom dames and blooming lasses, the wives, daughters, or sweethearts of the coachmen or guards, the fair passengers arrayed in coal-scuttle bonnets and in canary-coloured or scarlet silks. On this great occasion the guard was allowed two seats and the coachman two, no one allowed on the roof. But the great feature, after all, was that stirring note, so clearly blown and well drawn out, and every now and again sounded by the guards, and alternated with such airs as 'The Days when we went Gipsying,' capitally played on a key-bugle. Should a mail come late, the tune from a passing one would be, 'Oh, dear! what can the matter be?' This key-bugle was no part of the mail equipment, but was nevertheless frequently used.

"Heading the procession was the oldest-established

mail, which would be the Bristol. On the King's birthday, 1834, there were 27 coaches in the procession. They all wore hammer-cloths, and both guard and coachman were in red liveries, the latter being furnished by the mail contractor. They wore beaver hats with gold lace and cockades. Such a thing as a low billycock hat was not to be seen on any coach anywhere. Sherman's mails were drawn by black horses, and on these occasions their harness was of red morocco.

"The coaches were new each year. In these days brass mountings were rarely known; plated or silver only were in use. On the starting of the procession, the bells of the neighbouring churches rang out merrily, continuing their rejoicing peals till it arrived at the General Post-office. Many country squires, who were always anxious that their best horses should have a few turns in the mail-coaches in travelling, sent up their horses to figure in the procession.

"From Millbank the procession passed by St James's Palace, at the windows of which, above the porch, stood King William and his Queen. The Duke of Richmond (then Postmaster-General) and the Duke of Wellington stood there also. Each coach as it passed saluted the King, the coachman and guard standing up and taking off their hats.

The appearance of the smart coaches, emblazoned with the Royal arms, orders, &c., coachman and guard got up to every advantage, with their nosegays stuck in their brand-new scarlet liveries, was at this point strikingly grand. The inspectors of mail-coaches rode in front of the procession on horseback."

CHAPTER IV.

FOOT-POSTS.

"I know of no more universally popular personage than this humble official. Bearer of love-letters, post-office orders, cheques, little carefully tied packages, all the more charming that it is difficult to get at their contents, it is who shall be first to open the door to him. He is welcomed everywhere; smiling faces greet him at every door. In England, the postman is the hero of Christmas time; so he strikes the iron while it is hot, and on Boxing-day comes round to ask for a reward, which all are ready to give without grudging."—Max O'Rell in 'John Bull and his Island.'

THOUGH in former times foot-messengers—or, as they are called, post-runners—were employed to convey many of the principal mails over long stretches of country, their work in this way has been almost wholly superseded by the railway and by horse-posts; and while post-runners are perhaps now numerically stronger than they ever were, their work is principally confined nowadays to what may be termed the capillary service of the Post-office. They are chiefly employed in conveying correspondence between country towns and the outlying points forming the outskirts or fringes of inhabited districts. These men have in many cases very arduous work, being required to walk from sixteen to twenty-four miles a-day; and it is not improbable that the circumstances of these later times make the duties more trying in some respects than they were formerly. For the messengers are so timed for arrival and departure that they are prevented from taking shelter on occasions of storm, and are obliged to plod on in spite of the elements; whereas in remote times, when a runner took several days to cover his ground, he could rest and take refuge at one stage, and make up lost time at another. Be this, however, as it may, it is the fact that very many post-runners die from that insidious disease, consumption.

In the year 1590, the magistrates of Aberdeen established a post for conveying their despatches to and from Edinburgh, and other places where the royal residence might for the time be. This institution was called the "Council Post"; and the messenger was dressed in a garment of blue cloth, with the armorial bearings of the town worked in silver on his right sleeve. In the year 1715, there was not a single horse-post in Scotland, all the mails being conveyed by runners on foot; and the ground covered by these posts extended from Edinburgh as far north as Thurso, and westward as far as Inverary.

About the year 1750, an improved plan of forwarding the mails was introduced in Scotland by the horse-posts proceeding only from stage to stage—the mails being transferred to a fresh postboy at each point; but in the majority of cases the mails were still carried by foot-runners. Before the change of system the plan of proceeding was this, taking the north road as an example: "A person set out with the mail from Edinburgh to Aberdeen: he did not travel a stage and then deliver the mail to another postboy, but went on to Dundee, where he rested the first night; to Montrose, where he stayed the second; and on the third he arrived at Aberdeen; and as he passed by Kinghorn, it behoved the tide, and sometimes also the weather, to render the time of his arrival more late and uncertain."

The plan of conveying mails by the same runners over long distances continued much later, however; for we find that in 1799 a post-runner travelled from Inverness to Lochcarron—a distance across country as the crow flies of about fifty miles—making the journey once a-week, for which he was paid five shillings. Another messenger at the same period made the journey from Inverness to Dunvegan in Skye—a much greater distance—also once a-week, the hebdomadal stipend in this instance being seven shillings and sixpence.

As with the postboys, so with the runners; the surveyors seem to have had some trouble in keeping them to their prescribed duties, as will be gathered from the following report written in the year 1800: " I found it had been the general practice for the post from Bonaw to Appin to lodge regularly all night at or near the house of Ardchattan, and did not cross Shien till the following morning, losing twelve hours to the Appin, Strontian, and Fort William districts of country; and I consider it an improvement of itself to remove such private lodgings or accommodations out of the way of posts, which, as I have been informed, is sometimes done for the sake of perusing newspapers, as well as answering or writing letters."

Nor was the speed of the foot-posts—in some cases, at any rate—very much to boast of, these humble messengers being at times heavily weighted with the correspondence they had to carry. In the year 1805, before the Dumbarton to Inverary mail service was raised to the dignity of a horse-post, the surveyor, in referring to the necessity for the employment of horses, thus deplores the situation: " I have sometimes observed these mails, at leaving Dumbarton, about three stones or forty-eight pounds weight, and they are generally above two stones. During the course of last winter, horses were obliged to be occasionally employed; and it is often the case that a strong Highlander, with so great weight on him, cannot travel more than *two miles an hour*, which greatly retards the general correspondence of this extensive district of country."

In winter-time, and on occasions of severe storms, the post-runners have sometimes to endure great fatigue; and it is then that their loyalty to the service is put to the test. An instance of stern fidelity to duty on the part of one of these men, at the time of the snowstorm of 1836, formed the subject of a petition to the Postmaster-General from the inhabitants of Sheerness and the Isle of Sheppy.

The document recites that a foot-messenger named John Wright continued for nine days, from the 25th December 1836, to carry the mails between Sheerness and Sittingbourne—a distance for the double journey of about twenty-four miles. At the end of this time he was so completely exhausted and overcome by the effects of cold and exposure, that he had to give up duty for a time. The memorial sets forth that "the road is circuitous and crooked, through marshes, and very exposed, without any protection from the drift (in many places very deep), and with a ditch on either side—the water of which was frozen just sufficient to bear the weight of the snow, thereby rendering the travelling extremely hazardous, inasmuch as the dangers were in a great measure unseen; and had the postman mistaken his road (which from the frequent drifting of the snow and the absence of traffic at that time was often untracked), and fallen into one of these ditches, he must no doubt have perished." It appeared further, that between the two places there was a ferry which the postman had to cross, and that in making the passage on the night of the 25th December, the boat in which he was nearly swamped, and he "was compelled to escape through mud and water up to his waist." It is not an uncommon thing for messengers to lose their lives in the discharge of their duties, and a severe winter seldom passes without some fatality of this kind. In the winter of 1876-77, a sad accident befell a messenger employed in Northumberland. On a night of intense darkness and storm, this man turned off the usual road in order to avoid crossing a swollen stream; and subsequently losing his way, he sank down and died, overcome by exposure and fatigue. In another case a messenger at Lochcarron, in Scotland, being unable to pursue his usual route over a mountain 2000 feet high, on account of a heavy fall of snow, proceeded by water to complete his journey; but the boat which he had engaged capsized, and both the messenger and two other persons who accompanied him were drowned. A few years ago, on the evening of Christmas-day, a rural messenger at Bannow, in Ireland, while on his return journey along a narrow path flanked on each side by a deep ditch, is believed to have been tripped by a furze-root, and being precipitated into one of the ditches, was unfortunately drowned. The rural post-messengers having, moreover, to visit isolated houses along their route, are exposed to the attacks of dogs kept about the premises. A few years ago a rural messenger was delivering letters at a farmhouse, when he was severely bitten by a retriever dog, and he died six weeks afterwards from tetanus.

It is perhaps in the Western Highlands and Islands of Scotland that the most trying conditions for the rural messengers present themselves. From Ullapool to Coigach and Rieff in Ross-shire, for example, a journey of twenty-six miles, the messenger travels out one day, and back again the next. Proceeding from Ullapool, the main road is followed for about three miles, when the man strikes off into the hills, and after a time reaches a river. This he is enabled sometimes to cross by means of stepping-stones; but so often does the water cover these, that he is generally obliged to ford it, and in doing so gets himself thoroughly wet. Then he pursues a course along or over one of the most dangerous rocks in Scotland for a distance of three or four miles, the rock in some places being so precipitous that he is obliged to cling to it for dear life. After passing this rock he continues some distance farther over the hills, and ultimately regains the main road, by which he completes his journey. Apart altogether from the dangerous character of the road, the distance which the post-runner has to walk day after day must necessarily be severe and trying work.

From Lochmaddy to Castlebay there is a chain of posts seventy-five miles long, served partly by foot-messengers, partly by horse-posts, and partly by boats. The line is intersected by dangerous ferries, one between Kilbride and Barra being six miles wide, and exposed to the full force of the waves from the Atlantic. From Garrynahine to Miavaig, in the island of Lewis, there is another dangerous service, partly by foot-post and partly by boat, the distance being seventeen miles. The road lies all through bog—a dreary waste—while the sea portion is on a most exposed part of the coast.

These are a few instances of the laborious and dangerous services performed by the rural postmen. Their brother officers in the towns, though in many cases having quite hard enough work (Mr Anthony Trollope tells that the hardest day's work he ever did in his life was accompanying a Glasgow postman up and down stairs on his beat), have not the exposure of the men in the country; and as they are familiar to the eyes of every one, any special notice of them here would be out of place.

It may, however, be mentioned, that the men who formerly delivered letters in small towns were not always in the pay of the Post-office or under its control. This appears by an official report of 1810, relating to the town service of Greenock, which runs as follows: "As the Greenock letter-carrier is not paid by Government, nor *their* appointment properly in us, they are of course elected by the magistrates or inhabitants of the town, who have the right to choose their own carriers, or call for their letters at the office."

CHAPTER V.

MAIL-PACKETS.

THE employment of vessels for the conveyance of mails seems to have passed through three several stages, each no doubt merging into the next, but each retaining, nevertheless, distinct features of its own. First, there was the stage when Government equipped and manned its own ships for the service; then there was an age of very heavy subsidies to shipping companies who could not undertake regularity of sailing without some such assistance; and now there is the third stage, when, through the great development of international trade and the consequent competition of rival shipowners, regularity of sailing is ensured apart from the post, and the Government is able to make better terms for the conveyance of the mails.

It is curious to take a glimpse of the conditions under which the early packets sailed, when they were often in danger of having to fight or fly. The instructions to the captains were to run while they could, fight when they could no longer run, and to throw the mails overboard when fighting would no longer avail. In 1693, such a ship as then performed the service was described as one of "eighty-five tons and fourteen guns, with powder, shot, and firearms, and all other munitions of war." A poor captain, whose ship the Grace Dogger was lying in Dublin Bay awaiting the tide, fell into the hands of the enemy, a French privateer having seized his ship and stripped her of rigging, sails, spars, and yards, and of all the furniture "wherewith she had been provided for the due accommodation of passengers, leaving not so much as a spoone or a naile-hooke to hang anything on." The unfortunate ship in its denuded state was ransomed from its captors for fifty guineas. If we may judge from this case, the fighting of the packets does not seem always to have been satisfactory; and the Postmasters-General of the day, deeming discretion the better part of valour, set about building packets that should escape the enemy. They did build new vessels, but so low did they rest in the water that the Postmasters-General wrote of them thus: "Wee doe find that in blowing weather they take in soe much water that the men are constantly wet all through, and can noe ways goe below to change themselves, being obliged to keep the hatches shut to save the vessel from sinking, which is such a discouragement of the sailors, that it will be of the greatest difficulty to get any to endure such hardshipps in the winter weather." These flying ships not proving a success, the Postmasters-General then determined to build "boats of force to withstand the enemy," adopting the bull-dog policy as the only course open in the circumstances. It may be interesting to recall how these packets were manned. In May 1695 the crews of the packets between Harwich and Holland were placed on the following footing:—

	Per mensem.		Per mensem.
Master and Commander, . .	£10 0 0	Gunner's mate, .	£1 15 0
		Quartermaster, .	1 15 0
Mate, . . .	3 10 0	Captain's servant,	1 0 0
Surgeon, . .	3 10 0	11 Able seamen at	
Boatswain, . .	3 5 0	£1, 10s., . .	16 10 0
Midshipman, .	1 15 0	Agent's instrument,	2 0 0
Carpenter, . .	3 5 0		
Boatswain's mate,	1 15 0	In all, . .	£50 0 0

These wages may not have been considered too liberal considering the risks the men ran; and as an encouragement to greater valour in dealing with the enemy, and as an additional means of recompense, the crew were allowed to take prizes if they fell in their way. They also "received pensions for wounds, according to a code drawn up with a nice discrimination of the relative value of different parts of the body, and with a most amusing profusion of the technical terms of anatomy. Thus, after a fierce engagement which took place in February 1705, we find that Edward James had a donation of £5 because a musket-shot had grazed on the tibia of his left leg; that Gabriel Treludra had £12 because a shot had divided his frontal muscles and fractured his skull; that Thomas Williams had the same sum because a Granada shell had stuck fast in his left foot; that John Cook, who received a shot in the hinder part of his head, whereby a large division of the scalp was made, had a donation of £6, 13s. 4d. for present relief, and a yearly pension of the same amount; and that Benjamin Lillycrop, who lost the fore-finger of his left hand, had £2 for present relief, and a yearly pension of the same amount." Some other classes of wounds were assessed for pensions as follows: "Each arm or leg amputated above the elbow or knee is £8 per annum; below the knee is 20 nobles. Loss of the sight of one eye is £4, of the pupil of the eye £5, of the sight of both eyes £12, of the pupils of both eyes £14; and according to these rules we consider also how much the hurts affect the body, and make the allowances accordingly."

But between different parts of the United Kingdom, not a century ago, it is remarkable how infrequent the communications sometimes were. Nowadays, there are three or four mails a-week between the mainland and Lerwick, in Shetland, whereas in 1802 the mails between these parts were carried only ten times a-year, the trips in December and January being omitted owing to the stormy character of the weather. The contract provided that there should be used "a sufficiently strong-built packet," and the allowance granted for the service was £120 per annum. It may perhaps be worthy of notice that the amount of postage upon letters sent to Shetland in the year ended the 5th July 1802 was no more than £199, 19s. 1d. It was also stipulated, by the terms of the agreement, that the contractors should adopt a proper search of their own servants, lest they should privately convey letters to the injury of the revenue; and they were also required to take measures against passengers by the packet transgressing in the same way. On one occasion the good people in these northern islands, when memorialising for more frequent postal service, suggested that the packets would be of great use in spying out and reporting the presence of French privateers on the coast; but the Postmaster-General of the period took the sensible view that the less the packets saw of French privateers the better it would be for the packet service.

Difficulties are experienced even in the present

day in communicating with some of the outlying islands of the north of Scotland, weeks and occasionally months passing without the boats carrying the mails being able to make the passage. The following is from a report made by the postmaster of Lerwick on the 27th March 1883, with reference to the interruption of the mail-service with Foula, an outlying island of the Shetland group:—

"A mail was made up on the 8th January, and several attempts made to reach the island, but unsuccessfully, until the 10th March. Fair Isle was in the same predicament as Foula, but the mail-boat was more unfortunate. A trip was effected to Fair Isle about the end of December, but none again until last week. About 9th March the boat left for Fair Isle, and nothing being heard of her for a fortnight, fears were entertained for her safety. Fortunately the crew turned up on 23d March, but their boat had been wrecked at Fair Isle. During the twenty years I have been in the service, I have never been so put about arranging our mails and posts as since the New Year; we have had heavier gales, but I do not think any one remembers such a continuation of storms as from about the first week of January to end of February; indeed it could hardly be called *storms*, but rather one continued storm, with an occasional lull of a few hours. I cannot recall any time during the period having twenty-four hours' calm or even moderate weather. If it was a lull at night, it was on a gale in the morning; and if a lull in the morning, a gale came on before night. The great difficulty in working Foula and Fair Isle is the want of harbours; and often a passage might be made, but the men dare not venture on account of the landing at the islands." This statement gives a fair idea of the difficulties that have to be overcome in keeping up the circulation of letters with the distant fragments of our home country.

In the packet service deeds of devotion have been done in the way of duty, as has been the case on occasions in the land service. At a period probably about 1800, a Mr Ramage, an officer attached to the Dublin Post-office, being charged with a Government despatch, to be placed on board the packet in the Bay of Dublin, found, on arriving there, that the captain, contrary to orders, had put to sea. Mr Ramage, being unable to acquit himself of his duty in one way, undertook it in another; and hiring an open boat, he proceeded to Holyhead, and there safely landed the despatch. Another instance is related in connection with the shipwreck of the Violet mail-packet sailing between Ostend and Dover; the particulars being given as follows in the Postmaster-General's report for 1856:—

"Mr Mortleman, the officer in immediate charge of the mail-bags, acted on the occasion with a presence of mind and forethought which reflect honour on his memory. On seeing that the vessel could not be saved, he must have removed the cases containing the mail-bags from the hold, and so have placed them that when the ship went down they might float; a proceeding which ultimately led to the recovery of all the bags, except one containing despatches, of which, from their nature, it was possible to obtain copies."

It has already been mentioned that at the close of the seventeenth century a mail-packet was a vessel of some 85 tons—a proud thing, no doubt, in the eyes of him who commanded her. The class of ship would seem to have remained very much the same during the next hundred years; for, in the last years of the eighteenth century, a mail-packet on the Falmouth station, reckoned fit to proceed to any part of the world, was of only about 179 tons burthen. Her crew, from commander to cook, comprised only twenty-eight persons when she was on a war footing, and twenty-one on a peace footing; and her armament was six 4-pounder guns. The victualling was at the rate of tenpence per man per day; the whole annual charge for the packet when on the war establishment, including interest on cost of ship, wages, wear and tear of fittings, medicine, &c., being £2112, 6s. 8d.; while on the peace establishment, with diminished wear and tear, and reduced crew, the charge was estimated at £1681, 11s. 9d. The packets on the Harwich station, performing the service to and from the Continent, were much less in size, being of about 70 tons burthen.

During the wars with the French at this period the mail-packets were not infrequently captured by the enemy. From 1793 to 1795 alone four of these ships were thus lost—namely, the King George, the Tankerville, the Prince William Henry, and the Queen Charlotte. The King George, a Lisbon packet, homeward bound with the mails and a considerable quantity of money, was taken and carried into Brest. The Tankerville, on her passage from Falmouth to Halifax, with the mails of November and December 1794, was captured by the privateer Lovely Lass, a ship fitted out in an American port, and probably itself a prize, there having been some diplomatic correspondence with the United States shortly before on the subject of a captured vessel bearing that name. Before the Tankerville fell into the hands of the enemy, the mails were thrown overboard, in accordance with the standing orders which have already been referred to. The officers and crew were carried on board the Lovely Lass, and then the Tankerville was sunk. Soon afterwards the captive crew were released by the commander of the privateer, and sent in a Spanish prize to Barbadoes.

But though the mail-packets were intended to rely for safety mainly upon their fine lines and spread of canvas, and were expected to show fight only in the last resort, we may be sure that, when the hour of battle came upon them, they were not taken without a struggle. Nor, indeed, did they always get the worst of the fray, as will be seen by the following account of a brilliant affair which took place in the West Indies, copied from the 'Annual Register' of 1794:—

"The Antelope packet sailed from Port Royal, Jamaica, November 27, 1793. On the 1st of December, on the coast of Cuba, she fell in with two schooners, one of which, the Atalanta, outsailed her consort; and after chasing the Antelope for a considerable time, and exchanging many shots, at five o'clock in the ensuing morning, it being calm, rowed up, grappled with her on the starboard side, poured in a broadside, and made an attempt to board, which was repulsed with great slaughter. By this broadside, Mr Curtis, the master and commander of the Antelope, the first mate, ship's steward, and a French gentleman, a passenger, fell. The command then devolved on the boatswain (for the second mate had died of the fever on the passage), who, with the few brave men left, assisted by the passengers, repelled many attempts to board. The boatswain, at last observing that the privateer had cut her grapplings, and was attempting to sheer off, ran aloft, and lashed her squaresail-yard to the Antelope's fore-shrouds, and immediately pouring in a few vollies of small-arms, which did great execution, the enemy called for quarter, which was instantly granted, although the French had the bloody flag hoisted during the whole contest. The prize was carried into Annotta Bay about eleven o'clock the next morning. The Antelope sailed with 27 hands, but had lost four before the action by the fever, besides two then unfit for duty: so that the surgeon, being necessarily in the cockpit, they engaged with only 20 men, besides the passengers.

"The Atalanta was fitted out at Charlestown, mounted eight 3-pounders, and carried 65 men, French, Americans, and Irish, of whom 49 were killed or wounded in the action; the Antelope having only two killed and three wounded—one mortally.

"The House of Assembly at Jamaica, as a reward for this most gallant action, voted 500 guineas— 200 to be paid to the master's widow, 100 to the first mate's, 100 to the boatswain, and 100 among the rest of the crew."

' The packet-boats sailing from the ports of Harwich and Dover, being habitually in the "silver streak," were subject to frequent interruptions from

96   THE ROYAL MAIL.

English privateers and men-of-war frequenting these waters; and to lessen the inconvenience thus arising, the packets at one time carried what was called a "post-boy jack." An official record of 1792 thus describes the flag: "It is the Union-jack with the figure of a man riding post with a mail behind him, and blowing his horn." These flags were made of bunting, and cost £1, 2s. each.

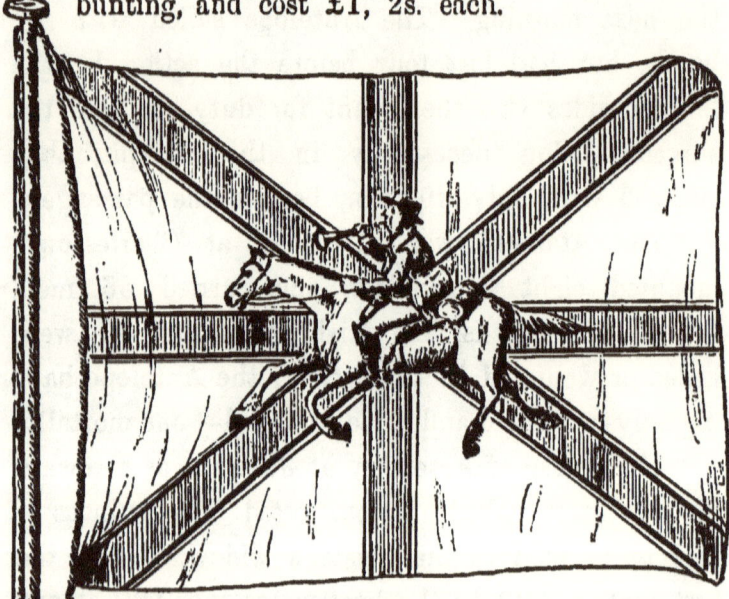

Happily there has not for a long time been any need for using fighting ships to convey the mails of this country over the high seas; and this is a danger which it has not been needful to provide against in the packet service of the present generation.

While in the eighteenth century but trifling advancement would seem to have been made in naval matters, what a contrast is presented by the achievements of the last eighty years! As compared with the Etruria and the Umbria, recent acquisitions of the Cunard Company, for the conveyance of the mails between Liverpool and New York, each of 8000 tons burthen and 12,500 horse-power, the pigmy vessels of the past almost sink into nothingness; and we cannot but acknowledge the rapidity with which such stupendous agencies have come under the control of man for the furtherance of his work in the world.

We would present a further contrast between the past and the present as regards the packet service. So late as 1829, and perhaps later still, the voyages out to the under-mentioned places and home again were estimated to take the following number of days—viz.:

	Days.		Days.
To Jamaica,	112	To Malta,	98
,, America,	105	,, Brazil,	140
,, Leeward Islands,	91	,, Lisbon,	28

There were then no regular packets to China, New South Wales, Sierra Leone, Cape Coast Castle, Goree, Senegal, St Helena, and many parts of South America; opportunity being taken to send ship letter-bags to these places as occasion offered by trading vessels.

Nowadays the transit of letters to the places first above-mentioned is estimated to occupy the following number of days:—

	Days.		Days.
To Jamaica,	18	To Malta,	4½
" America,	7	" Brazil,	21
" West Indies,	16	" Lisbon,	3

And the return mails would occupy a similar amount of time.

In nothing perhaps will the advantages now offered by the Post-office, in connection with the packet service, be more appreciated by the public than in the reduced rates of postage. The following table shows the initial rates for letters to several places abroad in 1829 and in 1884:—

	1829.	1884.		1829.	1884.
France,	2s. 1d.	2½d.	Gibraltar,	3s. 1d.	2½d.
Italy,	2s. 10d.	2½d.	Malta,	3s. 5d.	2½d.
Spain,	3s. 1d.	2½d.	United States,	2s. 5d.	2½d.
Sweden,	2s. 7d.	2½d.	Brazil,	3s. 9d.	4d.
Portugal,	2s. 9d.	2½d.			

If we were asked to point out a mail-packet of the present day as fulfilling all modern requirements in regard to the packet service, and showing a model of equipment in the vessels as well as order in their management, we would not hesitate to name the mail-steamers plying between Holyhead and Kingstown. It may not be generally known, but it is the case, that these vessels carry a post-office on board, wherein sorters perform their ordinary duties, by which means much economy of time is effected in the arrangement of the correspondence. In stormy weather, when the packets are tumbling about amid the billows of the Channel, the process of sorting cannot be comfortably carried on, and the men have to make free use of their sea-legs in steadying themselves, so as to secure fair aim at the pigeon-holes into which they sort the letters. But the departure of one of these ships from Kingstown is a sight to behold. Up to a short time before the hour of departure friends may be seen on the hurricane-deck chatting with the passengers; but no sooner is the whistle of the mail-train from Dublin heard than all strangers are warned off; in a few minutes the train comes down the jetty; the sailors in waiting seize the mail-bags and carry them on board; and the moment the last of the bags is thus disposed of, the moorings are all promptly cast off, and the signal given to go ahead: and with such an absence of bustle or excitement is all this done, that before the spectator can realise what has passed before his eyes, the ship is majestically sailing past the end of the pier, and is already on her way to England.

CHAPTER VI.

SHIPWRECKED MAILS.

OUTSIDE the Post-office Department it is probably not apprehended to what extent care is actually bestowed upon letters and packets—when, in course of transit through the post, their covers are damaged or addresses mutilated—in order to secure their further safe transmission; many envelopes and wrappers being of such flimsy material that, coming into contact with hard bundles of letters in the mail-bags, they run great risk of being thus injured. But the occasions on which exceptional pains are taken, and on a large scale, to carry out this work, are when mails from abroad have been saved in the case of shipwreck, and the contents are soaked with water. Then it is that patient work has to be done to get the letters, newspapers, &c., into a state for delivery, to preserve the addresses, and to get the articles dried. In certain instances the roof of the chief office in St Martin's-le-Grand has been used as a drying-green for shipwrecked newspapers, there being no sufficient space indoors to admit of their being spread out. The amount of patching, separating, and deciphering in such circumstances cannot well be conceived.

But perhaps the most curious difficulty arising out of a shipwrecked mail was that which took place in connection with the loss of the Union Steamship Company's packet European off Ushant, in December 1877. After this ship went down the mails were recovered, but not without serious damage, through saturation with sea-water. One of the registered letter-bags from Cape Town, on being opened in the chief office in London, was found to contain several large packets of diamonds, the addresses on which had been destroyed by the action of the water, and some 7 lb. weight of loose diamonds, which had evidently formed the contents of a lot of covers lying as pulp at the bottom of the bag, and from which no accurate addresses could be obtained. Every possible endeavour was made to trace the persons to whom the unbroken packets were consigned, and with such success, that after some little delay they reached the hands of the rightful owners. To discover who were the persons having claims upon the loose diamonds, which could not be individually identified, was a more serious matter, involving much trouble and correspondence. At length this was ascertained; and as the only means of satisfying, or attempting to satisfy, the several claims, the diamonds were valued by an experienced broker, and sold for the general behoof, realising £19,000. This means of meeting the several claimants proved so satisfactory, that not a single complaint was forthcoming.

CHAPTER VII.

AMOUNT OF WORK.

Correspondence.

THE amount of work performed by the Post-office in the transmission of letters and other articles of correspondence within the space of a year, may be gathered from the following figures, taken from the Postmaster-General's annual report issued in 1883 :—

The Letters numbered	1,280,636,200
Post-cards,	144,016,200
Books and circulars,	288,206,400
Newspapers,	140,682,600
Total,	1,853,541,400

These figures are, however, of little service in conveying to our minds any due conception of the amount of work which they represent. Nor, when the scene of the work is spread and distributed over the whole country, and the labour involved is shared in by a host of public servants, would any arrangement of figures put the matter intelligibly within our grasp. The quantity of paper used in this annual interchange of thought through the intermediary of the British Post-office, may perhaps be measured by the following facts: Supposing each letter to contain a single sheet of ordinary-sized note-paper; the post-cards taken at the size of inland post-cards; book-packets as containing on an average fifty leaves of novel-paper; and newspapers as being composed of three single leaves 18 inches by 24 inches,—the total area of paper used would be nearly 630 millions of square yards. This would be sufficient to pave a way hence to the moon, of a yard and a half in breadth; or it would give to that orb a girdle round its body 53 yards in width; or again, it would encircle our own globe by a band 14 yards in width. Another way to look at the magnitude of the Post-office work is as follows: Suppose that letters, book-packets, newspapers, and post-cards are taken at their several ascertained averages as to weight, the total amount of the mails for a year passing through the British Post-office, exclusive of the weight of canvas bags and small stores of various kinds, would exceed 42,000 tons, which would be sufficient to provide full freight for a fleet of twenty-one ships carrying

2000 tons of cargo each. What a burthen of sorrows, joys, scandals, midnight studies, patient labours, business energy, and everything good or bad which proceeds from the human heart and brain, does not this represent! Yet, after all, what are the figures above given, when put in the balance with the facts of nature? The whole paper, according to the foregoing calculations, although it would gird our earth with a band 14 yards wide, could only be made to extend hence to the sun by being attenuated to the dimensions of a tape of slightly over one-eighth of an inch in width!

Bearing in mind the great quantity of correspondence conveyed by the post, as well as the hurry and bustle in which letters are often written, it is not astonishing that writers should sometimes make mistakes in addressing their letters; but it will perhaps create surprise that one year's letters which could neither be delivered as addressed, nor returned to the senders through the Dead-letter Office, were over half a million in number! It is curious to note some remarks written by the Post-office solicitor in Edinburgh eighty years ago with respect to misdirected letters. He speaks of "the very gross inattention in putting *the proper* addresses upon letters—a cause which is more productive of trouble and expense to the Post-office than any other whatever. In fact, three out of four complaints respecting money and other letters may generally be traced to that source, and of which, from the proceedings of a few weeks past, I have ample evidence in my possession at this moment." Letters posted in covers altogether innocent of addresses, number 28,000 in the year; and the value in cash, banknotes, cheques, &c., found in these derelict missives is usually about £8000. Letters sent off by post without covers, or from which flimsy covers become detached in transit, number about 15,000; while the loose stamps found in post-offices attain the annual total of 68,000. The loose stamps are an evidence of the scrambling way in which letters are often got ready for the post, and probably more so of the earnest intentions of inexperienced persons, who, in preparing stamps for their letters, roll them on the tongue until every trace of adhesive matter is removed, with the result that so soon as the stamps become dry again they fall from the covers. Letters which cannot be delivered in consequence of errors in the addresses, or owing to persons removing without giving notice of the fact to the Post-office, are no less than 5,650,000, such being the number that reach the Dead-letter Office. But of these it is found possible to return to the writers about five millions, while the remainder fail to be returned owing to the absence of the writers' addresses from the letters. The other articles sent to the Dead-letter Office in a year are as follows, viz. :—

  Post-cards, nearly . . . 600,000
  Book-packets, ,, . . . 5,000,000
  Newspapers, ,, . . . 478,000

As regards the book-packets, it is well to know that a large part of the five millions is represented by circulars, which are classed as book-packets, and the addresses on which are not infrequently taken by advertisers from old directories or other unreliable sources.

There is one trifling item which it may be well to give, showing how the smallest things contribute to build up the great, as drops of water constitute the sea, and grains of sand the earth. Those tiny things called postage-stamps, which are light as feathers, and might be blown about by the slightest breeze, make up in the aggregate very considerable bulk and weight, as will be appreciated when it is mentioned that one year's issue for the United Kingdom amounts in weight to no less than one hundred and fourteen tons.

ST VALENTINE'S DAY.

> "The day's at hand, the young, the gay,
> The lover's and the postman's day,
> The day when, for that only day,
> February turns to May,
> And pens delight in secret play,
> And few may hear what many say."
>
> —Leigh Hunt.

The customs of St Valentine's Day have no direct connection with the saint whose name has been borrowed to designate the festival of the 14th of February. It is only by a side-light that any connection between the saint and the custom can be traced.

In ancient Rome certain pagan feasts were held every year, commencing about the middle of February, in honour of Pan and Juno, on which occasions, amid other ceremonies, it was the custom for the names of young women to be placed in boxes, and to be drawn for by the men as chance might decide. Long after Christianity had been introduced into Rome, these feasts continued to be observed, the priests of the early Christian Church failing in their attempts to suppress or eradicate them. Adopting a policy which has served missionaries in other quarters of the globe, the priests, while unable at once to destroy the pagan superstitions with the obscene observances by which they were accompanied, endeavoured to lessen their vicious character, and to bring them more into harmony with their religion; and one step in this policy was the substitution of the names of the saints for those of young women previously used in the lotteries. Now it happened that the fourteenth day of February was the day set apart for the commemoration of the saint named Valentine; and as the feasts referred to commenced, as has been seen, in the middle of February, a connection would seem to have been set up between the lotteries of the pagan customs (carried down to the time when Valentines were drawn for) and the saint's festival, merely through a coincidence of days. That St Valentine should have been selected as the patron of the custom known to us nowadays, is too unlikely, knowing as we do from history something of his life and death. He was a priest who assisted the early Christians during the persecutions under Claudius II., and who suffered a cruel martyrdom about the year 270, being first beaten with clubs, and then beheaded.

The customs of St Valentine's Day have passed through many phases, each age having its own variation, but all having a bearing to one idea. The following is an account of the ceremony in our own country as observed by "Misson," a learned traveller of the early part of last century: "On the eve of St Valentine's Day the young folks of England and Scotland, by a very ancient custom, celebrate a little festival. An equal number of maids and bachelors get together, each writes their true or some feigned name upon separate billets, which they roll up and draw by way of lots, the maids taking the men's billets, and the men's the maids'; so that each of the young men lights upon a girl that he calls his Valentine, and each of the girls upon a young man whom she calls hers. By this means each has two Valentines, but the man sticks faster to the Valentine that has fallen to him than to the Valentine to whom he has fallen. Fortune having thus divided the company into so many couples, the Valentines give balls and treats to their mistresses, wear their billets several days upon their bosoms or sleeves, and this little sport often ends in love." Pennant also, in writing of his tour in Scotland in 1769, refers to the observance of this custom in the north of Scotland in these words: "The young people in February draw Valentines, and from them collect their future fortune in the nuptial state."

In later times the drawing of a lady's name for a Valentine was made the means of placing the drawer under the obligation to make a present to the lady. The celebrated Miss Stuart, who became the Duchess of Richmond, received from the Duke of York on one occasion a jewel worth £800, in discharge of this obligation; and Lord Mandeville, who was her Valentine at another time, presented her with a ring worth some £300.

The term Valentine is no longer used in its more general application to denote the lady to whom a present is sent on the 14th of February, but the thing sent, which is usually a more or less artistic print or painting, surmounted by an image of Cupid, and to which are annexed some lines of loving import. Thirty years ago Valentines were generally inexpensive articles, printed upon paper with embossed margins. Their style gradually improved until hand-painted scenes upon satin grounds became common; and Valentines might be bought at any price from a halfpenny to five pounds. It should not be omitted to be noted that for many years Valentines have had their burlesques, in those ridiculous pictures which are generally sent anonymously on Valentine's Day, and which were often observed to be decked out in extraordinary guises, and having affixed to them such things as spoons, dolls, toy monkeys, red herrings, rats, mice, and the like. On one occasion a Valentine was seen in the post having a human finger attached to it.

But as every dog has its day, and each succeeding

period of life its own interests and allurements, so have customs their appointed seasons, and ideas their set times of holding sway over the popular mind. The wigs and buckled shoes of our forefathers, the ringlets of our grandmothers, which in their day were things of fashion, have lapsed into the category of the curious, and have to us none other than an antiquarian interest. The Liberal in politics of to-day becomes the Conservative of to-morrow; and the custom of sending Valentines, at one time so common, that afforded so great pleasure not only to the young, but sometimes to those of riper years, has already had its death-knell sounded; and at the present rate of decline, it bids fair very soon to be relegated to the shades of the past.

The rage for sending Valentines probably had its culmination some ten years ago, since when it has steadily gone down; and now the festival is no longer observed by fashionable people, its lingering votaries being found only among the poorer classes.

The following facts show how far the Post-office was called upon to do the *messenger's* part in delivering the love-missives of St Valentine when the business was in full swing. At the chief office in London on Valentine's Eve 1874, some 306 extra mail-bags, each 3 feet long by 2 feet wide, were required for the additional work thrown on the

Post-office in connection with Valentines, and at every post-office in the kingdom the staff was wont to regard St Valentine's Eve as the occasion of the year when its utmost energies were laid under requisition for the service of the public.

But the decay of the ancient custom of sending Valentines has probably not come about from within itself; it may rather be attributed to the progress made in what may be called the rival custom of sending cards of greeting and good wishes at Christmas-time. It would almost seem that two such customs, having their times of observance only a few weeks apart, cannot exist together; and it will probably be found that the new has been growing precisely as the old has been dying, the former being much the stronger, choking the latter. Valentines were sent by the young only—or for the most part, at any rate—while Christmas-cards are in favour with almost every age and condition of life. It follows, then, that a custom such as this, having developed great energy, and being patronised by all classes, must throw a larger mass of work upon the Post-office—the channel through which such things naturally flow—than Valentines did. And so it has been found. The pressure on the Post-office in the heyday of Valentines was small by comparison with that which is now experienced at Christmas. During the Christmas season of 1877, the number of letters, &c., which passed through the Inland Branch of the General Post-office in London, in excess of the ordinary correspondence, was estimated at 4,500,000, a large portion of which reached the chief office on Christmas morning; while in the Christmas week of 1882 the extra correspondence similarly dealt with was estimated at 14,000,000, including registered letters (presumably containing presents of value), of which there was a weight of no less than three tons. Everywhere similar pressure has been felt in the post-offices, and it is by no means settled that we have yet reached the climax of this social but rampant custom.

In the London Metropolitan district there are employed 4030 postmen; and taking their daily amount of walking at 12 miles on the average—a very low estimate—this would represent an aggregate daily journeying on foot of 48,360 miles, or equal to twice the circumference of our globe.

Articles of many curious kinds have been observed passing through the post from time to time, some of them dangerous or prohibited articles, which, according to rule, are sent to the Returned-letter Office—the fact showing that the Post-office is not only called upon to perform its first duty of expeditiously conveying the correspondence intrusted to it, but is made the vehicle for the carriage of small articles of almost endless variety. Some of these are the following, many of them having been in a live state when posted—viz., beetles, blind-worms, bees, caterpillars, crayfish, crabs, dormice, goldfinches, frogs, horned frogs, gentles, kingfishers, leeches, moles, owls, rabbits, rats, squirrels, stoats, snails, snakes, silk-worms, sparrows, stag-beetles, tortoises, white mice; artificial teeth, artificial eyes, cartridges, china ornaments, Devonshire cream, eggs, geranium-cuttings, glazier's diamonds, gun-cotton, horse-shoe nails, mince-pies, musical instruments, ointments, perfumery, pork-pies, revolvers, sausages, tobacco and cigars, &c., &c.

Occasionally the sending of live reptiles through the Post-office gives rise to interruption to the work, as has occurred when snakes have escaped from the packets in which they had been enclosed. The sorters, not knowing whether the creatures are venomous or not, are naturally chary in the matter of laying hold of them; and it may readily be conceived how the work would be interfered with in the limited space of a Travelling Post-office carriage containing half-a-dozen sorters, upon a considerable snake showing his activity among the correspondence, as has in reality happened.

On another occasion a packet containing a small snake and a lizard found its way to the Returned-letter Office. Upon examining it next day the lizard had disappeared, and from the appearance of the snake it was feared that it had made a meal of its companion. Another live snake which had escaped from a postal packet was discovered in the Holyhead and Kingstown Marine Post-office, and at the expiration of a fortnight, being still unclaimed, it was sent to the Dublin Zoological Gardens. In the Returned-letter Office in Liverpool, a small box upon being opened was found to contain eight living snakes; but we are not informed as to the manner in which they were got rid of.

The strike of the stokers employed by the Gas Companies of the metropolis in 1872 is remembered in the Post-office as an event which gave rise to a considerable amount of inconvenience and anxiety at the time. That the Post-office should be left in darkness was not a thing to be thought possible for a moment; for such a circumstance would almost have looked like the extinction of civilisation. On the afternoon of the 3d December in the year mentioned, intimation reached the chief office that the Gas Company could not guarantee a supply of gas for more than a few hours, in consequence of their workmen having struck work. The occasion was one demanding instant action in the way of providing other means of lighting, and accordingly an order was issued for a ton of candles. These were used at St Martin's-le-Grand and at the branch offices in the East Central district; while arrangements were made to provide lanterns and torches for the mail-cart drivers, and oil-lamps for lighting the Post-office yard. In the evening the sorting-offices presented the novel spectacle of being lighted up by 2000 candles; and this reign of tallow continued during the next three days. The total cost of this special lighting during the four days' strike was £58; but there was a saving of about 160,000 feet of gas, reducing the loss to something like £27.

CHAPTER VIII.

GROWTH OF CERTAIN POST-OFFICES.

WHEN the past history of the Post-office is looked into, at a period which cannot yet be said to be very remote, it is both curious and instructive to observe the contrast which presents itself, as between the unpretending institution of those other days, and the great and ubiquitous machine which is now the indispensable medium for the conveyance of news to every corner of the empire. To imagine what our country would be without the Post-office as it now is, would be attempting something quite beyond our powers; and if such an institution did not exist, and an endeavour were made to construct one at once by the conceits and imaginings of men's minds, failure would be the inevitable result, for the British Post-office is the child of long experience and never-ending improvement, having a complexity and yet simplicity in its fabric, which nothing but many years of growth and studied application to its aims could have produced.

But it is not the purpose here to go into the history of its improvements, or of its changes. It is merely proposed to show how rapidly it has grown, and from what small beginnings.

The staff of the Edinburgh Post-office in 1708 was composed of no more than seven persons, described as follows :—

	Salary.
Manager for Scotland,	£200 0 0
Accountant,	50 0 0
Clerk,	50 0 0
Clerk's Assistant,	25 0 0
Three Letter-carriers at 5s. a-week each.	

In 1736 the number of persons employed had increased to eleven, whose several official positions were as follows :—

    Postmaster-General for Scotland.
    Accomptant.
    Secretary to the Postmaster.
    Principal Clerk.
    Second Clerk.
    Clerk's Assistant.
    Apprehender of Private Letter-carriers.
    Clerk to the Irish Correspondents.
    Three Letter-carriers.

The apprehender of private letter-carriers, as the name implies, was an officer whose duty it was to take up persons who infringed the Post-office work of carrying letters for money.

The work continued steadily to grow, for in 1781 we find there were 23 persons employed, of whom 6 were letter-carriers; and in 1791 the numbers had increased to 31. In 1828 there were 82; in 1840, when the penny post was set on foot, there were 136; and in 1860, 244.

In 1884 the total number of persons employed in all branches of the Post-office service in Edinburgh is 939.

The Post-office of Glasgow, which claims to be the second city of the kingdom, shows a similar rapidity of growth, if not a greater; and this growth may be taken as an index of the expansion of the city itself, though the former has to be referred to three several causes—namely, increase of population, spread of education, and development of trade.

In 1799 the staff of the Glasgow Post-office was as follows—viz. :

	Salary.
Postmaster,	£200 0 0
First Clerk,	30 0 0
Second Clerk,	25 0 0
Four Letter-carriers at 10s. 6d. a-week each,	109 4 0
A Stamper or Sorter at 10s. 6d. a-week,	27 6 0

So that the whole expense for staff was no more than £391, 10s. per annum, and this had been the recognised establishment for several years. But it appears from official records, that though the postmaster was nominally receiving £200 a-year, he had in 1796 given £10 each to the clerks out of his salary, and expended besides, on office-rent, coal, and candles, £30, 2s. 8d. Somewhat similar deductions were made in 1797 and 1798, and thus the postmaster's salary was then less than £150 a-year in reality. It is worthy of note here that letters were at that time delivered in Glasgow only twice a-day.

Some ten years earlier—that is, in 1789—the indoor staff consisted of the postmaster and one clerk, the former receiving £140 a-year, and the latter £30.

A penny post, for local letters in Glasgow, was started in the year 1800, when, as part and parcel of the scheme, three receiving-offices were opened in the city. The revenue derived from the letters so carried for the first year was under £100, showing that there cannot have been so many as eighty letters posted per day for local delivery. After a time the experiment was considered not to have been quite a success, for one of the receiving-offices was closed, and a clerk's pay reduced £10 a-year, in order to bring the expense down to the level of the revenue earned. In 1803 matters improved, however, as in the first quarter of that year the revenue from penny letters was greater than the expense incurred.

At the present time, the staff of the Glasgow Post-office numbers 1267 persons, and the postmaster's salary is over a thousand pounds a-year.

At the end of last century and beginning of this —and indeed it may be said throughout the whole term of the existence of the Post-office—humble petitions were always coming up from postmasters for increase of pay, and from these we know the position in which postmasters then were.

The postmaster of Aberdeen showed that in 1763, when the revenue of his office was £717, 19s. 4d., with something for cross post-letters, probably about £400, his salary had been £93, 15s.; while in 1793, with a revenue of over £2500, his whole salary was only £89, 15s., and out of this he had to pay office-rent and to provide assistance, fire, wax, candles, books, and cord.

At Arbroath, now an important town, the revenue was, in 1763, £76, 12s. 8d., and the postmaster's salary, £20. At this figure the salary remained till 1794, though the revenue had increased to £367, 13s. 5d.; but now the postmaster appealed for higher pay, and brought up his supports of office-rent, coal, candles, wax, &c., to strengthen his case.

In Dundee, in the year 1800, the postmaster's salary was £50, and the revenue £3165, 9s. 5d. At Paisley, the postmaster's salary was fixed at £33 in 1790, and remained at that figure till 1800, when a petition was sent forward for what was called in official language an augmentation. In the memorial it is stated that the revenue for 1799 was £1997, 1s. 11d., and that the deductions for rent, coal, candles, wax, paper, pens, and ink, reduced the postmaster's salary to from £15 to £20 a-year!

To show how these towns have grown up into importance within a period of little more than the allotted span of man, and as exhibiting perhaps the yet more bounding expansion of the Post-office system, the following particulars are added, and may prove of interest:—

At Aberdeen, at the present time, the annual value of postage-stamps sold, which may be taken as a rough measure of the revenue from the carriage of correspondence alone, is little short of £30,000; the staff of all sorts employed numbers 191; and the postmaster's salary exceeds £600 a-year. Arbroath is less pretentious, being a smaller town; but the letter revenue is over £4000 a-year; the persons employed, 14; and the postmaster's salary nearly £200. Dundee shows a postage revenue of over £35,000; 193 persons are employed there; and the postmaster's salary is little short of £600. While at Paisley the revenue from stamps is nearly £10,000; the persons employed, 43; and the postmaster's salary, £300. Notwithstanding the vast decrease in the rates of postage, these figures show, in three of the cases mentioned, that the revenue from letters is now about twelve times what it was less than a century ago.

It will probably be found that one of the most mushroom-like towns of the country is Barrow-in-Furness, now a place of considerable commerce, and an extensive shipping-port. The following measurements, according to the Post-office standard, may repay consideration. Prior to 1847 there was nothing but a foot-postman, who served the town by walking thither from Ulverston one day, and back to Ulverston the next. Later on, he made the double journey daily, and delivered the letters on his arrival at Barrow. In 1869 the town had grown to such dimensions that the office was raised to the rank of a head-office, and three postmen were required for delivery. Now, in 1884, thirteen postmen are the necessary delivering force for the town.

About the year 1800 the Post-office had not as yet carried its civilising influence into the districts of Balquhidder, Lochearnhead, Killin, and Tyndrum, there being no regular post-offices within twenty, thirty, or forty miles of certain places in these districts. The people being desirous of having the Post-office in their borders, the following scheme was proposed to be carried out about the time mentioned :—

A runner to travel from Callander to Lochearnhead—fourteen miles—at 2s. a journey, three times a-week, ...	£15 12 0
Salary to postmaster of Lochearnhead, . . .	5 0 0
A runner from Lochearnhead to Killin—eight miles—at 1s. a journey, three times a-week, .	7 16 0
Salary to postmaster of Killin, ...	5 0 0
Receiving-house at Wester Lix, ...	2 0 0
Runner thence to Luib—four or five miles—1s. 6d. per week, ...	3 18 0
Office at Luib, ...	4 0 0
Total, .	£43 6 0

So that here a whole district of country was to be opened up to the beneficent operations of the Post at an annual cost of what would now be no more than sufficient to pay the wages of a single post-runner. It may be proper, however, to remark in this connection, that money then was of greater value than now; and since it has been shown that a messenger had formerly to travel as much as fourteen double miles for 2s., it is not surprising that Scotchmen, brought up in such a school, should like to cling to a sixpence when they can get it.

It were remiss to pass over London without remark, whose growth is a marvel, and whose Post-office has at least kept up in the running, if it has not outstripped, London itself. In 1796 the delivery of London extended from about Grosvenor Square and Mayfair in the west, to Shadwell, Mile End, and Blackwall in the east; and from Finsbury Square in the north, to the Borough and Rotherhithe in the south; and the number of postmen then employed for the general post-delivery was 126. London has since taken into its maternal embrace many places which were formerly quite separate from the metropolis, and nowadays the agglomeration is known, postally, as the Metropolitan district. In this district the number of men required to effect the delivery of letters in 1884 is no less than 4030. It may be mentioned that the general post-delivery above mentioned had reference to the delivery of ordinary letters coming from the country. Letters of the penny post—or local letters—and letters from foreign parts, were delivered by different sets of men, who all went over the same ground. In 1782 the number of men employed in these different branches of delivery work was as follows—viz.:

	Men.
For Foreign letters, ...	12 .
„ Inland letters, ...	99
„ Penny-post letters, . . .	44
Total, .	155

It was not till many years later that all kinds of letters came to be delivered by one set of postmen, and that thus needless repetition of work was got rid of.

At the same period—namely, in 1782—the other officers of all kinds employed in the London Post-office numbered 157. At the present time the officers of all kinds (exclusive of postmen who have been referred to separately) employed in the Metropolitan district are nearly 16,000 in number.

CHAPTER IX.

CLAIMS FOR POST-OFFICE SERVICE.

IN his Autobiography, Mr Anthony Trollope, many years a Post-office surveyor, records how he was employed in England, for a considerable period about the year 1851, revising and extending the rural-post service; and he there mentions the frequency with which he found post-runners to be employed upon routes where there were but few letters to deliver—while in other directions, where postal communication would have been of the utmost benefit, there were no post-runners at all. This state of things had no doubt had its origin in the efforts of influential persons, at some previous time, to have the services established for their own personal benefit; while persons in other districts, having less interest at headquarters, or being less imperious in their demands, were left out in the cold, and so remained beyond the range of the civilising influence. The posts in such cases, once established, went on from year to year; and though the arrangements were out of harmony with the surroundings, very often nothing was done—for in all likelihood no one complained loud enough, or, at any rate, in a way to prove effective.

But though the Department did wake up to the need for a better distribution of its favours in the country districts in 1851, there were earlier instances of surveyors attempting to lay down the posts for the general good, instead of for a select few, and in these cases the surveyors had sometimes a hard battle to fight. The following report from a surveyor in Scotland, written in the year 1800, will illustrate what is here mentioned. It is given at length, and will possibly be found worthy of perusal; for it not only shows both spirit and independence on the part of the surveyor, who was evidently a man determined to do his duty irrespective of persons, but it sheds some light on the practices of the post-runners of that period, and their relations with their superiors on the one hand, and the public on the other. It affords us, too, a specimen of official writing remarkable for some rather quaint turns and expressions. The report proceeds :—

" I am much obliged by the perusal of my Lord ———'s card to you of the 29th ultimo, with a copy of a fresh memorial from his lordship and other gentlemen upon the long-argued subject of the alteration of the course of the post betwixt Perth and Coupar-Angus.

"It is certainly one of those cases which hath become of tenfold more importance by the multiplicity of writing, than from any solid reasoning or essential matter of information to be drawn from it.

"It having fallen to my official duty to execute the alteration of this post proposed by my late colleague Mr ——, to whose memory I must bear testimony, not only of his abilities, but his impartiality in the duties of his office, and under the authority of the late respectable and worthy Postmaster-General Mr ——, whose memory is far above any eulogium of mine, I considered the measure as proper and expedient, equally for the good of the country in general, and the revenue under the department of the Post-office; and I can with confidence deny that it was 'hastily, inconsiderately, or partially' gone into, as this memorial would wish to establish. In this capacity, and under these circumstances, it is no wonder I could have wished the epithets used against this official alteration, of *ignorance, arbitrary and oppressive proceedings*, to have dropped from a person less honourable, respectable, and conspicuous than I hold the Honble. —— at the head of this memorial. Before this last memorial was presented, I understood from

Mr ——, Secretary, in the presence of Lord ——, that any further opposition upon the part of the Blairgowrie gentlemen to a re-alteration was now given up; indeed this cannot be surprising if they had learned, as stated in the memorial, page 9, that they had protested, did now protest, and would never cease to complain loudly of it, until they obtain redress. Whether this argument is cool or arbitrary I have not time nor inclination to analyse, but having been removed from this ancient district of road, and given my uniform opinion upon the merits of the alteration itself, I have no desire to fight the memorialists to all eternity. Before, however, taking final leave of this contest, and of a memorial said to be unanswerable, I consider myself in duty and honour called upon to vindicate the late Mr ——, as well as myself, from the vindictive terms of '*ignorance, arbitrary, and oppressive*' implied in the memorial, and which, if admitted *sub silentio*, might not be confined to the mismanagement of the Post-office, but to every other department of civil government. In order to this, I shall as briefly as I can follow the general track of the memorial, as of a long beaten road in which, if there is not safety, there is no new difficulty to encounter. It is needless to go over the different distances,—I am ready to admit them—they have

not formed any material part of the question,—
and the supposed ignorance of the surveyor here
is not to the point. The alteration neither did
nor should proceed upon such mathematical nicety.
The idea of posts is to embrace the most extensive
and most needful accommodation. In establishing
a post to Blairgowrie it was neither *ignorant nor
arbitrary* to take the line by Isla Bridge, which
was the centre of the country meant to be served
by it—that is, the Coupar and the Stormont and
Highland district. It is of some consequence to
observe here, that with all the great and rapid
improvements mentioned in the memorial, of the
lower or Coupar district, the upper or Stormont
district was, upon the first year's trial, above one-
half of its revenue to the Post-office, the second
nearly or about three-fourths, and continuing to increase in proportion. Coupar-Angus revenue for the
year ending 10th October last was £159, 3s. 7d.,
and Blairgowrie £123, 4s. 10d. Now, if the
Coupar district of country, which contains in it a
populous market-town, can produce no more than
this proportion for the whole district, it is evident
that the district of Stormont, with only as yet a
little village for its head town, has more correspondence in regard to its state of agriculture and improvement as an infant district, than the parent

district with its antiquity can lay claim to, and equally well entitled at least to be protected and nourished. Much is said of the memorialists' line of road, and of its being one from time immemorial. I have said in a former paper that this may be the case; many of the roads in Scotland, God knows, are old enough. But unless the feudal system should still exist upon any of them, I know of no law, no regulation, no compulsion, that can oblige the post, more than any other traveller, to take these old beaten tracks where they can find any other patent or better road. Nay, more,—as a traveller, I am entitled to take any patent road I choose, good or bad; and the moment this privilege is doubted in regard to the post, you resign at once the power of all future improvements so far as it belongs to your official situation to judge it, and let or dispose of in lease the use of your posts to particular and local proprietors of lands, who will be right to take every advantage of it in their power, and include it specifically in the rental of their estates, as I have known to be the case with inns in which post-offices had formerly been kept.

"There are three great roads to the north of Scotland from Perth (besides one by Dunkeld)—viz., one by Dundee, &c., one by Coupar, &c., and one by Blairgowrie, which run not at a very great distance in general from each other in a parallel line. The great post-line or mail-coach road is by Dundee; and there is little chance, I believe, of this being departed from, as there is no other that can ever be equally certain. The next great road to the westward is by Coupar and Forfar, &c., and is supplied by branch-posts from the east or coast line. And the third or upper line is by Blairgowrie and Spittal of Glenshee, which have no post for 50, 60, or 70 miles; and if ever that part of the country is to have the blessing of a regular post, it surely ought not to be by branching from the coast-line through all the different centres, but by the more immediate and direct line through Blairgowrie. Every one will call his own line the great line; but surely, if I am to travel either, I should be allowed to judge for myself; and I believe it would be thought very *arbitrary* indeed, if, before I set out, a proprietor or advocate for any of these great lines should arrest my carriage or my horse, and say, You shall not proceed but upon my line. I confess myself so stupid that I can see no difference betwixt this and taking it out of the power of the Post-office to judge what line they shall journey mails. If this is not the case, then all the present lines of the post, however absurd and ridiculous they now are or may become, must, as they were at the beginning and now are, remain so for ever. And I would expect next to see legal charters and infeftments taken upon them as post-roads merely, and travellers thirled to them as corn to a mill. But in regard to the voluminous writings already had upon this subject, and now renewed in this last memorial, it may be necessary to be a little more particular.

"Setting the distances aside, which no persons should have a right to complain of except the inhabitants of Coupar and beyond it, by any delay occasioned on that account, what is the whole argument founded upon? That, by the alteration, the memorialists, some of them in the near neighbourhood of Coupar-Angus, but betwixt Perth and it, have had the privilege from time immemorial, as it is said, of receiving their letters by the post from Perth, and sending them back by the same conveyance to Perth, without benefiting the Revenue a single sixpence, which would accrue to it by such letters being either received from or put in at the office at Coupar-Angus, as they ought to be. For, so far as I understand the regulations of the office, they are to this purpose, that if any letters shall be directed for intermediate places, at least three-fourths from any post-office, they shall be put into the bag and conveyed (if conveved at all by post) to the post-office nearest them, or at which they shall be written, one-fourth of the distance of the whole stage, and rated and charged accordingly. The Post-office could not be ignorant of this rule not being observed, for it was evident that very few letters for this populous and thriving district were put into the bag, except such as behoved to go beyond Coupar or Perth, and bearing the name of 'short letters.' It was impossible to convict the posts of fraud in carrying them without opening the letters, a privilege which cannot be exercised without much indelicacy as well as danger. But it required no penetration to discover that this was a very commodious and cheap way of corresponding, though it did not augment the revenue. It was an ancient privilege, and in that view it might be considered *arbitrary* and *oppressive* to meddle with or interrupt it. It is a little curious that the memorialists are principally gentlemen of property upon the road short of Coupar, and who require to be supplied daily with their small necessary articles from Perth. I have seen no remonstrance or complaint from the town of Coupar itself as to this alteration, nor of the consequent lateness of arrival and danger it is said to have occasioned, nor from a number of gentlemen beyond, whose letters come in the bag for the delivery of Coupar. The noise has chiefly been made by gentlemen who pay nothing for this post to Coupar-Angus, and it puts me in mind of an anecdote I met with of a gentleman who had influence enough with a postmaster in the country to get the post by his house, and deliver and receive his letters, proceeding by a line of road in which he avoided an intermediate office, and thereby saved an additional postage both ways.

"This line was also a very ancient one, and from time immemorial a line too upon which our forefathers had fought hard and bled; but their children somehow or other had discovered and adopted what they thought a much better line. I said the delivery of short letters was not all the advantages privately had by the old plan of the post to Coupar-Angus. This post was in the known and constant habit of carrying a great deal more than letters for the inhabitants short of, as well as for Coupar itself; and in the delivery of various articles upon the road, and receiving reimbursements for his trouble one way or other, he lost one-fourth of his time; and if, as the memorialists assert, there are fewer places to be served on the Isla road, it is a demonstration that the longest way is often all the nearest, and upon this head I have already ventured to assert, and still do, that by a regular management which may be easily accomplished, the post may come sooner by Isla to Coupar than ever it did formerly by the ancient road; and if it was possible to watch and hunt after the irregularity of the post as established upon the old system, the memorialists would find themselves in no better situation than they now are. I beg to mention here a specimen I met of this old system of private accommodation, with the consequence that followed, which may illustrate a little upon which side the imputation of *ignorance, arbitrary*, and *oppression* may lie. Having met this post with a light cart full of parcels, and a woman upon it along with the mail, I charged him with the impropriety of his conduct as a post, and threatened that he should not be longer in the service. 'Oh,' says he, 'sir, you may do as you please; I have served the country so long in this way, that if you dismiss me, the principal gentlemen on the road have determined to support me, and I can make more without your mail than I do by it.' He was dismissed. He was supported by a number of names which it is not now in my power to recollect, but which are well known in Coupar-Angus, and he issued in consequence hand-bills that, being now dismissed as a post, he would continue to carry on as before; and it was not till the *arbitrary* hand of the Solicitor of the Post-office fell upon him, that he would either have been convicted or discouraged from his employ.

"In this view, therefore, and not from ignorance, I know it is better for the Revenue in some instances to pay for 19 miles of a post, than 14 or 15, and to pay for three short runners than one long one. We have no greater faith in Blairgowrie than Coupar posts, and they were both put upon the same footing; and notwithstanding all the arguments stated against the measure, or upon the *absurdity, arbitrary*, and *oppression*, so much insisted on, I am still humbly of the opinion, which was maturely weighed and decided, that the system now in practice was best for the Revenue, whatever it might be to particular individuals; and in this decision I only followed the coincident opinion of judgments much superior to my own.

"A great deal is said upon the danger of committing care of bags or letters to two separate runners instead of one. With regard to carrying letters privately, or executing commissions, it may be so. This is the great inconvenience felt from the change. But is there any instance where posts have opened any of the bags containing letters, and thereby committed felony? Is there any instance where a wilful and felonious delay has happened here more than may be natural to any change of bags anywhere else in the kingdom? I have heard of their not meeting sometimes so regularly in very bad or stormy weather. This will happen to the most regular mail-coaches and horse-posts in Britain; and before such general objections are to be founded upon, wilful and corrupt misconduct should be proved, such as I am able to do upon the old system of one post only.

"The poor blacksmith is next brought forward. I do not know that a man's character is to be decided by his calling. He was engaged by the Office to keep a receiving-house for the runners. He is paid for his trouble by Government, and is as much under the confidence and trust of the Office, till he proves himself unworthy of it, as the postmasters of Perth, Coupar-Angus, or Blairgowrie. It is not surprising, however, that this poor blacksmith should be in general terms decided unfit for such duty, when officers who should have been much better acquainted with the *hammer and nails of office*, do not know how to drive them!

"A very short explanation to the idea mentioned by the memorialists that the opposition by the Blairgowrie gentlemen rose from the supposition that they were to be cut out of their post altogether. I never heard of this before, nor do I know this idea to have existed. The Blairgowrie district did not interfere with the Post-office, nor the Office with them, more than has happened in writing; nor, so far as consists with my knowledge, have I heard or understood that the Coupar district wished to deprive Blairgowrie of an office. That Coupar wishes to have Blairgowrie subservient to and passing through it is clear enough. But they do not advert that, as both Coupar and Blairgowrie are within one stage of Perth; had Coupar gone through Blairgowrie or Blairgowrie through Coupar, the law might say that one of them must pay an additional rate from Perth—that is, 4d. instead of 3d.; and which both Mr Edwards and I were clearly of opinion would rather have injured than improved the Revenue, as has been experienced in some similar cases. This legal distinction my Lord —— does not appear to have observed. It is, however, stated, that by this plan of going through Coupar to Blairgowrie a very easy and direct communication would be established betwixt the two places. This I have no doubt of for private business-parcels, money, &c., &c.; because it would be easier for Blairgowrie to communicate in this way by one runner, by one with Coupar and two to Perth, than by two to Coupar and two to Perth, and for Coupar to communicate with Perth by one than two each way. This is harping on the old key. But it is a reduction of service, like the shortening of the road here, I do not wish to see. I do not want a reconciliation of this kind; and whatever obloquy I may endure, with imputation of *ignorance* and other general epithets of a similar kind, I believe the memorialists, upon cool reflection, may be more inclined to ascribe these observations to proceed from honest zeal rather than wanton opposition. If it should be otherwise, I shall remain very satisfied that I have given my judgment of it according to conscience; and I cannot be afraid, if it is necessary, that the whole writings upon the subject should be again submitted to the final decision of his Majesty's Postmaster-General. In regard to the power of altering the course of the posts, I am decidedly of opinion the question ought to go to their lordships' judgment; but as to any personal opposition to the memorialists, I disclaim it; and as they say they are determined to fight till they conquer, I would now retire from the contest, with this observation, that, though such doctrines and resolutions may be very good for the memorialists, they would, in my humble opinion, if generally expressed and followed, be very bad for the country."

It is really surprising how some of the ideas and practices of the feudal times still survive, ancient arrangements coming up from time to time for revision, as those who suffer acquire greater independence or a truer conception of their position in the State. Quite recently the Postmaster-General was called upon to settle a dispute between the Senior Magistrate of Fraserburgh and Lord —— (the local seigneur) as to who had the right to receive letters addressed to "The Provost" or "Chief Magistrate" of Fraserburgh, both parties claiming such letters. His lordship had hitherto obtained delivery of the letters, on the ground of his being "heritable provost" or baron-bailie, titles which smell strongly of antiquity; but the modern Provost and Chief Magistrate, being no longer disposed to submit to the arrangement, appealed to headquarters, and obtained a decision as follows—viz., that he being Senior Police Magistrate, should receive all communications addressed to "The Provost," "The Chief Magistrate," or "The Acting Chief Magistrate," and that Lord —— should have a right to claim any addressed to the "Baron-Bailie." The surprise is, that the ancient method of disposing of the letters should have been endured so long, and that a town's Provost should have been so slighted.

Personal interest, unfortunately, often steps in to prevent or hinder the carrying out of reforms for the general good; even the selfishness of mere pleasure placing itself as an obstacle to the accomplishment of things of great consequence in practical life. The Post-office being called upon to consider the question of affording a daily post to a small place in Ireland which until then had had but a tri-weekly post, a gentleman called upon the postmaster to urge that things might be left as they were, stating as his reason that the change of hours, as regards the mail-car, rendered necessary in connection with the proposed improvements, would not suit himself and some other gentlemen, who were in the habit of using the car when going to fish on a lake near the mail-car route! Is not this a case showing a sad lack of public spirit?

CHAPTER X.

THE TRAVELLING POST-OFFICE.

TRAVELLERS who are in the habit of journeying over the principal railway lines, must at some time or other have noticed certain carriages in the express trains which had an unusually dull and van-like appearance, though set off with a gilded crown and the well-known letters V.R., and that generally these carriages appeared to have no proper doors, and were possessed of none but very diminutive windows—on one side, at any rate. It will have been observed, also, that sometimes two, three, or more of such carriages are placed end to end in certain trains, and that a hooded gangway or passage enables those inside one carriage to visit any or all of the other carriages. When the small square holes or dwarf doorways which communicate with the outside are open, a glare of light is seen within, which reveals a variety of human legs and much canvas—the latter in the shape of mail-bags, either

K

suspended from the walls of the carriage or lying on the floor. These carriages are what are called in the Post-office the "Travelling Post-office"; or, when brevity is desirable—as is often the case—

Travelling Post-office.

the "T.P.O." There are several travelling post-offices of more or less importance pursuing their rapid flight during the night in different quarters of the country; but the most important, no doubt, are the "London and North Western and Caledonian," running from London to Aberdeen; the "Midland," running from Newcastle diagonally across England to Bristol; and the "London and Holyhead" travelling post-office, by which the Irish mails to Dublin are conveyed as far as Holyhead.

If a stranger were allowed to travel in one of these carriages, the first thing that would probably take his notice would be the brilliant light which fills the interior; and the necessity for a good light to enable men, standing on a vibrating and oscillating floor, to read quickly all sorts of manuscript addresses, will be understood by whoever has attempted to peruse writing by the light derived from the ordinary oil-lamps of a railway carriage. Yet for years the light supplied in the Travelling Post-office has been given by improved oil-lamps, though more recently gas has been introduced in some of the carriages. The next thing he would notice would likely be the long series of pigeon-holes occupying the whole of one side of the vehicle, divided into groups—each box having a name upon it or a number, and a narrow table running along in front of the boxes, bearing a burden of letters which the sorters are busily disposing of by putting each one in its proper place—that is, in the pigeon-hole, from which it will afterwards be despatched. Then hanging on the walls or lying under the table will be seen canvas bags and canvas sacks, each having its name stencilled in bold letters on its side; and somewhere about the floor great rolls of black leather, with enormously strong straps and buckles—the expanse of leather in each roll being almost sufficient to cover an ox. The use of these hides of leather will be described further on.

The *raison d'être* of the travelling post-office is to circumvent time,—to enable that to be done on the way which, without it, would have to be done before the train started or after it arrived at its destination, at the expense of time in the doing, and to collect and dispose of correspondence at all points along the route of the train—which correspondence would otherwise in many cases have to pass through some intermediate town, to be detained for a subsequent means of conveyance. The T.P.O. is one of the most useful parts of the machinery of the Post-office. Among the smaller things that might be observed in the carriage would be balls of string for tying bags or bundles of letters, cyclopean sticks of sealing-wax, a chronometer to indicate sure time, a lamp used for melting the wax, and various books, report-forms, seals, &c.

The stranger would be surprised, also, to see with what expedition an experienced sorter can pass the letters through his hands, seldom hesitating at an address, but reading so much of it as is necessary for his purpose, and, without raising his eyes, carrying his hand to the proper pigeon-hole, just as a proficient on a musical instrument can strike with certainty the proper note without taking his eye off his music. In some cases — as in dealing with registered letters—a sorter has much writing to do; but, standing with his feet well apart, and holding a light board on his left arm on which to write, and further, by accommodating his body to the swinging of the carriages, he is able to use his pen or pencil with considerable freedom and success.

As the duties in the T.P.O. are for the most part performed during the night, the sorters employed have a great deal of night-work, and in some cases their terms of duty are very broken and irregular. Thus, with the hardships they have to endure in periods of severe frost, when no heating apparatus is supplied except a few warming-pans, they live a life of duty far removed from ease or soft idleness.

The large pieces of leather with stout straps attached, already referred to, called pouches, are used as a protection to mail-bags which have to be delivered by what is commonly known as the apparatus. The mail-bags to be so disposed of are rolled up inside one of these pouches; the ends of the leather are folded in; the whole is bound round with the strong leather straps; and, the buckles being fastened, the pouch is ready for delivery. But, first, let the apparatus itself be described. This consists of two parts: an arm or arms of stout iron attached to the carriage, which can be extended outwards from the side, and to the end of which the pouch containing the bag is suspended when ready; and a receiving net, also attached to the side of the carriage, which can likewise be extended outwards to catch the mails to be taken up—this portion acting the part of an aerial trawl-net to capture the bags suspended from brackets on the roadside. The apparatus on the roadside is the counterpart of that on the carriage, the suspending arm in each case fitting itself to the nets on the carriage and roadside respectively. Now the use of this apparatus demands much attention and alacrity on the part of the men who are in charge of it; for arms and net must not, for fear of accidents, be extended anywhere but at the appointed places, and within 200 or 300 yards of where the exchange of mails is to take place. The operators, in timing the delivery, are guided by certain features of the country they are passing through—a bridge, a tree on a rising ground which can be seen against the sky, a cutting along the line through which the train passes with much clatter, a railway station, and so on—as well as by their estimate of the speed at which the train is running. When the nights are clear, a trained operator can easily recognise his marks; but in a very dark night, or during a fog, his skill and experience are put to the test. On such occasions he seems to be guided by the promptings of his collective senses. He puts his face close to the window, shutting off the light from the carriage with his hands, and peers into the darkness, trying to recognise some wayside object; he listens to the noise made by the train, estimates its speed of travelling, and by these means he judges of his position, and effects the exchange of the mails.

It is indeed marvellous that so few failures take place; but this is an instance of how, by constant application and experience, things are accomplished which might at first sight be considered wellnigh impossible. When the exchange takes place, it is the work of a moment—"thud, thud." The arm which bore the bag springs, disengaged, to the side of the carriage; the operator takes the inwards bag from the net, draws the net close up to the side of the vehicle, and the whole thing is done, and we are ready for the next exchange.

The blow sustained by the pouch containing the mail-bag at the moment of delivery, on occasions when the train is running at a high speed, is exceedingly severe, and sometimes causes damage to the contents of the bags when of a fragile nature and these are not secured in strong covers. A bracelet sent by post was once damaged in this way, giving rise to the following humorous note:—

"Mr —— is sorry to return the bracelet to be repaired. It came this morning with the box smashed, the bracelet bent, and one of the cairngorms forced out. Among the modern improvements of the Post-office appears to be the introduction of sledge-hammers to stamp with. It would be advisable for Mr —— to remonstrate with the Postmaster-General," &c.

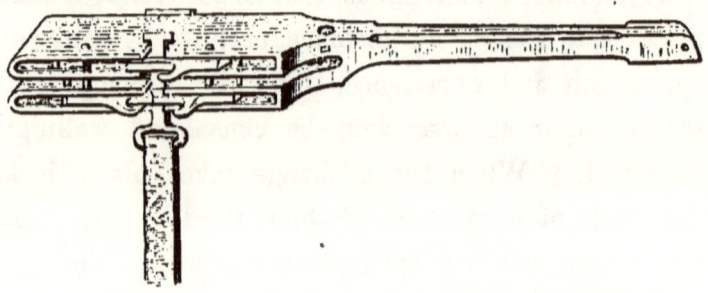

Delivering Arm, showing how the Pouch is suspended.

The Travelling Post-office apparatus is said to have been originally suggested by Mr Ramsay of the General Post-office; but his machinery was not very satisfactory when brought into practice. The idea was, however, improved upon by Mr Dicker, who was able to bring it into working condition; and for his services in this matter he was awarded a sum of £500 by the Lords of the Treasury, and the Postmaster-General conferred upon him an appointment as Supervisor of mail-bag apparatus. Some further improvements were carried out by Mr Pearson Hill, as, for example, the double arm, so that two pouches might be discharged at once from the same carriage-door. The apparatus first came to be used about thirty years ago, and there are now in the United Kingdom some 250 points or stations at which this magical game of give and take is carried on daily, and in many cases several times a-day. At certain places not merely one or two pouches are discharged at a time, but a running fire is sometimes kept up to the extent of nine discharges of pouches. By the limited mail proceeding to the North, nine pouches are discharged at Oxenholme from the three Post-office carriages, the method followed being this: Two pouches are suspended from the arms at each carriage-door, and upon these being discharged, three of the arms are immediately reloaded, when the pouches are caught by a second set of roadside nets, distant only about 600 yards from the first. It is necessary that great care should be taken in adjusting the nets, arms, and roadside standards to their proper positions in relation to one another, for any departure from such adjustment sometimes leads to accident. The pouches occasionally are sent bounding over hedges, over the carriages, or under the carriage-wheels, where they and their contents get cut to pieces. Pouches have been found at the end of a journey on the carriage-roof, or hanging on to a buffer. In November last, a pouch containing several mail-bags was discharged from the Midland Travelling Post-office at Cudworth, near Barnsley; but something going wrong, the pouch got cut up, and the contents were strewn along the line as far as Normanton. Some of these were found to be cheques, a silver watch, a set of artificial teeth, &c.

The following is a list of the Travelling Post-offices in the United Kingdom, most of which travel by night, distributing their freight of intellectual produce through all parts of the country:—

North-Western and Caledonian.	St Pancras and Derby.
Birmingham and Stafford.	Midland.
London and Holyhead.	Bristol and Newton Abbot.
Bangor and Crewe, and Normanton and Stalybridge.	South-Western.
	South-Eastern.
London and Exeter.	Great Northern.
Bristol and Exeter.	London and Bristol.
York and Newcastle.	London and Crewe.
Dublin and Belfast.	Midland (Ireland).
Belfast and Northern Counties.	Gt. Southern and Western.
Ulster.	Dublin to Cork.

There are, besides, a great many other Travelling Post-offices of minor importance throughout the country, designated Sorting Tenders.

CHAPTER XI.

SORTERS AND CIRCULATION.

POST-OFFICE sorters, unlike men who follow other avocations, are a race unsung, and a people unknown to fame. The soldier of adventure, the mariner on the high seas, the village blacksmith, the tiller of the soil, the woodman in the forest—nay, even the tailor on his bench,—all of these have formed the theme of song, and have claimed the notice of writers of verse. It is otherwise with the men who sort our letters. This may possibly be due to two causes—that sorters are comparatively a modern institution, and that their work is carried on practically under seal. In times which are little beyond the recollection of persons now living, the lines of post were so few, and the division and distribution of letters so simple, that the clerks who examined and taxed the correspondence also sorted it: and the time taken over the work would seem to show much deliberation in the process; for we find that in 1796, when correspondence was very limited, it took above an hour at Edinburgh "to tell up, examine, and retax" the letters received by the mail from England for places in the north; and that, when foreign mails arrived, two hours were required; and further time was necessary for taxing and sorting letters posted in Edinburgh for the same district of country—the staff employed in the business being two clerks. In those days there were really no sorters, unless such as were employed in the chief office in London. As to the work being carried on under seal, it is not going beyond the truth to say that, to the great majority of persons, the interior of the Post-office is a *terra incognita*, their sole knowledge of the institution being derived from the pillar and the postman.

Yet the sorters of the present age, forming a very large body, are ever engaged in doing an important and by no means simple duty. As letters arrive in the morning, and are handed in at the breakfast-table, speculation arises as to their origin; a well-known hand is recognised, interest is excited by the contents, or the well-springs of emotion are opened—joy is brought with the silvered note, or sorrow with the black insignia of death; and thus, absorbed in the matter of the letters themselves, no passing thought is spared to the operators whose diligent hands have given them wings or directed their line of flight.

When most men are enjoying the refreshment of nature's sweet restorer, which it is the privilege of the night-hours to give, the sorters in a large number of post-offices throughout the country are hard at work, and on nearly all the great lines of railway the travelling post-offices are speeding their wakeful flight in every direction, carrying not only immense quantities of correspondence, but a large staff of men who arrange and sort it in transit. Unconsciously though it may be, these men by their work are really a most powerful agency in binding society together, and promoting the commercial enterprise of the country. It lies in the nature of things that sorters' duties should largely fall into the night. Like a skilful mariner who bends to his use every wind that blows, the Post-office avails itself of every opportunity to send forward its letters. To lay aside till morning, correspondence arriving at an intermediate stage at night, would not consort with the demands of the age we live in; despatch is of the first consequence, and hence it is that to deal with *through* correspondence, many offices are open during the night. Some offices are never closed: at all hours the round of duty goes on without intermission; but in these, as also in many other cases where the periods of duty are long, relays of sorters are necessarily employed. Much might be said of the broken hours of attendance, the early risings, the discomforts and cold of the travelling post-offices in winter, and the like, which sorters have to endure; and something might also be said of their loyalty to duty, punctuality in attendance, and readiness to strain every nerve under the pressure of occasions like Christmas. But these things would not, perhaps, be of general interest, and our object here is rather to show what a sorter's work really is.

Does it ever occur to an ordinary member of the community how letters are sorted? And if so, what has the thinking member made of it? We fear the idea would wear a somewhat hazy complexion. This is how it is done in Edinburgh, for example. The letters when posted are of course found all mixed together, and bearing addresses of every kind. They are first arranged with the postage-stamps all in one direction, then they are stamped (the labels being defaced in the process), and thereafter the letters are ready to be sorted. They are conveyed to sorting frames, where a first division is carried out, the letters being divided into about twenty lots, representing roads or despatching divisions, and a few large towns. Then at these divisions the final sortation takes place, to accord with the bags in which the letters will be

SORTERS AND CIRCULATION.

enclosed when the proper hour of despatch arrives. This seems a very simple process, does it not?

But before a sorter is competent to do this work, he must learn "circulation," which is the technical name for the system under which correspondence flows to its destination, as the blood courses through the body by means of the arteries and veins. By way of contrast to what will be stated hereafter, it may be convenient to see how letters circulated less than a hundred years ago. In 1793 the London mail arrived at Glasgow at 6 o'clock in the morning, but the letters for Paisley did not reach the latter place till 11 A.M.—that is, five hours after their arrival in Glasgow, though the distance between the places is only seven miles. A couple of years before that, letters arriving at Edinburgh on Sunday morning for Stirling, Alloa, and other places north thereof, which went by way of Falkirk, were not despatched till Sunday night; they reached Falkirk the same night or early on Monday morning, and there they remained till Tuesday morning, when they went on with the North mail—so that between Edinburgh and Falkirk two whole days were consumed. In the year 1794 the London mail reached Edinburgh at 6 A.M., unless when detained by bad weather or breakdowns. The letters which it brought for Perth, Aberdeen, and places on that line, lay in Edinburgh fourteen hours—viz., till 8 P.M.—before being sent on. The people of Aberdeen were not satisfied with the arrangement, and as the result of agitation, the hour was altered to 1 P.M. This placed them, however, in no better position, for the arrival at Aberdeen was so late at night, that the letters could only be dealt with next day. It was not easy to accommodate all parties, and there was a good deal of trouble over this matter. The Edinburgh newspapers required an interval, after the arrival of the London mail, for the printing of their journals and preparing them for the North despatch. The Aberdeen people thought that an interval of three hours was sufficient for all purposes, and urged that the North mail should start at 9 A.M. In one of their memorials they write thus: "They think that the institution of posts was, in the first place, to facilitate commerce by the conveyance of letters with the quickest possible despatch from one end of the kingdom to the other, and, in the next place, to raise a revenue for Government; and they cannot conceive that either of those ends will be promoted by the letters of two-thirds of the kingdom of Scotland lying dormant for many hours at Edinburgh."

In another of the petitions from the people of Aberdeen, they strangely introduce their loyalty as a lever in pressing their claims: "Were we of this city," say they, "to lay claim to any peculiar merit, it might perhaps be that of a sincere attachment to order and good government, which places us, in this respect at least, equal to the most dignified city in Britain."

From a Post-office point of view the memorialists appeared to be under some mistake as to the gain to be derived from the change desired, for there was something connected with the return mails which did not fall in with the plan, and the surveyor made some opposition to it. In one of his reports he makes this curious observation: "I am persuaded that some of them, as now appears to be the case, may be very well pleased to get free from the obligation of answering their letters in course—and particularly in money matters"!

These facts show what a poor circulation the Post-office had at the period in question, and what splendid intervals there were in which to sort the correspondence. Nowadays, in any office pretending to importance, the letters pour in all day long (and all night too, possibly), and they pour out in a constant stream at the same time—letters being in and out of an office in certain instances within the space of a few minutes. A good sorter will sort letters at the rate of 25 to 40 a minute. But let us look at what a sorter has to learn to do

Towns.	Counties.	How Sent.						
		10 A.M.	2.40 P.M.	4.15 P.M.	5.50 P.M.	7.20 P.M.	9.0 P.M.	10.0 P.M.
Martock, R.S.O. (Ilminster)	Somerset	Birmingham	Midland T.P.O., F. 3	..	G. & C. S. T.	..	B. & E.T.P.O.	London
Maryport	Cumberland	Carlisle	Carlisle 2.0 P.M.	..	Carlisle	..	Carlisle	..
Matlock Bath	Derby	..	Derby	Derby	G. & C. S. T.	..	Derby	Leeds
Melksham	Wiltshire	Birmingham	Midland T.P.O., F. 2	..	G. & C. S. T.	London	London, G.W. Div.	London
Melton Mowbray	Leicester	..	Midland T.P.O., No.3	..	G. & C. S. T.	..	Leicester	Leeds
Menai Bridge, R.S.O. (Bangor)	Anglesea	..	..	..	G. & C. S. T.	..	Liverpool	Manchester
Merthyr Tydvill	Glamorgan	Birmingham	Gloucester	..	G. & C. S. T.	..	Gloucester	Manchester
Micheldever Station	Hants	London	London, S.W. Div.	..	London, S.W. Div.	London	London, S.W. Div.	London
Middlesborough	York	Darlington	..	..	..	..	..	Bag
Middleton - on - the - Wolds, S.O. (Beverley)	York	York	Normanton	..	..	Hull	..	York
Middlewich	Chester	Liverpool	..	..	G. & C. S. T	..	N. W. T.P.O.	Liverpool
Midhurst	Sussex	London	London, S.W. Div.	..	London, S.W. Div.	London	London, S.W. Div.	London
Milford Haven	Pembroke	Birmingham	Gloucester	..	G. & C. S. T.	..	Gloucester	Manchester
Milnthorpe	Westmorland	Carlisle	..	..	G. & C. S. T.	..	Cal. T.P.O.	Manchester
Milverton, R.S.O. (Taunton)	Somerset	Birmingham	Midland T.P.O., F. 3	..	G. & C. S. T.	..	B. & E.T.P.O.	London
Minehead, R.S.O. (Taunton)	Somerset	Birmingham	Midland T.P.O., F. 1	..	G. & C. S. T.	..	B. & E.T.P.O.	London
Mitcham	Surrey	London	London Sub.	..	London Sub.	London	London Sub.	London
Mitcheldean, R.S.O. (Ross)	Gloucester	Birmingham	Gloucester	..	G. & C. S. T.	..	Gloucester	Manchester

this. A leaf of the circulation book in use at Edinburgh for places in England is here inserted (p. 162), which will be of assistance in understanding the matter. It will be observed that there are seven times in the day at which despatches are made to England. Letters for Martock, in Somersetshire, for example, in accordance with the hour at which they may be posted, would be sent thus: to Birmingham at 10.0 A.M.; to the Midland Travelling Post-office Forward, third division, at 2.40 P.M.; no circulation at 4.15 P.M.; to the Glasgow and Carlisle Sorting Tender (a sorting carriage running between these towns) at 5.50 P.M.; no circulation at 7.20 P.M.; to the Bristol and Exeter Travelling Post-office at 9.0 P.M.; and to London at 10.0 P.M. Then if we take Mitcheldean, at the foot of the sheet, its circulation is this: to Birmingham at 10.0 A.M.; to Gloucester at 2.40 P.M.; to the Glasgow and Carlisle Sorting Tender at 5.50 P.M.; to Gloucester at 9.0 P.M.;. and to Manchester at 10.0 P.M. And so on throughout the book, which contains the names of some 1300 places in England. Nor, as regards England, is this all. The sorters have to divide letters into the several London districts by reference to the street addresses which the letters bear. Again, these men have to know the circulation for Scotch towns and Irish towns, and many of them have, besides, such a knowledge of the streets of their own city, Edinburgh, as enables them to sort letters for delivery into the several postmen's districts. Thus it will be seen that the sortation of letters is no mere mechanical process, but demands considerable head-work, as well as activity of body.

With some men it is impossible for them ever to become good sorters, even with the most earnest desire on their part to do so. There are certain qualities necessary for the purpose, and if they are not united in the person, he will never come to the front as a good sorter. These are: self-command—necessary when working against time; activity in his person so as to meet any sudden strain of work; a methodical habit; and, the *sine quâ non* of a sorter, a quick, prehensile, and retentive memory. So much has a sorter to learn, that a man without a head can never distinguish himself; and an educational test, except as a measure of acquirements in a collateral way, is of very little use. A sorter's success rests chiefly upon natural aptitude.

In the circulation of letters, we may discover the paradox that "the longest road is often the shortest;" the explanation of which is, that by a roundabout way letters may sometimes arrive sooner than by waiting the next chance by a more direct route. Post-office circulation is not tied down by any strait-laced lines of geographical science, nor by any consideration but that of the economy of time.

For example, at certain periods letters from Edinburgh for places in Norfolk and Suffolk go on to London, to return north to those counties by the mails out of London; similarly, letters for places north of Manchester are at certain hours sent on to that city, to be returned part of the way by next opportunity. It will no doubt seem a puzzle that letters for Ireland should, at a certain time of day, be forwarded from Edinburgh to Leeds in Yorkshire! Yet this is so, and with good results,—the fact being that, after the more direct despatches for the day, Irish letters are sent by the last evening train to Leeds, whence early next morning they are sent across the country, reaching a travelling post-office proceeding from London to Holyhead, and then catching the day-mail packet for Ireland. Thus they arrive in the sister isle by the time they would otherwise be only leaving Scotland. In the travelling post-offices the plan of carrying letters away from their destinations in order that time may be gained for their sortation, and afterwards sending them back by a Post-office carriage proceeding in the reverse direction, is largely practised, and with the greatest advantage. Again, letters from Newcastle-on-Tyne for Glasgow, forwarded by the night-mail, take what might be thought to be a very wide circuit—namely, by way of Normanton in Yorkshire, and Manchester and Wigan in Lancashire; yet that circulation is found to be best at the hour at which the night-mail despatch is made. In one more case that may be cited, letters from Berwick-on-Tweed for Carlisle are, at a certain time of the day, forwarded through Edinburgh as the most expeditious route. There is such a complexity of arrangement in the matter of circulation, and so great a dependence of any one part on a great many other surrounding parts, that comparatively few persons ever thoroughly understand it, and only those who can master it should meddle with it.

In one aspect the process of sortation bears some resemblance to digestion. This is observed in connection with the strange courses which letters run if, by a first misreading of the address, they happen to get out of their proper line or direction. A day seldom passes but some letter addressed to Edenbridge in Kent reaches the city of Edinburgh, either from London or some other English town. There is, of course, a strong resemblance between the names of the two places as written, yet the missent letters must have passed through the hands of two or three sorters before reaching Edinburgh. But though this might seem to suggest carelessness, there is this to be said, that whenever a letter for Edenbridge gets out of its own course, and into the stream of letters for Edinburgh, the sorters have a predisposition to assimilate it as an Edinburgh letter, and so it gets forwarded to that city. The same thing applies in regard to letters for Leek, Leith, and Keith, and for Musselburgh and Middlesborough—especially when, as is too often the case, the writing is not good; and many other similar instances might be given. Letters for Fiji frequently reach Edinburgh from London and the South, being missent as for Fife in Scotland; and we have it on the authority of the Colonial Postmaster of Fiji, that numbers of letters, papers, &c., directed to Fife, reach the Fiji Islands. Two letters posted at Hamilton, Bermuda, and addressed to Edinburgh, Saratoga Co., N.Y., were recently observed to perform a curious circuit before reaching their destination. Instead of being sent direct to the United States from Bermuda, they were forwarded to London in England; and here, getting into the current of inland correspondence, they were sent to Edinburgh in Scotland. At this stage their wild career was stopped, and they were put in proper course to recross the Atlantic. It is near the truth to say, that similarity of names and bad writing are the causes of very many of the irregularities which befall letters in their transit through the post.

CHAPTER XII.

PIGEON-POST.

THE intellectual superiority of man has enabled him to bend to his purposes the various physical powers of the lower animals—as, for example, the strength of the ox and the fleetness of the horse—and his observation has taught him also to turn to his use some of the instincts of the lower creation, though these gifts may lie hidden beyond the reach of his understanding. Thus the keen scent of the bloodhound, and the sense which enables the "ship of the desert" to sniff the distant spring, are equally become subservient to the interests of man; but it is with reference to another instinct not less remarkable that this chapter is written—the homing instinct of the carrier-pigeon. This gentle bird has long been known as a messenger capable of conveying news from one place to another over considerable distances. It is asserted that "Hirtius and Brutus, at the siege of Modena, held a correspondence by pigeons; and Ovid tells us that Taurosthenes, by a pigeon stained with purple, gave notice to his father of his victory at the Olympic games, sending it to him at Ægina." In Persia and Turkey pigeons were trained for this service, and it is stated that every bashaw had some of these birds reared, in order swiftly to convey news to the seraglio on occasions of insurrection or other emergency. In somewhat modern times the best birds were said to be those of Aleppo, which served as couriers at Alexandretta and Bagdad; but many years ago their services in this line had to be given up, owing to the Kurd robbers killing the pigeons in the course of their journey. It does not appear, however, that, until quite recent times, any great use has been made of these birds by Western nations, at any rate under any extended scheme for commercial or peaceful ends. Yet, by what may seem an incongruity, the dove, which is *par excellence* the emblem of love and peace, has of late years been trained for purposes of war by the great Continental States; and it is impossible to predict how far the fate of nations may be determined hereafter by the performances of these naturally harmless creatures. The following particulars from one of the annual reports on the Post-office will show to what extent service was rendered by carrier-pigeons in keeping up postal communication with Paris when that city was invested during the Franco-German war of 1870-71:—

"As the war proceeded and the hostile forces approached Paris, the risk of interruption to our Indian mails became more and more imminent, and caused serious uneasiness to the Post-office. This feeling, which was not long in communicating itself to the public, the subsequent investment of the capital served to enhance. The mails had now to branch off at Amiens, and go round by Rouen and Tours, at a cost, in point of time, of from thirty to forty hours; but even this circuitous route could not long be depended upon, and nothing remained but to abandon Marseilles altogether as the line of communication for our Indian mails. There was only one alternative—to send them through Belgium and Germany by the Brenner Pass to Brindisi, and thence by Italian packets to Alexandria.

"But it was in respect to the mails for France herself, and especially for Paris, that the greatest perplexity prevailed. As soon as Amiens was threatened—Amiens, the very key-stone of our postal communication with the interior and south of France—it became evident that the route *viâ* Calais would not remain much longer. The alternative routes that presented themselves were *viâ* Dieppe, and *viâ*

Cherbourg or St Malo, and no time was lost in making the necessary arrangements with the Brighton and South-Western Railway Companies. By both Companies trains were kept in constant readiness at the terminus in London, and vessels remained under steam at Newhaven and Southampton, prepared to start at the shortest notice, according to the course events might take. Late in the evening of the 26th of November, intelligence was received in London that the line of communication through Amiens was closed, and the mails were diverted from Calais to Cherbourg; within the next four days Cherbourg was exchanged for Dieppe, and Dieppe soon afterwards for St Malo. As to the means adopted for maintaining communication with Paris, the pigeon-post has become matter of history. Letters intended for this novel mode of transmission had to be sent to the headquarters of the French Post-office at Tours, where, it is understood, they were all copied in consecutive order, and by a process of photography transferred in a wonderfully reduced form to a diminutive piece of very thin paper, such as a pigeon could carry, the photographic process being repeated on their arrival in Paris, for the purpose of obtaining a larger impression. They were essential conditions that these letters should be posted open without cover or envelope, and that they should be registered; that they should be restricted to twenty words; that they should be written in French in clear and intelligible language, and that they should relate solely to private affairs, and contain no allusion either to the war or to politics. The charge was fixed at 5d. for each word (the name and address counting as one word), and 6d. for registration. During the investment, from November 1870 to January 1871, the number of letters sent from London to Tours, for despatch by pigeon-post to Paris, was 1234."

Profiting by the example furnished during the progress of the Franco-German war, the good people of the Fiji Islands have quite recently established a pigeon-post, to serve them in the peaceful pursuits of trade. The colony of Fiji is a group of 225 islands, between which the communications by sailing-vessels or steamers are not very regular, the former being frequently becalmed or retarded by head-winds, while the latter are of small power and low speed. An important part of the trade of the Islands consists in exporting fruit and other produce to Australia and New Zealand, the largest portion consisting of bananas, of which a single steamer will sometimes carry about 12,000 bunches. It is desirable not to cut the bananas till the steamers from Australia and New Zealand arrive at Fiji, and consequently early news of the event is most important to planters in the more remote islands; for if the small schooners or cutters which carry the fruit between the islands arrive too late for the steamer, the poor planters lose their whole produce, which, being perishable, has to be thrown overboard. In these circumstances a pigeon-post has been called into operation; and should this method of communication be extended to all the important islands, as it has already been to some, many a cargo will be saved to the poor planters which would otherwise be wholly lost.

Subjoined is a copy of news by "Pigeon-post," taken from the 'Polynesian Gazette' of the 10th June 1884. It was conveyed by pigeon from Suva to Levuka, a distance as the crow flies of about 40 miles, and the time occupied in transit was 42 minutes, the actual flight to the home of the pigeon taking but 30 minutes :—

"LATEST NEWS FROM SUVA.

"*Per Pigeon-post.*

"The following despatch, dated Suva, Sunday, 3 P.M., was received at Nasova at 3.42 same day:—

" Hero arrived midnight, left Melbourne 26th, Newcastle 29th. Passengers — Mrs Fowler and child, Mrs Cusack and family, Mrs Blythe and child, Messrs F. Hughes, Fullarton, J. Sims, J. B. Matthews, T. Rose, and A. H. Chambers.

"Agents-General of Queensland and Victoria gone to France to interview Ministers *in re* recidivistes question. Marylebone won match, one innings and 115 runs; Australians have since defeated Birmingham eleven. Gunga, Capt. Fleetwood, leaves Sydney 24th ult. New Zealand football team beat N.S. Wales, 34 points to *nil*. Cintra at Newcastle, loading coal for Melbourne, same time as Hero. A.S.N. Co. bought Adelaide Simpsons Birkgate and Fenterden.

".Wairarapa and Penguin just arrived, further news when admitted to pratique.

"*Monday*, 5 P.M.

"Penguin may be expected in Levuka mid-day to-morrow, Tuesday.

"Wairarapa leaves for Levuka at daylight on Wednesday. Hero leaves at 10.30 on Tuesday, for Deuba, and may be expected to arrive in Levuka on Wednesday night."

It is right to add that the "Pigeon-post" of Fiji is not connected with the Postal Department, but is carried on as a private enterprise.

CHAPTER XIII.

ABUSE OF THE FRANKING PRIVILEGE, AND OTHER PETTY FRAUDS.

Abuse of the Franking Privilege.

WHEREVER the use of anything of value is given without the check of a money or other equivalent, the use is sure to degenerate into abuse; and in the experience of the Post-office this has been proved to be the case, both as regards letters and telegrams. In regard to the first, the franking privilege was long found to be a canker eating into the vitals of the Revenue; and its abolition on the introduction of the penny postage in 1840 came none too soon. Had the privilege been longer continued, it is impossible to conceive to what extent the abuse of it might have grown; but what might have occurred here has, in some measure, taken place in the United States, as is shown by the following statement made by the Postmaster-General of that country, about twenty years after the abolition of the privilege in this:—

"Another potent reason for the abolition of the franking privilege, as now exercised, is found in the abuses which seem to be inseparable from its existence. These abuses, though constantly exposed and animadverted upon for a series of years, have as constantly increased. It has been often stated by my predecessors, and is a matter of public notoriety, that immense masses of packages are transported under the Government frank which neither the letter nor the spirit of the statute creating the franking privilege would justify; and a large number of letters, documents, and packages are thus conveyed, covered by the frank of officials, written in violation of law, not by themselves, but by some real or pretended agent; while whole sacks of similar matter, which have never been handled nor even seen by Government functionaries, are transported under franks which have been forged. The extreme difficulty of detecting such forgeries has greatly multiplied this class of offences; whilst their prevalence has so deadened the public sentiment in reference to them, that a conviction, however ample the proof, is scarcely possible to be obtained. The statute of 1825, denouncing the counterfeiting of an official frank under a heavy penalty, is practically inoperative. I refer you to the case reported at length by the United States attorney for the district, as strikingly illustrating this vitiated public opinion, reflected from the jury-box. The proof was complete, and the case unredeemed by a single palliation; and yet the offender was discharged unrebuked, to resume, if it should please him, his guilty task. This verdict of acquittal is understood to have been rendered on two grounds: first, that the accused said he did not commit the offence to avoid the payment of the postages; and second, that the offence has become so prevalent that it is no longer proper to punish it. These are startling propositions, whether regarded in their legal, moral, or logical aspects."

The unblushing way in which the British Post-office in its earlier days was called upon to convey not only franked letters, but, under franks, articles of a totally different class, will be perceived from the following cases. It is not to be understood, however, that the things consigned actually passed through the Post-office, but rather that they were admitted for transport on board the special packet-ships of Government, sailing for the purposes of the Post-office. The cases are taken from the first annual report of the Postmaster-General:—

"Fifteen couples of hounds going to the King of the Romans with a free pass."

"Some parcels of cloth for the clothing colonels in my Lord North's and my Lord Grey's regiments."

"Two servant-maids going as laundresses to my Lord Ambassador Methuen."

"Doctor Crichton, carrying with him a cow and divers other necessaries."

"Three suits of cloaths for some nobleman's lady at the Court of Portugal."

"A box containing three pounds of tea, sent as a present by my Lady Arlington to the Queen-Dowager of England at Lisbon."

"Eleven couples of hounds for Major-General Hompesch."

"A case of knives and forks for Mr Stepney, her Majesty's Envoy to the King of Holland."

"One little parcell of lace, to be made use of in clothing Duke Schomberg's regiment."

"Two bales of stockings for the use of the Ambassador of the Crown of Portugal."

"A box of medicines for my Lord Galway in Portugal."

"A deal case with four flitches of bacon for Mr Pennington of Rotterdam."

The Post-office always had a great deal of trouble in controlling and keeping in check this system of franking; and withal, the privilege was much abused. Before the year 1764, members of Parliament had merely to write their names on the covers to ensure their correspondence free passage through the post; and packets of such franks were furnished by the members to their friends, who laid them past for use as occasion required. Nay, more,—a trade was carried on in franks by the servants of members, whose practice it was to ask their masters to sign them in great numbers at a time. It was even suspected, and probably with sufficient reason, that franks were forged to a large extent; and, had postage been paid on all franked correspondence, it is estimated that the Revenue would have been increased by £170,000. In the hope of imposing some greater check on the evil, it was enacted in 1763 that the whole superscription must be in the handwriting of the member; but even this proved inadequate, and further restrictions were imposed in 1784 and 1795. Some very difficult and troublesome questions arose from time to time in dealing with members' letters. For example, when a member of Parliament had no place of residence in London, and was living out of the United Kingdom, if he had his letters addressed to a public office, or to any solicitor, banker, or other agent, he was not entitled to have his letters free of postage, but, if so directed and delivered, the postage had to be paid. Again, when a member kept up a residence in London, but had his letters directed to another place, the member ceased to enjoy the privilege as regards such letters; as he also did when letters were addressed to his residence in the country, and he happened to be elsewhere at the time of their delivery. Then a Catholic peer dying, who had never taken his seat, and being succeeded by his brother, who was a Protestant, the question is raised whether the latter could claim to use the franking privilege before the issue of the writ calling him to the House of Peers; and the legal decision is given that he could not so exercise the privilege. Keeping the members within proper bounds must evidently have been a task for the officers of the Post-office requiring both vigilance and determination.

But there was another kind of fraud carried on under the privilege granted to soldiers. A surveyor in Scotland thus referred to the irregularity as observed in Scotland in 1797 :—

"As there is so much smuggling of letters already in Scotland, and reason to suspect it will increase from the additional rates, it is matter of serious concern to the Revenue to obtain a clear legal restriction; and I wish you to represent it to the Board at London, in case it may not be too late to offer any hints from the distant situation we are in.

"I have had occasion formerly to observe to you

that a very great evasion of the Post Revenue has taken place—particularly in the north of Scotland—from the privilege granted to soldiers, under cover of which not only a very general opportunity is taken by the common people there to have their letters carried by soldiers to be freed by their officers, and having them again in return under soldiers' addresses; but even in several instances which I observed and detected, persons in higher ranks have availed themselves of this circumstance."

The Post-office has also been exposed to frauds in other ways. Thus it was a common device to take a newspaper bearing the newspaper frank, prick out with a pin certain words in the print making up a message to be sent, and the newspaper so prepared served all the purposes of a letter as between the sender and receiver. Or a message would be written on the cover of a newspaper with the first of all fluids known to us—milk—which, when dry, was not observed, but developed a legible communication subsequently when held to the fire.

The following anecdotes of the evasions of postage are told by the late Sir Rowland Hill :—

"Some years ago, when it was the practice to write the name of a member of Parliament for the purpose of franking a newspaper, a friend of mine, previous to starting on a tour into Scotland, arranged with his family a plan of informing them of his progress and state of health, without putting them to the expense of postage. It was managed thus: He carried with him a number of old newspapers, one of which he put into the post daily. The postmark, with the date, showed his progress; and the state of his health was evinced by the selection of the names from a list previously agreed upon, with which the newspaper was franked. Sir Francis Burdett, I recollect, denoted vigorous health."

"Once on the poet's [Coleridge's] visit to the Lake district, he halted at the door of a wayside inn at the moment when the rural postman was delivering a letter to the barmaid of the place. Upon receiving it she turned it over and over in her hand, and then asked the postage of it. The postman demanded a shilling. Sighing deeply, however, the girl handed the letter back, saying she was too poor to pay the required sum. The poet at once offered to pay the postage; and in spite of some resistance on the part of the girl, which he deemed quite natural, did so. The messenger had scarcely left the place when the young barmaid confessed that she had learnt all she was likely to learn from the letter; that she had only been practising a preconceived trick—she and her brother having agreed that a few hieroglyphics on the back of the letter should tell her all she wanted to know, whilst the letter would contain no writing. 'We are so poor,' she added, 'that we have invented this manner of corresponding and franking our letters.'"

In asserting its monopoly in the carriage of letters in towns, or wherever the Post-office had established posts, there was always trouble; and so much attention did the matter require, that special officers for the duty were employed, called "Apprehenders of Private Letter-carriers." The penalties were somewhat severe when infringements were discovered, and the action taken straight and prompt, as will be seen by the following, which is a copy of a letter written in 1817 to a person charging him with breaking the law:—

"SIR,—His Majesty's Postmasters-General have received an information laid against you, that on the 18th ultimo your clerk, Mr ——, for whom you are answerable, illegally sent three letters in a parcel by a stage-coach to you at Broadstairs, Kent, contrary to the statute made to prevent the sending of letters otherwise than by the post.

"I am commanded by their lordships to inform you that you have thereby incurred three penalties of £5 each, and that they feel it their duty to proceed against you to recover the same.

"Should you have any explanation to give, you will please to address the Postmaster-General.—I am," &c.

In August 1794, at the Warwick Assizes, a carrier between Warwick and Birmingham was convicted of illegally collecting and carrying letters, when penalties amounting to £1500 were incurred; but the prosecution consented to a verdict being taken for two penalties of £5 each, with costs of the suit. A report of the period observed that "this verdict should be a warning to carriers, coachmen, and other persons, against taking up letters tied round with a string or covered with brown paper, under pretence of being parcels, which, the learned judge observed, was a flimsy evasion of the law."

The very cheap postage which we now enjoy has removed the inducement in a large measure to commit petty frauds of this kind on the Post-office Revenue, and the commission of such things may now be said to belong to an age that is past.

Frauds on the Public.

The Post-office, while it is the willing handmaid to commerce, the vehicle of social intercourse, and the necessary helper in almost every enterprise and occupation, becomes at the same time a ready means for the unscrupulous to carry on a wonderful variety of frauds on the public, and enables a whole army of needy and designing persons to live upon the generous impulses of society. While these things go on, —and Post-office officials know they go on,—the Department is helpless to prevent them; for the work of the Post-office is carried on as a secret business, in so far as the communications intrusted to it are concerned, and the contents of the letters conveyed are not its property or interest. There are men and women who go about from town to town writing begging-letters to well-to-do persons, appealing for help under all sorts of pretences; and these persons are as well known, in the sense of being customers to the Department, as a housekeeper is known at her grocer's shop. There are other persons, again, who carry on long-firm swindles through the post, obtaining goods which are never to be paid for; and as soon as the goods are received at one place, the swindlers move on to another place, assume new names, and repeat the operation. The schemes adopted are often very deeply laid; and the police, when once set upon the track, have hard work to unravel the wily plans. But tradespeople are not infrequently themselves very much to blame, as they show themselves too confiding, and too ready to do business with unknown persons.

The following is an instance of a fraud upon well-to-do persons in this country, attempted by an American in the year 1869 :—

The Rev. Mr Champneys, of St Pancras, London, received a letter posted at Florence, Burlington County, New Jersey, U.S., which upon being opened seemed to be not intended for him, but was a communication purporting to be written from one sister to another. The letter made it appear that the writer was highly connected, had fallen into the greatest distress owing to the death of her husband, that her feelings of self-respect had restrained her from telling her griefs till she could no longer withhold them, and making free use of the deepest pathos and high-sounding sentiments, and finally appealing for an immediate remittance. Mr Champneys, not suspecting a fraud, and desiring to help forward the letter to the person who, as he supposed, should have received it, inserted the following advertisement in the 'Times' newspaper :—

"A letter, dated Florence, Burlington County, New Jersey, U.S., intended for Mrs Lucy Campbell, Scotland, has been misdirected to Rev. W. Champneys, 31 Gordon Square. Will Mrs Campbell kindly communicate her address immediately ? "

In response to this inquiry, what was Mr Champney's surprise but to find that a large number of persons had received letters in identical terms and in precisely the same circumstances! This of course caused him to reflect, and then the facts became clear to him—which were, that under the guise of a trifling mistake, that of placing a letter in the wrong envelope, a set of dire circumstances were placed before persons who were likely to be kind-hearted and generous, in the hope that, though the writer was unknown to them, they might send some money to cheer a poor but respectable family steeped in calamity!

How far the attempt succeeded does not appear, but Mr Champneys very properly at once wrote a letter to the 'Times' exposing the fraud, and it is to be hoped that some generous souls were in consequence saved from folly.

One more instance—but one coming within the class of the "confidence trick." In several country newspapers the following advertisement made its appearance:—

"An elderly bachelor of fortune, wishing to test the credulity of the public, and to benefit and assist others, will send a suitable present of genuine worth, according to the circumstances of the applicant, to all who will send him 17 stamps—demanded merely as a token of confidence. Stamps will be returned with the present." And then the address followed, which was not always the same in all the advertisements.

The advertiser alone would be able to say how far he profited by this little arrangement, but some idea of the simplicity of mankind may be derived from the fact that between 300 and 400 letters for this person, each containing 17 stamps, reached the Dead-letter Office—owing doubtless to his having "moved on" from the places where he had lived, in consequence of their becoming too warm to hold him. Specimens of the letters written by the dupes are as follows:—

1. "The Rev. —— encloses 17 stamps. He is a clergyman with very limited means, and the most useful present to him would be five pounds. If his application be not agreeable, he requests that the stamps be returned."

2. "I have enclosed the 17 stamps, and shall be very pleased to receive any present you will send me. As I am not very well off, what I would like very much would be a *nice black silk dress*, which I should consider a rich reward for my credulity."

3. "Mrs —— presents her compliments to the 'elderly bachelor,' and in order to amuse him by her credulity encloses 17 stamps, and thus claims the promised present. Her position and circumstances are good, she mixes in gay society,

and is quite an adept at dancing the polka mazourka. These details may determine the suitability of the present."

4. "Having read your advertisement testing the 'credulity of the public,' I feel disposed on my part to test the upright and honourable intentions of a stranger, contrary to the opinion of some, who tell me it is only a hoax, or, worse, a mere take-in. I therefore, with the honesty of an Irishman, beg to say I am a clergyman's wife, mother of nine children,—the six eldest fine enterprising sons; the three youngest, engaging, intelligent girls. We Irish generally have larger hearts than purses. I therefore lay these facts before you, an Englishman, knowing that a Briton's generosity and capabilities are proverbially equal.—Hoping I may be able to prove I have formed a correct opinion of advertiser's truthfulness, I am," &c.

After this we may afford to smile, and use the words of a very old author with every confidence of their freshness: "Oh where shall wisdom be found? where is the place of understanding?"

CHAPTER XIV.

STRANGE ADDRESSES.

THE addresses of letters passing through the post have often very curious features, arising from various causes: sometimes the whole writing is so bad as to be all but illegible; sometimes the orthography is extremely at fault; sometimes the writer, having forgotten the precise address, makes use of a periphrase; sometimes the addresses are insufficient; and sometimes the addresses are conjoined with sketches on the envelopes showing both artistic taste and comic spirit. Post-office sorters, who constantly have passing through their hands writing of every style and every degree of badness, acquire an aptitude for deciphering manuscript; and writing must be bad indeed, if to be read at all, when it fails to be deciphered in the Post-office. A very large collection might be made of the vagaries of writers in the addresses placed by them on letters; but the following will give some idea, though not a complete idea, of one of the troubles met with in dealing with post-letters.

STRANGE ADDRESSES.

Some time ago the Danish and Norwegian Consul at Ipswich, being struck by the ever-varying way in which the word "Ipswich" was spelt in the addresses of letters reaching him from abroad, took the pains to make a record of each new style of spelling, and after a time he was able to collect together fifty-seven incorrect methods of spelling the word "Ipswich," which had been used upon letters addressed to him. They are given as follows, viz. :—

Elsfleth, Epshvics, Epshvidts, Epsids, Epsig, Epsvet, Epsvidts, Epwich, Evswig, Exwig, Hoispis, Hvisspys, Ibsvi, Ibsvig, Ibsvithse, Ibwich, Ibwigth, Ispsich, Ie yis wich, Igswield, Igswig, Igswjigh, Ipesviok, Ipiswug, Ipswitis, Ipsiwisch, Ipsovich, Ipsveten, Ipsvick, Ipsvics, Ipsvids, Ipsvidts, Ipsvig, Ipsvikh, Ipsyits, Ipsvitx, Ipsvoigh, Ipsweh, Ipsweich, Ipswgs, Ipswiche, Ipswick, Ipswict, Ipswiceh, Ipswig, Ipswigh, Ipswight, Ipswish, Ipswith, Ipswitz, Ispich, Ispovich, Ispwich, Ixvig, Iysuich, Uibsvich, Vittspits.

Letters so addressed generally reached the Consul in direct course of post, though some of them were occasionally delayed by being first sent to Wisbeach. In other cases assistance was given in reading the addresses by the northern version of the county "Suffolg" following the word intended for Ipswich.

The address,
    23 Adne Edle Street, London,
proved to be intended for
    2 Threadneedle Street, London.

In another case,

           No. 52 Oldham & Bury, London,

was written for

           No. 52 Aldermanbury, London.

On another occasion the following address appeared on a letter:—

        too dad Thomas
           hat the ole oke
              Otchut
                    10 Bary. Pade.
Sur plees to let ole feather have this sefe ;

the address being intended for

        The Old Oak Orchard,
            Tenbury.

A further odd address was as follows, written, it is presumed, by a German :—

Tis is fur old Mr Willy wot brinds de Baber in Lang Kaster ware ti gal is. gist rede him assume as it cums to ti Pushtufous ;

the English of the address being—

This is for old Mr Willy what prints the paper in Lancaster where the jail is. Just read him as soon as it comes to the Post-office.

The next address is one made use of, apparently, owing to the true and particular addresses being lost, but the directions given served their purpose, and the letter was duly delivered :—

STRANGE ADDRESSES. 193

For a gentleman residing in a street out of the —— Road, London.

He is a shopkeeper, sells newspapers and periodicals to the trade, and supplies Hawkers, and others with cheap prints, some of which are sold by men in the street. he has for years bought the waste of the Illustrated —— their prints printed in colours particularly. he is well known in the locality, being wholesale. Postman will oblige if he can find this.

Similar cases are as follows, but we are unable to say whether the addresses given served their intended purpose :—

Mr ——. Travelling Band, one of the four playing in the street.
     Persha [Pershore],
        Worcestershire.
Please to find him if possible.

To E——, a cook as lived tempery with a Mrs L——, or some such a name, a shoemaker in Castle St. about No. —— Hoburn in 1851 ; try to make this out. She is a Welsh person about 5 feet 1—stoutish. Lives in service some ware in London or naboured. London.

This is for her that maks dresses for ladies, that livs at tother side of road to James Brocklip.
     Edensover,
        Chesterfield.

This is for the young girl that wears spectacles, who minds two babies.
     30 Sherriff St.,
       Off Prince Edwin St,
         Liverpool.

In two further instances the indications sufficed, and the letters were duly delivered. Thus—

> To my sister Jean,
> Up the Canongate,
> Down a Close,
> Edinburgh.
> She has a wooden leg.

And—

> My dear Ant Sue as lives in the Cottage by the Wood near the New Forest.

In this case the letter had to feel its way about for a day or two, but Ant Sue was found living in a cottage near Lyndhurst.

Another letter was addressed thus :—

> This letter is for Mrs ——. She lives in some part of Liverpool. From her father John ——, a tailor from ——; he would be thankful to some Postmaster in Liverpool if he would find her out.

Unfortunately, in this instance the directions given failed to trace the person to whom it was sent, and it had to go to that abyss of "rejected addresses," the Dead-letter Office.

It occasionally happens that when the eye is unable to make out an address, the ear comes to the rescue. In London a letter came to hand directed to

> Mr Owl O'Neil,
> General Post Office.

But no one was known there of that name. A clerk, looking at the letter, commenced to repeat aloud, "Mr Owl O'Neil, Mr Owl O'Neil," when another clerk, hearing him, exclaimed, " Why ! that must be intended for Mr Rowland Hill," — which indeed proved to be the case. A similar circumstance happened in Edinburgh with a letter from Australia, addressed to
>Mr ———
>Johns. 7.
>Scotland.

It proved to be intended for Johnshaven, a village in the north of Scotland.

Two odd addresses are as follows, one being from America, the other from Ireland :—

>Little Alice,
>>Serio-Comic Singer,
>>>London, England.

>to Edinburgh City, Scotland,
>>For Pat Feeley, Katie Kinnigan's Son,
>>>Ould fishmarket close,
>>>>Number 42, send this with speed.

An American gentleman having arrived in England, and not knowing where a sister was residing at the time, addressed a letter to her previous residence thus—

>Upper Norwood,
>>or Elsewhere.

The letter having been delivered to the lady, the writer intimated to the Post-office that he had received a reply in ordinary course, and explaining that the letter had been delivered to her on the top of a stage-coach in Wales. In admiration of the means taken to follow up his sister, the writer ventured to add, "that no other country can show the parallel, or would take the trouble at any cost."

It would be impossible to explain in words the difficulties that are met with, and the successes which are obtained, in deciphering badly written addresses; and facsimiles of the directions upon some such letters are therefore appended to enable the reader to appreciate the facts. In the London Post-office indistinctly addressed letters are at once set aside, so as not to delay the work of sortation, and are carried forthwith to a set of special officers who have an aptitude for deciphering indistinct writing. These officers, by a strange contradiction in the sense of things, are called the "blind officers"; and here the letters are rapidly disposed of, either by having the addresses read and amended, or marked with the name of a post-town for which the letters may be supposed to be intended. To facilitate this special work, the blind officers are furnished with a series of gazetteers and other books containing the names of gentlemen's seats, farms, and the like, throughout the country, and many a letter reaches

STRANGE ADDRESSES. 197

the hands of the person addressed through a reference to these books.

In addition to instances of indistinctly addressed letters, a few specimens of addresses of an artistic and humorous character are furnished in this chapter.

> E C ——
> Seaman H. M. S. Danae
> Sanlaryhon Cape cash
> ancel orelo whine
>
> Read
> E.C. ————
> Sierra Leone
> Cape Coast Castle
> or elsewhere

> Mers ——
> 50 Wilewham
> Scotlend Road
> Jeverlebool
>
> Read
> 50 .... Lane?
> Scotland Road
> Liverpool

> mrs S   at mr Nows
> grasling man the forle S Raa
> Guegeulscutt de laghi
>   Mg sachi
>
> Read
>   Hugglescote
>   Ashby de la Zouch
>   Warwickshire

> Mr chole ———
> I should late palce
> good Street give to
>   London him
>
> Read
> Mr C ———
>   7 Charlotte Place
>   Gooage Street W

Read
    No 1306 Pvt W———
    No 2 Section 1st Oxfordshire
        Light Infantry
    Convalescent Depôt
        Madras, East Indies

Read
    Mrs ———
    103 Minories
    Nr Aldgate Church
        London

> Mr W. —————
> at Joe gregrey
>
> harayr Wile
> haroeyr
>   middlesex
>
> Read
>   Harrow Weald
>   Harrow

> gunner John —————
>   of battery
> b brigade royl
> horse tileryworloyg
> kent
>
> Read
>   Gunner John
>   "G" Battery, B Brigade
>   Royal Horse Artillery
>   Woolwich

> *Miss* ―――
> 37 Queen St
> 3 Tratje ord
> Newfarm Essex
>
> Read
> 37 Queen Street
> Stratford New Town
> E

> Wᵐ ―
>
> 60 Olena Rd
>
> (Read
> Forest Gate)
> Hunter Gate

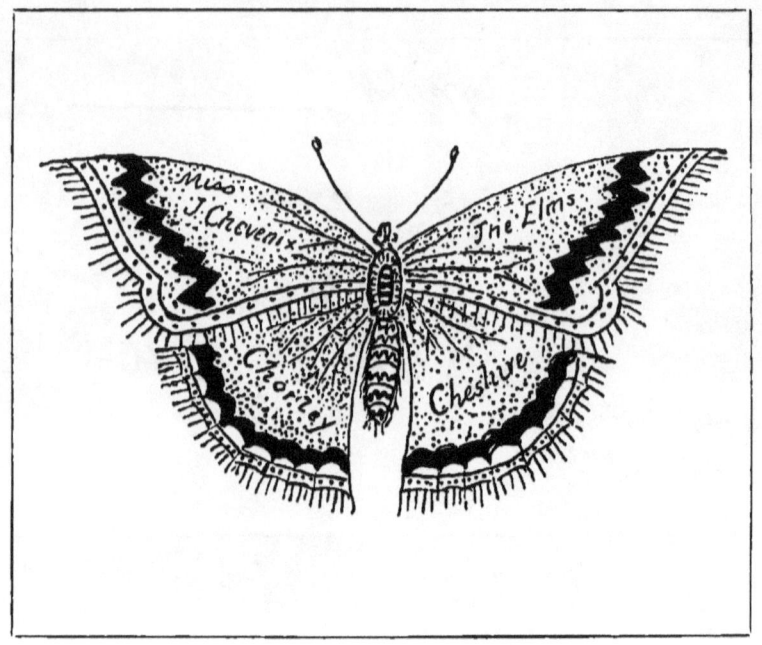

STRANGE ADDRESSES.

STRANGE ADDRESSES. 207

The letter, of which the above represents the address, was posted in a town in the north of England, and delivered to the editor of the 'Courant' in Edinburgh. A facsimile of a portion of the communication enclosed is given on the following page, which will give an idea of the interest attaching to editorial work, and afford some valuable information to the reader!

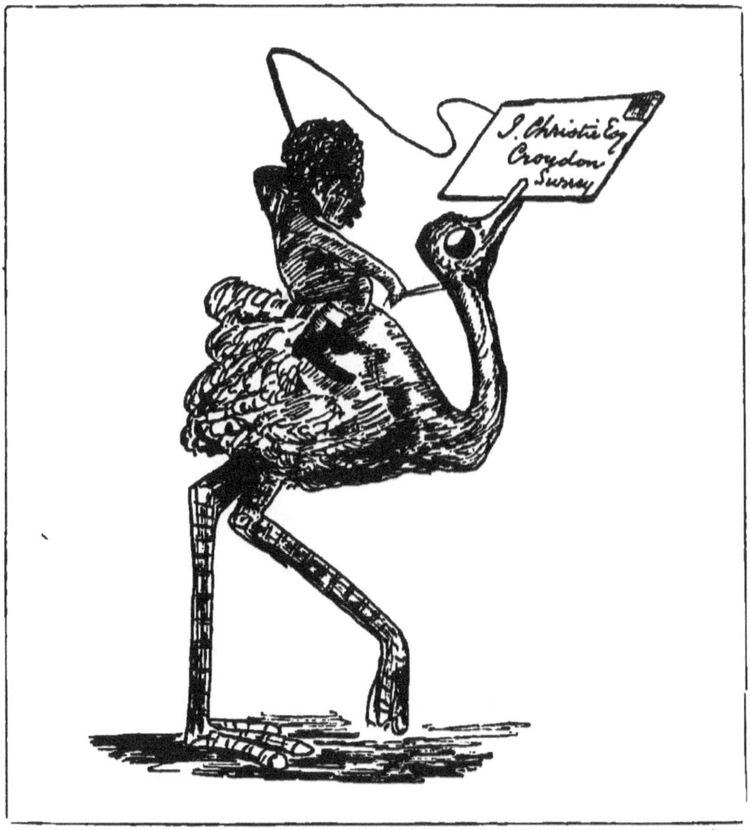
J. Christie Esq
Croydon
Surrey

J.B.ROSS ESQ.
RAVELSTONE
ALNWICK
NORTHUMBERLAND

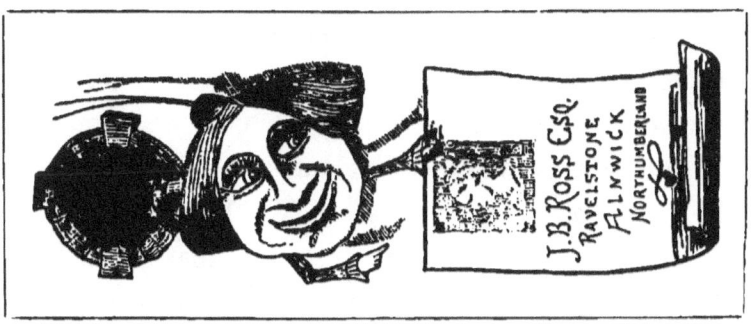

CHAPTER XV.

POST-OFFICE ROBBERIES.

IF records are not now forthcoming of all the robberies which have been committed upon the Post-office from the earliest times, we may be assured that an institution such as it is, maintaining agencies all over the country, and having to keep up communications between those agencies, would be exposed at all times and at all points to the risk of robbery, whether by the dashing boldness of the highwayman, or the less pretentious doings of the town housebreaker. To us who live in an age when the public roads are generally safe to travellers, it is difficult to realise the dangers that lurked in the highways at no more remote a period than last century; nor can we well realise a state of things under which mail-coaches in this our quiet England had to be protected by guards armed to the teeth. We have it handed down, however, as a historical fact, that when, in 1720, Belsize House, Hampstead, was opened as a place of public resort, the programme announcing its attractions contained the following item: "And for the security of its guests, there are twelve stout fellows completely armed, to patrol betwixt London and Belsize, to prevent the insults of highwaymen or footpads which may infest the road." Yet that statement does not give the whole truth, for the road between these two places became so much more dangerous, that after a time "the patrol had to be increased from twelve to thirty stout fellows completely armed, independently of two tall grenadiers who mounted guard over the gate of the mansion."

Again, it is recorded that "even the toll-house keepers in London were so liable to be robbed, that they had to be furnished with arms, and enjoined to keep no money in their houses after eight o'clock at night. The boldness with which street robberies still continued to be committed was evinced so late as 1777, when the Neapolitan ambassador was robbed in his coach in Grosvenor Square by four footpads armed with pistols."

Thus it will be seen that the roads leading out of London were infested by disorderly characters; and robberies of the mails proceeding to and from London were of frequent occurrence, as appears from official records referring to the close of last century and the commencement of this.

In the coaching days very frequent robberies of the mails took place, though they were protected by armed guards, and some of these robberies have been described in the chapter relating to mail-coaches.

The passengers who travelled in the mail-coaches, with the knowledge of these molestations going on around them, must have been kept in a constant state of alarm; and the circumstance could not fail materially to discourage travelling in days when the facilities for exchanging visits were few compared with what we now enjoy.

The state of things already described as regards the mail-coaches, extended also to the horse-posts, the riders being attacked probably more freely than the coaches; for while the plunder to be had would be less, the postboys were not in a position to make so great a show of defence. Nor did the severity of the laws restrain evil-doers, either in England or Scotland, where sentences of execution were from time to time carried out upon the delinquents.

On the 7th of July 1685, the post-rider who was proceeding through the extreme north of England, on his way from London to the Scottish metropolis, was known to have been twice stopped, and to have been robbed of his mail, the scene of the occurrence being near Alnwick, in Northumberland. In connection with this event, of which an account has been handed down by Lauder of Fountainhall, a curious and romantic anecdote has been told by Wilson in his 'Tales of the Borders,' and by Chambers as one of his Scottish traditional stories.

Sir John Cochrane of Ochiltree, in Ayrshire, was one of Argyle's chief associates in that unfortunate and abortive attempt, made by the exiles in the year above named, to compass the overthrow of the reigning monarch, James II., so far as Scotland was concerned, which attempt was only part of the more general scheme of the exiles abroad—both English and Scotch—and the disaffected at home, to drive the king from his throne, and to place the Duke of Monmouth thereon in his stead. After a variety of disasters experienced by the limited following which Argyle and his party had been able to bring together, and when hope of a successful issue could no longer secure cohesion, there ensued a general break-up of the party, accompanied by what is to be looked for in similar situations—a general flight and *sauve qui peut*. Sir John Cochrane sought refuge in the house of a relative in Renfrewshire, where, however, he was discovered by his pursuers at the end of June; and on the 3d of July, Sir John, his son, and another traitor were brought into Edinburgh, " bound and barefooted, by the hangman," and cast into the Tolbooth to await their doom.

What daring enterprises may not flow from a woman's love and devotion, when a parent's liberty is imperilled or his life is at stake! Sir John had a daughter called Grizel, who fondly loved him, and who, on visiting him in prison, had not failed to show the intensity of her filial regard; nor was Sir John slow to reciprocate these feelings on his part. Being then but eighteen years of age, she nevertheless conceived the daring thought of intercepting the mail-packet coming from the South, which was supposed to contain a warrant for the execution of her father; and with this object in view, she proceeded to Berwick-on-Tweed alone. Here she habited herself in male attire; and being armed, and mounted on a fleet horse, she set out upon her extraordinary and perilous adventure.

On Tweedmouth Moor, it is narrated, she fell in with the postboy, who, under threats of immediate death, gave up his charge, Grizel riding off with the mail-packet and the postboy's horse, from which he had been unseated.

Under these circumstances, the warrant not reaching its destination, it could not be put into execution, and the delay which took place before another could be procured was turned to account by Sir John's friends, who exerted themselves on his behalf. Sir John was the younger son of a rich family, from whom a ransom was to be had; and it is stated that a bribe of £5000 by Lord Dundonald, Cochrane's father, to the priests of the Royal household, was the means of securing a pardon. Sir John lived to become Earl of Dundonald, while Grizel became the wife of John Kerr of Morriston, in Berwickshire; and there can be little doubt that she afterwards exhibited as a wife all the amiable and affectionate qualities of which she proved herself possessed as a daughter.

Unfortunately for the authenticity of the story, so far as Grizel Cochrane's connection with it is concerned, the dates hardly bear the matter out; for if Sir John was lodged in the Tolbooth of Edinburgh on the 3d July, a warrant for his execution could barely have reached Northumberland from London by the 7th: and again, while the story relates that Sir John Cochrane was confined in the Tolbooth, Macaulay states that he " was taken, and sent up to London."

The following story of the robbery of a mail carried by a postboy, is taken from Chambers's 'Domestic Annals of Scotland,' under the date 16th August 1690:—

"Andrew Cockburn, the postboy who carried the packet or letter-bag on that part of the great line of communication which lies between Cockburnspath and Haddington, had this day reached a point in his journey between the Alms-house and Hedderwick Muir, when he was assailed by two gentlemen in masks; one of them mounted on a blue-grey horse, wearing a stone-grey coat with brown-silk buttons—the other riding on a white horse, having a white English grey cloak-coat with wrought silver-thread buttons. Holding pistols to his breast, they threatened to kill him if he did not instantly deliver up the packet, black box, and bag which he carried; and he had no choice but to yield. They then bound him, and leaving him tied by the foot to his horse, rode off with their spoil to Garlton House, near Haddington. As the packet contained Government communications, besides the correspondence of private individuals, this was a crime of a very high nature, albeit we may well believe it was committed on political impulse only. Suspicion seems immediately to have alighted on James Seton, youngest son of the Viscount Kingston, and John Seton, brother of Sir George Seton of Garlton; and Sir Robert Sinclair, the sheriff of the county, immediately sought for these young gentlemen at their father's and brother's houses, but found them not. With great hardihood, they came to Sir Robert's house next morning to inquire, as innocent men, why they were searched for; when Sir Robert, after a short examination in presence of the postboy, saw fit to have them disarmed and sent off to Haddington. It was Sunday, and Bailie Lauder, to whose house they came with their escort, was about to go to church. If the worthy bailie is to be believed, he thought their going to the sheriff's a great presumption of their innocence. He admitted, too, that Lord Kingston had come and spoken to him that morning. Anyhow, he concluded that it might be enough in the meantime if he afforded them a room in his house, secured their horses in his stable, and left them under charge of two of the town-officers. Unluckily, however, he required the town-officers, as usual, to walk before him and his brother magistrates to church—which, it is obvious, interfered very considerably with their efficiency as a guard over the two gentlemen. While things were in this posture, Messrs Seton took the prudent course of making their escape. As soon as the bailie heard of it he left church, and took after them with some neighbours, but he did not succeed in overtaking them. The Privy Council had an extraordinary meeting to take measures regarding this affair, and their first step was to order Bailie Lauder and the two town-officers into the Tolbooth of Edinburgh as close prisoners. A few days afterwards the magistrate was condemned by the Council as guilty of plain fraud and connivance, and declared incapable of any public employment. William Kaim, the smith at Lord Kingston's house of Whittinghame, was also in custody on some suspicion of a concern in this business; but he and the town-officers were quickly liberated.

"John Seton was soon after seized by Captain James Denholm on board a merchant vessel bound for Holland, and imprisoned in the castle of Edinburgh. He underwent trial in July 1691, and by some means escaped condemnation. A favourable verdict did not procure his immediate liberation; but, after three days, he was dismissed on caution, to return into custody if called upon. This final result was the more remarkable, as his father was by that time under charge of having aided in the betrayal of the Bass."

Other instances of such gentlemanlike performances in waylaying the post were not unknown in the primitive days of the Post-office, for about the year 1658 the following notice was issued for the discovery of a gentleman of the law who had taken to evil ways by intercepting the mail: " Whereas Mr Herbert Jones, attorney-at-law in the town of Monmouth, well known by being several years together under-sheriff of the same county, hath of late divers times robbed the mail coming from that town to London, and taken out divers letters and writs, and is now fled from justice," &c.

In August 1692, the postboy riding the last stage towards Edinburgh with the mail from England, was robbed on the 13th of that month, at a short distance from Edinburgh. A record of the period relates that the robbery was committed by "a person mounted on horseback with a sword about him, and another person on foot with a pistol in his hand, upon the highway from Haddington to Edinburgh, near that place thereof called Jock's Lodge (a mile from town) about ten hours of the night." The robbers took "the packet or common mail, with the horse whereon the boy rode." A proclamation was issued by the Scottish Privy Council, offering a reward of a hundred pounds for the apprehension of the offenders, with a free pardon to any one of them who should inform upon the rest; but with what result is not known.

On the 13th September 1786, the mail-rider from the North charged with the conveyance of mails for Edinburgh, having reached Kinross about midnight, proceeded to change horses as usual in a stable-yard at that place. The mail-bags he deposited on the back of a chaise in the yard until he should be ready to resume his journey. As was his custom, he then went into the stable to give a feed of corn to his horse; but while so engaged, the bags were abstracted and the contents stolen. Two brothers, who were proved to have been in the neighbourhood at the time, and to whom some of the stolen property was traced, were arraigned for the crime before the High Court of Justiciary in Edinburgh, and being found guilty, were sentenced to be executed.

The following is a somewhat fuller account of a post robbery on the public road, which occurred a few years later:—

In 1802, the mails between Edinburgh and Glasgow were still conveyed by men travelling on horseback—the route taken being by way of Falkirk—the hour of despatch from Glasgow being 9 P.M., and the hour of arrival in Edinburgh about 6 A.M. or 7 A.M. The riders of this mail seem to have had sections of the road apportioned to them — one rider covering the road from Glasgow to Falkirk, the other taking the stage from Falkirk to Edinburgh. On the morning of the 1st of August in that year, the rider for the east stage — named William Wilson — received the Glasgow mail-bag entire and duly sealed at Falkirk, and thereafter set out towards Edinburgh. When he approached a rising ground called Sighthill—probably a wooded knoll bearing that name, about three miles from Linlithgow, on the road to Polmont—he observed two men coming down towards him, and who, so soon as they got near him, placed themselves one on each side of his horse, and immediately seized him. One of the two men held something in his hand, and threatened Wilson that if he offered to speak his brains would be blown out. Then he was led away into a field of corn, where he was blindfolded by one of the men with his own handkerchief, and his hands tied behind his back; thereupon he was thrown down, and his legs bound together to prevent his getting away. Meanwhile the other man led away his horse and rifled the mail. The post-rider remained in his unhappy position for about an hour, when he managed to extricate himself, and proceeding to the first house he could reach, implored the inmates "for God's sake" to let him in, as he had been robbed. Having been admitted and obtained assistance, he returned to the scene of his adventure, and found the empty mail-bag at the foot of a haystack, while the horse was recovered a little distance away. The mail contained bills, &c., for something like £1300 or £1400.

The robbery of the mail caused great excitement in Edinburgh so soon as it became known, and no long time elapsed before the perpetrators were in the hands of the authorities. The two men concerned in it proved to be James Clark, *alias* Alex. Stewart, and Robert Brown, formerly privates in the Foot Guards. No sooner had they got back to Edinburgh—where they had previously lodged—than they commenced to change some of the bank-notes taken from the mail-bag, and got the worse of drink; and being once suspected, the evidence soon accumulated and became strong against them. They were tried for the offence before the High Court of Justiciary in Edinburgh in November following, and being found guilty, were sentenced to be executed.

This robbery would appear to have had the effect of stirring up the public mind to demand a means of conveying the mails between the two cities affording greater security; for an agitation immediately followed for the setting up of coaches or diligences to carry the mails between those cities. Owing, however, to difficulties and disagreements between the merchants and traders as to the hours of departure and arrival, and to wranglings over the particular route to be journeyed, the idea was abandoned, and the horse-post as of old was meanwhile continued. The robbery seems not to have been soon forgotten, however; for we find that towards the close of 1802 a proposal was made to enter into an agreement for the service with "an officer of the Mid-Lothian Cavalry, and master of the Riding Academy in Edinburgh," who offered to conduct and carry on the service in a masterly and military manner for an allowance of £450 per annum — the riders to be employed being none other than able and active dragoons. But in the nature of things such a mail-service could not continue, and negotiations still proceeded for the employment of diligences—not resulting in success, however, until the year 1805, when the first mail-coach between Edinburgh and Glasgow was put upon the road.

A somewhat similar attack upon a postboy was made in Yorkshire in the year 1798, when the rider's life was threatened by a highwayman single-handed, and the mails stolen from him. The case is interesting owing to the fact that traces of the robbery were obtained so recently as 1876, though at the period of its occurrence no trace of the highwayman or of his plunder could be discovered.

The official account of the robbery, when it happened, was as follows :—

"The postboy coming from Selby to York was robbed of his mail between six and seven o'clock this evening. About three miles on this side of Selby he was accosted by a man on foot, with a gun in his hand, who asked him if he was the postboy, and at the same time seized hold of the bridle. Without waiting for any answer, he told the boy he must immediately unstrap the mail and give it him, pointing the muzzle of the gun at him whilst he did it. When he had given up the mail, the boy begged he would not hurt him; to which the man replied he need not be afraid, and at the same time pulled the bridle from the horse's head. The horse immediately galloped off with the boy, who had never dismounted.

"He was a stout man, dressed in a drab jacket, and had the appearance of being a heckler. The boy was too much frightened to make any other remark on his person, and says he was totally unknown to him. The mail contained the bags for Howden and London, Howden and York, and Selby and York."

Although a reward of £200 was offered for the discovery of the robber, and a free pardon to any accessory who might turn accuser, nothing was heard of the matter at the time, though suspicion, it is said, pointed to some of the inhabitants of Selby. The robbery might perhaps have remained forgotten, but that, upon a public-house situated on the Church-hill, Selby, being pulled down in 1876, a suit of clothes, a sou'-wester hat, and an old mail-bag marked "Selby" were found in the roof. There is little doubt that these were the clothes worn by the robber on the occasion under notice, and that the bag (which is a sort of waterproof-pouch, furnished with two straps to pass over the shoulders) is the identical bag which contained the mails stolen in 1798. When the foundations of this old public-house were turned up, the discovery was made of several coffins containing bodies in a good state of preservation—a circumstance, when taken in connection with the traces of the mail-robbery and the public character of the house, ominous in the extreme. The case is one which might be taken as somewhat proving the suggestion put forward by Smollett in ' Roderick Random' as to the intimate relations which existed between the *personnel* of the innkeepers and the common highwaymen—the former being well aware of the profession followed by the latter, if not actually sharers in their plunder.

On Wednesday the 23d October 1816, at half-past nine in the evening, the postboy carrying the mail-bags from Teignmouth and neighbouring places to Exeter, was assaulted " in a most desperate and inhuman manner" near the village of Alphington, and plundered of the Teignmouth and Exminster bags. The poor man was attacked with such fury that he was felled from his horse, came to the ground on his head, which was fractured in two places, and in consequence of his injuries, he remained insensible for some time. When he regained consciousness in the Exeter Hospital, whither he had been conveyed, he was able to explain that, at the time of the attack, he was walking his horse up a hill, that the assailant was a young man, and that he was mounted on a grey horse. This horse was supposed afterwards to be traced, though the robber failed to be discovered, notwithstanding that a reward of £50 was offered for his discovery and conviction. "A horse exactly answering the description," says an official record, " was taken from a field near Dawlish on the Wednesday night, and turned back to the same place before daybreak on Thursday, having evidently been rode very fast, and gored very much in the sides." The owner of the horse could give no assistance in the matter, nor had he suspicions against any one; so that it would appear the robber had taken the horse surreptitiously for his purpose. The mail-bags were afterwards recovered, with some few of the letters opened; but it did not appear that any property was missing. The unfortunate rider, whose name was "Caddy," remained in hospital till the January following, when he was discharged; but in the month of May his wounds broke out afresh, and he had to return to hospital, being now become subject to epileptic fits owing to his injuries. As he was no longer able for service, he was granted a gratuity by the Post-office; and it is not probable that he survived very long thereafter. With the mere expectation of getting some little gain from the robbery, the marauder had all but killed the poor postboy, who had a wife and two children dependent on him; and he has in his evil-doing given a good example of what Burns calls " man's inhumanity to man," that " makes countless thousands mourn."

In the year 1797 the deputy-postmaster of the Orkneys and his son, a lad of about sixteen years of age, were tried at the High Court of Justiciary, Edinburgh, on a charge of breaking open certain post-letters while in their custody in course of transit, and therefrom abstracting money. The indictment contained a further charge of forgery against the elder prisoner, the deputy having endorsed another person's name upon a money-order contained in one of the stolen letters. The thefts were committed at different times in 1794 and 1796, and the specific cases upon which evidence was led were in respect of the following letters—viz., two letters sent at different times to Orkney by a seaman in the Royal Navy, one containing a guinea-note and half a guinea in gold, the other containing either a guinea in gold or a note for that amount; a letter from London for Orkney, containing a money-order for £5, 5s.; and a letter from Perth for Orkney, enclosing a note for a guinea: the whole amount involved being under £9.

In the course of the trial it was proved that the deputy was guilty, certain of the missing letters having been found in his house, and the son had already confessed to what was charged against him. The whole cases were clearly made out to the satisfaction of the jury, who returned a verdict accordingly against both prisoners, but with a recommendation of mercy towards the son of the deputy, on the score of his tender years. Sentence was pronounced on the 5th September, and the date of execution fixed for the 18th October. By the exercise of the Royal prerogative, George III. granted a free pardon to the deputy's son, who was forthwith set at liberty; but it is a melancholy reflection, that for delinquencies involving the loss of so small a sum as £9, the deputy-postmaster should, on the date fixed for his execution, have actually been led forth to his doom. In a report of the circumstance written at the time, it is stated "that he was attended by the Rev. Mr Black of Lady Yester's, and Mr Struthers of the Relief congregation, and behaved in a manner suitable to his unhappy situation"! God forbid that there should be a standard of deportment for occasions like this, where, to our more humane notions, the punishment so fearfully outweighs the offence.

Early in the year 1849 a sad blow fell upon the

postmaster of a certain town in Wales, on its being discovered that an assistant in his office, a daughter of his own, had been stealing post-letters. In the course of investigations made into her misdoings, it was discovered that the thefts had been going on for a period of seven years, during which time she had accumulated as much jewellery and haberdashery as would have stocked a small shop—and besides, money to the amount of £95. The letters from which the property had been taken were between two and three hundred, and these she had kept, so that it was possible to restore to the owners, in many cases, the stolen articles. On the 20th March the unfortunate and misguided creature was tried, on the charge of stealing a particular letter, and was convicted—the sentence passed upon her being *transportation for ten years.*

It was afterwards ascertained that the motive underlying this long career of thieving was a desire to amass such a dowry as would improve her prospects in the matter of obtaining a husband.

Hatton Garden Robbery.

On Thursday the 16th November 1881, the whole country was made aware, through the daily papers, that a most daring Post-office robbery had been committed in London the previous afternoon, the scene of the event being the Hatton Garden Branch Office, situated in the busy district of Holborn. The time and plan of carrying out the undertaking were not such as are usually chosen for attempts of this kind, the hour at which the robbery was effected being 5 P.M., when the office was thronged with the public purchasing stamps, or doing other business in view of the night-mail despatch. Nor was there any furtive mode of proceeding in the ordinary sense, but a bold and dashing stroke for the chances of success or failure.

On the afternoon of the day of the robbery, a murky fog, such as Londoners know so well and heartily dislike, hung over the metropolis. The street lamps afforded but a dull light in the thoroughfares; shops and offices were lighted up for the evening's business; and the afternoon's work in the Hatton Garden Post-office was at its height (the registered-letter bag, containing some forty registered letters, having just been deposited in an ordinary bag hanging from a peg in the office), when suddenly, and without apparent cause, the whole of the lights in the office went out, and the place was plunged in almost total darkness. Consternation took possession of the female clerks behind the counter, while young clerks and boys from warehouses and offices, conceiving the occasion to be one for noise and merriment, helped to increase the confusion by clamour and hubbub outside the counter. No long time elapsed before matches were obtained and tapers lit, when it was immediately discovered that the tap of the gas-meter in the basement had been turned off; but on the tap being turned on again, the jets in the office were relit, and the place resumed its wonted appearance. The young ladies in the office being now able to see around them, soon detected the absence of the bag, which had been left hanging on the peg, and which they knew had not yet been despatched by them. It did not take long to realise that the bag had vanished—in fact, had been stolen; and to this day the property contained in the lost registered letters has not been recovered, nor have the persons concerned in the theft been traced.

It is believed that two or more individuals were engaged in the robbery, the supposition being that one person got down into the basement without attracting attention, and turned off the gas, while another, so soon as darkness supervened, got by some means within the counter, and, unobserved, took the bag from the peg—all concerned making good their escape in the midst of the stir and noise by which they were surrounded. The whole adventure bears the impress of having been carefully planned and cleverly executed, and there is little doubt that the robbery was carried out by men who were experts in their nefarious calling.

The value of the articles contained in the forty registered letters was about £15,000; and as the scene of the robbery lay in the midst of diamond merchants and jewellers, it is not surprising that precious stones and jewellery were the principal contents of these letters. Besides watches, bracelets set with pearls and diamonds, ear-rings, rings, &c., the following articles were among the property stolen— viz., eight parcels of rough diamonds, 147 turquoises, a quantity of small emeralds, 6000 drilled sapphires, 2000 pairs of garnet bores, 240 pairs of sapphire bores, a quantity of sapphires weighing 695 carats, several rubies and sapphires weighing 546 carats, &c., &c.

A reward of £200 was offered by the Postmaster-General, and a further reward of £1000 by certain insurance companies who had insured the valuable letters, for the conviction of the delinquents and the recovery of the stolen property; but the robbery remains to this day one of those which have baffled the skill of the Metropolitan police and the officers of the Post-office to unravel or to bring home to the evil-doers.

Cape Diamond Robbery.

The greater portion of the diamonds found in Griqualand West, in South Africa, are sent weekly to England through the Post-office, made up in packets, which are forwarded as registered letters—the value of these remittances being collectively from £60,000 to £100,000. In April 1880, the sailing of the mail-steamer from Cape Town having been delayed until the day after the arrival of the up-country mails, the bag containing the registered correspondence was left in the registered-letter office of the Cape Town Post-office; not, however, locked up in the safe, where it ought to have been, but carelessly left underneath one of the tables. During the night the office was broken into, and the whole of the diamonds stolen, valued at £60,000. Who the robbers were appears never to have been discovered, and they have doubtless since been in the enjoyment of the fruits of their villanous enterprise. As it is the practice of people in the diamond trade to insure packets of diamonds sent by them, the senders did not suffer anything beyond inconvenience by this robbery; but the insurance companies were involved in the loss, and had to pay claims amounting to £60,000.

The following is an account of a robbery attempted upon a postman in London in July 1847, as officially reported at the time:—

"An attempt was this morning made to murder or seriously to maim Bradley, the Lombard Street letter-carrier, with a view of obtaining possession of the letters for his district. He was passing through Mitre Court, a narrow passage between Wood Street and Milk Street, when the gate of the Court was closed and locked behind him with a skeleton key by, it is believed, three men, who followed him a few yards farther on in the passage. On Bradley getting to a wider part of the Court, one of them felled him to the ground by a heavy blow from a life-preserver; he attempted to rise, but was again knocked down in a similar manner. He then felt that they tried to force from him his letter-bags, but fortunately the mouths of them were, for security, twisted round his arm. They continued their blows; but Bradley retained sufficient consciousness to call out 'Murder!' so as to be heard by some of the porters in the adjoining warehouses, who ran to see what was the matter, but unluckily the villains escaped. Poor Bradley is most seriously injured—so much so that he may be considered in some danger."

An idea of the amount of property the thieves would have obtained had Bradley not held the bags tightly (even under such circumstances), may be formed from the fact that he had in his possession thirty-seven registered letters containing property, besides all the other letters for Messrs Overend, Gurney, & Co., Robarts, Curtis, & Co., Glynn & Co., the London and County Bank, as well as those for thirty-four other houses in Lombard Street. It was believed at the time that the value of the property in Bradley's possession amounted to hundreds of thousands of pounds.

A daring robbery of a Berlin postman occurred not very long ago, when the outrage was accompanied by a still more atrocious crime—the murder of the postman. The man was one of a class who deliver money remittances at the addresses of the persons to whom they are sent, under a system which prevails in some countries of the Continent, and he had with him cash and notes to the amount of some £1500. The robber and murderer, a man of great bodily strength, had so arranged that a small remittance would fall to be delivered at his address on Monday morning—an occasion when a large number of remittances are received; and on the postman reaching the place, and proceeding to pay the requisite sum, the occupier of the premises felled him with a hammer, and with repeated blows killed him outright. It was evident from the circumstances that the murderer had duly planned the outrage, for the room rented was near to the starting-point of the postman, so that he should not have paid away any portion of his charge when he reached the room. The body of the poor postman was found afterwards cold and stiff, lying in a pool of blood, with his empty and rifled bag beside him; and the weapon with which the perpetrator had achieved the murder, remained there as a witness of the crime. The murderer was said to have previously served in a cuirassier regiment. Before decamping, he had turned the key in the door of his room; and the discovery was only made after a search by the Post-office authorities at the addresses at which the postman had to call, on his failing to return later in the day.

Some years ago the following extensive robbery of letters occurred in London. An unusually large number of complaints were found to be reaching the General Post-office, of the non-receipt by merchants, bankers, and others carrying on business in Lombard Street and its neighbourhood, of letters containing bank-notes, cheques, advices, and important correspondence, sent to them from all parts of the kingdom. The circumstance naturally gave rise to careful inquiry on the part of the Post-office authorities, with the result that suspicion fell upon a young postman of nineteen years of age, through whose hands many of the missing letters would in ordinary course have to pass. Certain Bank of England notes, which had been contained in some of the letters, were found to have been cashed; and the names endorsed upon them, though fictitious, were in a handwriting resembling that of the young man suspected. Thereupon he was arrested and searched, when in a pocket-book on his person were found two £5 notes, which had been forwarded from Norfolk to a banking-house in London, but had failed to reach their destination. In a pocket in his official coat were found also some thirty-five letters of various dates, which he had neglected to deliver, to the inconvenience or loss no doubt of the persons addressed; but the most astonishing part of the business is, that when his locker or cupboard at the General Post-office was examined, about 1500 letters were found there which he had stopped, the dates upon the envelopes showing that his delinquencies had extended over several months. This young man, upon being tried for the offences named, was convicted, and with the usual severity observed in similar circumstances, the judge passed upon the prisoner a sentence of six years' penal servitude.

The following curious instance of the wholesale misappropriation of post-letters also came under the notice of the Post-office authorities in London a few years ago:—

A man was observed one day carrying off some boards from a building in course of erection in the Wandsworth Bridge Road, Fulham, and being pursued by a constable, he dropped the timber and made off. The man was, however, captured and taken to the police-station, whereupon the place where he lived was searched for other stolen property. His habitation was situated upon a waste piece of ground on the banks of the Thames, the erection being of wood built upon piles, and so placed as to be almost entirely surrounded by water. Here this man, who was a barge-owner, and who was passing under an assumed name, had lived in isolation for about a year; the position selected for his home being one calculated to afford him that complete seclusion from social intercourse which would seem to have been his aim. In the course of their examination of the contents of the hut, the police found not only more stolen timber, but various other articles, the chief of which, in the present connection, were a large lot of post-letters, mail-bags, and articles of postmen's clothing, besides milk-cans and a case of forty rifles. As the inquiry proceeded, it became known that the prisoner was a Post-office pensioner, having been superannuated from his office of postman some three years previously, after having served in that capacity a period of fifteen years. It would seem that his official delinquencies had extended over some six or eight-years; but so far as the letters showed, theft in the ordinary sense could hardly have been the man's purpose, inasmuch as the letters had not been opened, with one exception, and in this instance the person for whom the letter was intended could not be found. The motive underlying this free departure from the ways of honesty seems to have had its root in simple acquisitiveness; the hundredweight of letters, book-packets, &c., the old mail-bags, discarded uniforms, and waste official papers (not to mention the thirty milk-cans, supposed to have been picked up when going his rounds as a postman, and the case of rifles), having been turned to no profitable account. Had the superannuated postman opened the letters found in his premises, the punishment which would have followed would necessarily have been severe. As the case stood, however, he was merely charged under the Post-office Acts with their unlawful detention, and sentence was passed upon him of eighteen months' imprisonment with hard labour. It seems astonishing that this postman should have had the folly to retain about him so long the evidences of his errors, which might at any time have been brought up against him; but perhaps the feeling prompting this may be akin to that which leads criminals to visit the scenes of former iniquities, even when incurring the risk of discovery, and if discovered, of certain punishment.

The following is a case of robbery which occurred in 1883, as reported by the newspapers of the day, the culprit being quite a young person:—

"The most destructive and important case of robbery in connection with Mr Fawcett's plan, introduced some two or three years ago, for facilitating the placing of small sums, by means of postage-stamps, in the Post-office Savings Bank, came before the Bristol magistrates to-day, when Ellen Hunt, a domestic servant, about sixteen years of age, was charged with stealing a large number of letters, some of them containing cheques, the property of the Postmaster-General. Mr Clifton, who prosecuted, said the robberies were of a very extensive character, and might have been fraught with the direst consequences. They had been discovered in a singular manner, no money having been missed; but a large number of circular letters, addressed by the Bristol clerk to officials requiring to be sworn in connection with the School Board election this week, miscarried. Inquiries were made by the Postal authorities, when it was found that all these circulars had been posted at the Redcliffe district office, where the prisoner was the servant of the postmaster, Mr Devine. It was the custom of Mr Devine to place the key of the letter-box in a secret place for the use of himself and his assistants; but the prisoner discovered it, and the circular letters were found in her possession with the postage-stamps off them. They had been removed for payment into the Post-office Savings Bank on the forms by which a shilling's worth of postage-stamps saved up by school-children and others is now accepted by the Savings Bank department of the Post-office; but the most serious part of the case was the fact that in the prisoner's box were discovered the bundles of opened letters now produced by Detective Short, and containing cheques already discovered to the amount of £74, 16s., all of which had been sent through the same post-office. The charge was laid under the 27th section of the Act, but formerly a prisoner would have been liable for such an offence to transportation for life. Some evidence having been given, the girl, who was hysterical throughout the hearing, was remanded. Apparently no effort had been made to deal with the cheques, but the detective stated that the numerous letters had been opened."

Tale of a Banker's Letter.

Towards the close of last century, or early in the present century, a tradesman of the better class carrying on business in a certain town of the west of England, which we shall here call X——, and who also added to his ordinary business that of the agency of a bank, posted a bulky letter containing heavy remittances in notes, addressed to the Bank of England. This letter never reached its destination, and the loss, being of a most serious kind, was soon bruited about, and became the theme, locally, of general conversation. As it happened, the sender was a man of strong political opinions, and having courage to express them, there were many persons holding opposite views who not only regarded him with feelings akin to dislike, but were ready to take up any missile which chance might place in their way to damage their adversary's fair name. While, therefore, the bank agent maintained that he had posted the letter in question, insinuations were set afloat to the effect that he had not done so, and that the object of his allegations was to fend off pressing calls in matters of account. He suffered greatly in reputation from these unsupported stories, though there was nothing else in his circumstances to create suspicion. Time, the great anodyne of scandal, had somewhat assuaged the sufferings of the unfortunate banker, and probably softened the unkind feelings of those who had been disposed to think hardly of him; the loss of the letter itself had ceased to attract attention; and as yet nothing was heard of the letter, or the valuable enclosures which it had contained.

At length, however, the agent received intimation that one of the missing notes — a Bank of England note for £50—which was *stopped* at that establishment, had been presented in London. As the result of inquiries which were made, it was now traced to an old-established silversmith somewhere in the city of London; but beyond this point the search failed, for all the account the silversmith could give was, that he had received the note some time previously from a man of respectable appearance, who had the exterior and conversation of what might be a well-to-do west-country farmer. This man was accompanied to his shop by a young woman of the flash type, to whom the stranger presented two or three rings; purchasing for himself some heavy gold seals, such as were in vogue at the period, a silver tankard or two, and several punch-ladles. In payment of these articles the £50 note was passed, but the silversmith could give no further help;

though hope was not yet extinct, for he added that he should certainly recognise his customers, were they ever to come under his observation again.

The man of X—— was a man of determination, and, still smarting under the loss of means and honour, he resolved that sooner or later he should discover by whom his letter had been stolen. The silversmith, readily entering into these views, cordially offered his personal services, and it was arranged between the banker and himself that they should ransack London, visiting the Ranelahs, the Vauxhalls, the Parks, the theatres—indeed every place where gay women and men of pleasure might be found together. This was an arduous task; but in the end their perseverance was rewarded by the discovery of the young woman to whom the farmer had presented the rings. On being questioned, this young person, while frankly stating what she knew, had little to tell. She had, she said, been in Snow Hill or Holborn one morning at the hour of the arrival of the west of England mail-coach. Among the passengers who got down was a youngish, fresh-looking farmer, whose acquaintance she then made, and whose constant companion she was for several days thereafter. She still wore the articles of jewellery which had been presented to her; but she declared that she had never seen the man since, nor did she know his name. And here the inquiry again seemed to exhaust itself, in the vague discovery of a *west-country farmer*.

The acquaintance between the banker and the silversmith, which had come about in the way already stated, soon ripened into friendship. They had, in a greater or less degree, a common interest in the matter of the stolen note, but they soon found out that there was other common ground for the growth of amity between them—they were both disciples of Izaak Walton. It became the custom of the silversmith to visit at the house of his friend in the west every season, when the two men would go out fishing together in the neighbouring streams, enjoying each other's society, and frequently, no doubt, going over again the old story of the lost letter. One day, during such a visit, the silversmith went out alone to try a stream not many miles distant from his friend's residence, and while so engaged a heavy shower swept across the scene. The angler sought shelter in a roadside inn, from which, as it happened, he was not far distant. The house was well known, and the proprietor was of the half-farmer, half-publican type, the business of innkeeper in such a situation not affording a sufficient living by itself. Feeling somewhat peckish, the visitor called for lunch. He was waited upon by the landlord in person. While the bread and cheese and cider were being carried in, the landlord apologised for the absence of the female folks, who were for the moment engaged elsewhere; and during this brief conversation, the silversmith (still instinct with professional taste) studied a bunch of heavy seals hanging from a watch in the landlord's fob. The landlord perceived that these articles had attracted the stranger's notice, and when he again came into the room the fact was observed by the other that they had been left aside or placed out of sight.

This incident set the stranger thinking; and while so engaged, his eye fell upon an old-fashioned glass-fronted cupboard occupying a corner of the room, in which were exhibited the inn treasures — old crystal vessels, china bowls, and the like—together with the plate of the establishment. A sudden thought struck him. He proceeded to examine the contents of the repository; and, standing upon a chair to explore the upper shelves, what was his amazement when he there recognised the silver tankards and the silver punch-ladles which he had sold to the west-country farmer many years before! Then, eagerly turning over the whole matter in his mind, the features of the landlord came back upon him, and in this man he recognised the person who in London had purchased these articles and paid to him the stolen £50 Bank of England note. The silversmith lost no time in communicating the facts to the banker, who at once obtained a warrant, and, with two constables, proceeded the same evening to the inn to put it into execution. The landlord was called into a room, there and then he was charged with having stolen the note, and was forthwith conveyed into X—— a prisoner.

It transpired in the course of inquiries that in his early days—before the period of the robbery—this man had been employed as a servant or assistant by the postmaster at X——. He left that situation, however, and became coachman to one of the neighbouring gentry. While in this service it was very frequently his duty to drive the family into town, where they would rest some portion of the day in their town house, and return to the country seat in the evening. In these intervals it sometimes happened that the coachman would go to the post-office, and there chat and gossip with his old fellow-servants. He visited the post-office on the day when the stolen letter was posted; he and his former comrades smoked and drank together; and in the end he volunteered to assist with the letters. He did so; and while thus engaged he managed to abstract the banker's letter, which, owing to its bulky nature and the address which it bore, he suspected to contain value. His visit on that particular day was verified by circumstances in the recollection of the persons at the post-office, and other evidence of his guilt accumulated against him; but this testimony was not really necessary, for the farmer-publican himself confessed to the theft of the letter, and explained how he had obtained possession of it.

The course usual in such circumstances followed. The offence was visited with the severity which characterised the period — the man suffered the extreme penalty of the law.

CHAPTER XVI.

TELEGRAPHIC BLUNDERS.

ALTHOUGH the work of sending and receiving telegraphic messages may be regarded in a general way as partaking largely of a merely mechanical nature, yet it is work to which the operator who is to achieve credit in his sphere must bring much tact, good sense, intelligence, a knowledge of the world, and a considerable amount of patience. Not only are the terms in which telegrams are frequently written so far devoid of context in themselves, owing to the curt way in which they are worded, as to render the sense of little assistance in estimating the correctness of a message received, but the letters of the telegraphic alphabet, being nothing more than little groups of dots and dashes variously arranged, are extremely susceptible of mutilation, owing to any lack of exact spacing on the part of the sending operator. Nor does the liability to error lie only in these directions. The dots and dashes frequently fail or run together, owing either to feeble signals, contact of the wires with one another, with trees, or other objects, or to the instruments not being in perfect adjustment. A grain of grit or of dust getting between the points of contact in a delicate instrument will sometimes do much mischief in the way indicated. There is liability to mistakes, too, in consequence of the handwriting of the senders, or of the operators at a transmitting point where messages have to be again taken down, not being very plain. Yet over and above these tendencies to error, there is the fallibility of human nature, which will sometimes lead a person to write "no" where "yes" is intended, or "black" where "white" is meant; and of such mistakes probably no explanation can be given. So that the work of a telegraphist is beset with pitfalls, and he requires all his wits and a fair share of intelligence to keep him right in his work. It may further be remarked that many errors in telegrams, which might be supposed by the public to be gross or inexcusable, have occurred in the most simple way, or have been shown to be due to failures of the most trifling kind.

The following are illustrations of such mistakes:—

A pleasure-party, telegraphing to some friends,

stated that they had "arrived all right," but the message was rendered, "We have arrived all tight." The words "right" and "tight" in the Morse code are as follows:—

```
r       i       g       h       t
. — .   . .     — — .   . . . .   —

t       i       g       h       t
—       . .     — — .   . . . .   —
```

In another case, a poor person, desiring to state that her daughter was ill, wrote in her message "Mary is bad." This was rendered, "Mary is dead," the sense being changed by a slight imperfection of spacing, thus—

```
    d       e       a       d
    — . .   .       . —     — . .
```

instead of—

```
    b           a       d
    — . . .     . —     — . .
```

In a third case, owing to failing signals, possibly from so simple a cause as the intermittent contact of the wire with a wet branch of a tree, or a particle of grit or dust finding its way between the points of the instrument, the import of the message was altogether changed. Thus, " Alfred doing well, enjoyed egg to-day," was received, " Alfred dying, enjoyed GG to-day."

A gentleman telegraphed from London to his brother in the country to send a hack to meet him at the station; but when the gentleman arrived at the station he found a *sack* waiting for him. A firm in London telegraphed, " *Send rails ten foot lengths;* " but the message was delivered, " *Send rails in foot lengths.*"

A person telegraphed to a friend to "take two stalls at the Haymarket," but the message conveyed directions to secure "two stables at the Haymarket." In another telegram, the intimation, "mother is no worse," was changed to "mother is no more." Again, "You will be glad to hear that your sister has accepted an engagement with your father's approval," was rendered, "that your sister has accepted an engagement with your father's apostle." In another case a plain business message, thus—" Come to me as early as you can, that we may arrange Wednesday," was given a matrimonial turn by being delivered as, "that we may arrange wedding." The next case is one in which a hungry man would doubtless be made an angry man in consequence of the mistake which occurred. His message, which was written thus,—" Shall arrive by train to-morrow *morning;* provide a good *supply* of bread, butter, eggs, milk, and potatoes,"—was delivered as " provide a good *supper* of bread," &c. In another instance the notice that "Mr —— will come to-night with me at 7 to tea,'" was rendered, "Mr ——- will come to-night with me, get 7 to tea;" the only argument in favour of the mistake being "the more the merrier." Then, on another occasion, a telegram sent by a person in the country to "Madame ——, Costumier," at an address in London, conveying an order for a fancy dress, was presented to the maker of costumes as "Madame ——, Costermonger." In a telegram directed to "——, M.P., House of Commons," the address somehow got changed to "——, M.P., House of Correction;" but the member not being found there, the clerks at the delivering office suggested that it should be tried at the "House of Detention,"— a not unlikely place for successful delivery of such a message as things were at the time.

It has been left to America to produce a mistake in telegraphing which, while it is very amusing, could not result in hurt or disappointment to any one. Here it is, just as received from the other side of the "ferry":—

A St Louis merchant, while in New York, received a telegram notifying that his wife was ill. He sent a message to his family doctor asking the nature of the sickness, and if there was any danger, and promptly received the answer—"*No danger; your wife has had a child; if we can keep her from having another to-night she will do well.*" The mystification of the agitated husband was not removed until a second inquiry revealed the fact that his indisposed lady had had a *chill*.

CHAPTER XVII.

HOW LETTERS ARE LOST.

IN dealing with the vast numbers of letters and other post articles which daily flow through the capacious veins of the British Post-office, the officials of the department come to learn many strange things connected with the wanderings of letters from their proper courses; they learn much in regard to the blunders made by the senders of letters in writing their addresses, and of the supreme folly frequently shown by individuals in transmitting valuables in carelessly-made-up packets: and this experience not only has the effect of causing complaints made by the public to be sometimes met by doubts and misgivings on the part of the Post-office, but is of great use in tracing home the blame to the right quarter, which is found to be, not infrequently, where the complainer had least reason to suspect it. The following facts will probably establish what is here advanced, besides proving of interest to the reader.

It is quite a common occurrence for letters—especially letters of a small size—which are dropped into a letter-box, to slip inside newspapers or book-packets, and to be carried, not only out of their proper course, but to places abroad, thus getting into the hands of the wrong persons. Such letters are returned from time to time from every quarter of the globe, but what proportion of those which go astray are duly returned it is impossible to say; for there are persons who, on receiving letters in this way not intended for them, proceed to open the envelopes through sheer curiosity, and having thus violated the letters, do not hesitate to destroy them. Others again, through dishonest motives, open letters of this class in the hope of gain. But there are others who, through no such interest, but merely from the want of a neighbourly spirit, refuse to take any trouble to put an errant letter in its proper course. This spirit was displayed in the case of a letter which had been misdelivered by the postman at a given address on the first floor of a tenement (it being intended for a person occupying the ground floor), the person who had received it stating, when questioned, that he had torn up the letter because he would not be troubled to send it down-stairs! Letters are sometimes, too, carried away to wrong addresses by sticking to the backs of other letters.

Again, through a great want of sense, or perhaps a redundancy of stupidity, letters are deposited occasionally in the most extraordinary places, in the idea that they are being posted. A servant-girl being sent out to post a letter, drops it into the letter-box of an empty shop, where it is found when an intending tenant goes to look at the premises. In a town in the north of Scotland a person was observed to deposit a letter in a disused street hydrant, and on the cover of the box being removed, three other letters were found, the senders of which had similarly mistaken the water-pillar for a letter-box. The letters had been passed into the box through the space formerly occupied by the tap-lever. A somewhat similarly absurd thing happened some time ago in Liverpool, where two letters were observed to have been forced behind the plate indicating the hours of collection on a pillar letter-box—the person who had placed them there no doubt thinking he was doing the correct thing.

It must be that many individuals entertain the greatest confidence in the servants of the Post-office, or they would not send money and valuables as they do. They also perhaps regard the Department as a fit subject on which to perpetrate petty frauds, by sending things of intrinsic value enclosed in books and newspapers. Instances of this kind are frequent.

Within the folds of a newspaper addressed to a person in Ireland were found two sovereigns, yet there was no writing to show who the sender was.

A brown-paper parcel, merely tied with string, unsealed, and not even registered, was found to contain six sovereigns, one half-crown, two sixpences, and three halfpenny-pieces, wrapped up in small articles of ladies' dress.

In the chief office in London, two gold watches were found inside an unregistered book-packet addressed to New Zealand, the middle portions of the leaves having been cut out so as to admit of the watches being concealed within. On another occasion, but in a Scotch post-office, a packet containing a book bound in morocco, was on examination discovered to have the inner portion of the leaves hollowed out, while still retaining the appearance of an ordinary book, and inside this hollow were found secreted a gold watch and a silver locket. At another time, a £20 Bank of England note was observed pinned to one of the pages of a book addressed to the initials of a lady at a receiving-house in the London Metropolitan District.

A packet done up in a piece of brown paper, unsealed but tied with string, was found to contain a small quantity of trimming, a collar-box with a few paper-collars, and inside the box were two £1 notes and 10s. in silver. A halfpenny wrapper was used to serve as a covering for the transmission of a letter, a bill of sale, and four £5 Bank of England notes. In a newspaper which reached the Dead-letter Office were found four sovereigns, and in another a gold locket. A packet carelessly rolled up was seen to contain a sovereign, two half-sovereigns, and a savings-bank book. In several instances coins have been found imbedded in cake and pieces of toast; and on one occasion gold coins of the value of £1, 10s. were discovered in a large seal at the back of a letter, the gold pieces having come to light through the wax getting slightly chipped. But the most flattering act of confidence in the probity of the Post-office fell to be performed by a person at Leeds, who, desiring to send a remittance to a friend, folded a five-pound note in two, wrote the address on the back of it, and, without cover or registration, consigned it to the letter-box. Petty frauds are committed on the Post-office to a large extent by the senders of newspapers, who infringe the rules by enclosing all sorts of things between the leaves—such as cigars and tobacco, collars, sea-weed, ferns and flowers, gloves, handkerchiefs, music, patterns, sermons, stockings, postage-stamps, and so on. People in the United States and Canada are much given to these practices, as shown by the fact that in one-half of the year 1874, more than 14,000 newspapers were detected with such articles secreted in them.

Occasionally letters of great value are very carelessly treated after delivery, through misconception as to what they really are. A person alleging that a registered letter containing a number of Suez Canal coupons had not reached him, the Post-office was able to prove its delivery; and on search being then made in the premises of the addressee, the coupons were found in the waste-paper basket, where they had been thrown under the idea that they were circulars. In another instance a registered letter, containing Turkish bonds with coupons payable to bearer, was misdirected to and delivered at an address in the west end of London, though it was really intended for a firm in the city. The value of the enclosures was more than £4000. When inquiry came to be made at the place of delivery, it was found that the bonds had been mistaken for foreign lottery-tickets of no value, and were put aside for the children of the family to play with.

Cases come to light, too, involving a history—or at least suggesting a history without affording particulars—or leaving us entirely in the dark as to the circumstances of the matter. Thus, two packets which had been addressed to Australia, and had been forwarded thither, were returned to England with the mark upon them, " unclaimed." On being opened, one of them was found to contain 100 sovereigns, and the other 50 sovereigns; yet there was no communication whatever in either to show who had sent them. It was supposed, by way of explanation, that a person proceeding to Australia had directed the packets to himself, intending to reach the colony by means of another ship; and that, having died upon the passage, or his ship having been lost, no application was ever made for them at the office to which they had been directed.

On one occasion a cheque for £9, 15s. was found loose in a pillar letter-box in Birmingham. The owner was traced through the bank upon which the cheque was drawn, but he was unable to give any explanation of the circumstances under which it had passed from his possession.

The following are a series of instances in which letters have got out of their proper bearings,—chiefly in the hands of the senders or the persons addressed, or through the carelessness of the servants of those persons; and the cases show how prone the public are to lay blame upon the Post-office when anything goes wrong with their letters, before making proper search in their own premises. A number of cases are added, in which the servants of the senders or of the persons addressed have been proved dishonest, when the blame had first been laid upon post-office servants; and one or two cases are given where the Department has been held up as the delinquent, merely to afford certain individuals an excuse for not paying money due by them, or otherwise to shirk their obligations.

"A person applied at the Leeds post-office and stated that two letters (one of which contained the half of a bank-note) which he had himself posted at that office had not reached their destination—mentioning at the same time some circumstances associated with the alleged posting of the letters. After some conversation, he was requested to produce the letter which had informed him of the non-receipt of the letters in question; but instead of producing it, he, to his own great astonishment, took from his pocket the very letters which he believed he had himself posted."

"Inquiry having been made respecting a letter sent to a person residing at Kirkcudbright, it appeared that it had been duly delivered, but that the addressee having left the letter on a table during the night, it had been devoured by rats." Another case of the depredations of rats upon letters is as follows:—

Certain letters which ought to have reached a bookseller in a country town not having been received, it was concluded, after inquiry, that they had been duly delivered, but had subsequently been withdrawn from under the street door, which was furnished with a slit to receive letters, but without a box to retain them. During subsequent alterations in the shop, however, when it was necessary to remove the flooring under the window, the discovery was made of thirty-one letters, six post-cards, and three newspapers, which had been carried thither by rats! The corners of the letters, &c., bearing the stamps, were nibbled away, leaving no doubt that the gum upon the labels was the inducement to the theft. Several of the letters contained cheques and money-orders.

But rats are old enemies to letters, as is known in the Post-office; for in the olden times, when sailing-ships were in use as mail-packets, sad complaints were made of the havoc caused by "ratts" to the mails conveyed in these ships.

Nor are rats the only dumb creatures which have shown a "literary" turn, in getting possession of post-letters. Some years ago a postman was going his rounds delivering letters in Kelvedon, in Essex, carrying a registered letter in his hand ready to deliver it at the next house, when a tame raven—a worthy compeer, if not a contemporary, of the Jackdaw of Rheims—suddenly darted down, snatched it from his grasp, and flew off with it. The bewildered postman could only watch the bird while it made a circuit over the town, which it did before alighting; and so soon as it got to a suitable place, it set to work to analyse the composition of the missive by tearing the letter to pieces. The fragments were shortly afterwards collected and put together, when it was found that part of them were the remains of a cheque for £30, which was afterwards renewed when the singular affair was made known.

Another curious incident in which birds are concerned occurred in the spring of 1884 at Shewbridge Hall, near Nantwich, in Cheshire. For the convenience of the people at the Hall, a letter-box is placed by the gate at the roadside, into which the post-runner drops the correspondence addressed to Shewbridge Hall. Mr Lockett, the occupier of the house, expecting a letter from Liverpool containing a cheque for £10, went to the box, where, as it happened, he found the letter, but in a mutilated state, and the cheque gone. Believing that a robbery of his box had been committed, or that the letter had been violated before being deposited therein, he forthwith rode into Nantwich to report the matter at the post-office and to the police. Returning later on, he examined the box more closely,

HOW LETTERS ARE LOST.

and discovered tomtits inside; and further investigation led to the discovery of the cheque lying twenty yards away on the turnpike road, whither it had evidently been carried for examination. The

cheque was folded small, and could therefore be easily carried by these small birds. The tomtits had taken possession of the box for nesting purposes, and perhaps they found the letter to be in the way, and accordingly made an effort to remove it. In the spring of the previous year a pair of tomtits built

Letter-box taken possession of by Tomtits.

their nest in this letter-box (possibly the same pair), and reared a brood of young, though letters were being dropped into the box every day.

A very similar circumstance occurred in the same season at a place near Lockerbie, where a letter-box is affixed to the trunk of a tree bordering on the main road, for the convenience of the people living at Daltonhook farm, which occupies a site some distance from the highway. The letter-box is about fifteen inches square, with the usual slit to admit of letters being dropped in, and a door to the front the full size of the box, to allow the postman to clear it or to place larger packets within. A pair of tomtits, considering the box an eligible place for bringing up a family, built their nest in it, obtaining ingress and egress by the letter-slit, and choosing that portion of the interior farthest from the door for their purpose. In contrast to the ruthlessness and cruelty of many who show no love to God's creatures unless they contribute in some way to their comfort or profit, the post-runner and the family who use the box, in a kind-hearted way took every care to disturb these objects of interest as little as possible, and in due time the nest was complete, and eight tiny eggs were deposited therein. While the female was sitting on the eggs during the term of incubation, she did not rise from the nest when the post-runner opened the door, but would make a peculiar noise and peck at his hand as he put it forward to take out or deposit letters. But after a time the two became more friendly, and kindness on the one side begetting confidence on the other, the bird at length became so familiar, that while it continued to sit on the nest it would peck crumbs from the man's hand, instead of showing displeasure, as it formerly had done. At length seven young birds became the joy of the parents. These, however, did not find the box altogether free from drawbacks; for letters, in being deposited through the slit, sometimes fell on the top of the youngsters, and so excited the wrath of the old birds. This was proved on one occasion when a servant dropped a letter into the box, for when the post-runner next visited the receptacle, he found the letter so mutilated, either through sheer rage on the part of the tomtits, or in their endeavours to eject it by the slit, that he took it back to the farmhouse rather than send it forward in its badly damaged state. However, the brood at length got through the troubles of their infantile days; and we may indulge the hope that they have since lived to join in the antiphonies of the grove, or to adorn the roadside spray with their neat figures and glowing colours.

It may be added that these little birds are very

eccentric in the choice of their nesting-places. In one case they selected the inside of a weathercock on the top of a steeple for their breeding-place, and in another the interior of a beehive in full work. Here they set up house and reared their young, neither injuring the bees, nor being molested by them in return.

"A gentleman at Archerstown, county Westmeath, complained of a letter, containing half bank-notes and post-bills amounting to £400, addressed to Dublin, not having come to hand; but when the matter came to be fully examined, it was ascertained that the letter was in a drawer in the house of the very person to whom it had been directed, but by whom it had been entirely overlooked."

A banker residing in a country town in Scotland reported that a letter containing two £20 notes and two £1 notes, addressed to him by another banker, and posted at a town ten miles distant, had not come to hand. On inquiry, the sender could not state either the numbers or the dates of the notes. He had, moreover, allowed upwards of two months to elapse before taking any steps to ascertain whether his letter had reached its destination. "As this valuable letter had been posted without the precaution of registration, and had the words 'county rates' on the envelope, it was supposed to have excited the cupidity of some one connected with one or other of the two post-offices concerned, and an officer was immediately despatched to investigate the case. The complainant reiterated the statement that the letter had not reached him; but within half an hour of the officer's departure, an inmate of the house having made a fresh search, found the letter among some papers in a press, where it had apparently been placed unopened when received."

"A bank agent sent a letter containing valuable enclosures to another bank agent. The letter was presumed to have been lost by the Post-office; but no trace of it could be obtained there, and the applicant was informed accordingly. It subsequently appeared that the son of the person to whom the letter had been addressed had called at the Post-office and received the letter, and that he had afterwards left the town for the holidays, carrying the letter away with him in his pocket, where it had remained."

"A letter supposed to contain a £10 note was registered at Moffat, and in due course delivered to the addressee, who, however, declined to sign a receipt for it, as the £10 note was missing. The sender was written to, but he asserted that the note had been enclosed. The postmaster chiefly concerned (who had been more than fifty years in the service) was greatly distressed at the doubt thus cast upon his honesty; but on further inquiry, the sender admitted that he had obtained a trace of the £10 note, and stated that the fault had not been with the Post-office. On being pressed for fuller information, he stated that when writing his letter he had placed the £10 note in an envelope and affixed a postage-stamp thereon, when a lady came hurriedly into his shop, also to write a letter, and he had assisted her by getting an envelope and placing a postage-stamp on it; that he had placed this envelope beside that which contained the bank-note; and that when the lady had finished her letter, he gave her by mistake the envelope with the £10 note in it, and put his own letter into the empty envelope. He had carried the two letters to the Post-office; and his own, which he supposed contained the £10, he had registered. Both letters were safely delivered; and the £10 having been returned as evidently sent in error, the lady who had forwarded it brought it to the complainant, and thus the mystery was cleared up."

During a snowstorm which occurred a year or two ago, a London firm put up for posting, among others, a letter to a Glasgow firm containing a cheque for a sum little short of £1000. The cheque not reaching its destination in due course, payment was stopped at the bank, and notwithstanding that every inquiry was made, nothing was heard of the letter at the time. Eventually, however, the cheque was brought to the firm who had drawn it, together with the letter, by a police inspector, who had found the letter adhering to a block of ice floating in the Thames off Deptford. The supposition is, that when the letters of the day were being carried to the Lombard Street Post-office, this letter was dropped in the street, that it was carted off in the snow to the Thames, and there, after a week's immersion in the river, got affixed to the block of ice, as already stated.

On the 27th February 1885, a medical gentleman residing at Richmond, Surrey, when going his usual round of visits, found on the carriage floor two letters, one addressed to a person in Edinburgh, the other to a lady residing near Castle Douglas. The letters had been duly prepared for the post, each bearing an undefaced postage-stamp, but nothing in their appearance indicated that they had ever been posted. The finder was at first puzzled at the discovery, but on reflection, he remembered having a few minutes previously opened a large newspaper, the 'Queen,' which had reached him from

Edinburgh two or three days before, but had till then remained unopened in his carriage. It occurred to him that the letters might have come concealed within the folds of the newspaper, and he was good enough to forward a note with each to the persons addressed, explaining the circumstances under which he had found them. Subsequent investigation by the Post-office brought to light the fact that one of the two letters, and the copy of the 'Queen' from which they were supposed to have dropped, had been deposited in different pillar-boxes in Edinburgh, but in the same collector's district; and there can be no doubt that this letter, and probably also the other letter, were shaken inside the folds of the newspaper during their conveyance to the head-office in the collector's bag. In one of the notes which the doctor sent with the letters, he made this remark: " I cannot help feeling that the postal authorities and the public should both have their eyes opened to what a serious danger such a letter-trap as a large newspaper might prove." He omitted to add, however, that the sender of the 'Queen' had tied it up very carelessly without a wrapper, and in a way that could hardly fail to render it a dangerous travelling companion for letters. Had the letters fallen into dishonest hands, their loss would certainly have been attributed to the Post-office, and the case is one which aptly illustrates a means by which letters sometimes get out of their proper course, or are lost altogether.

A firm of solicitors in Leith wrote a letter to a client in the same town, enclosing a cheque for £102; and this letter, although it was alleged to have been duly posted, failed to reach the person for whom it was intended. The usual inquiries were made, but unsuccessfully, no trace being discovered of the letter. Some days afterwards the firm received the letter and cheque, minus the envelope, from a farmer near Tranent, in one of whose fields a ploughman had picked them up. This man was engaged spreading town-refuse upon the field when he found the letter, which he opened, and thereupon threw away the cover. For the purposes of investigation, it was very essential that this should be produced; but it happened that meanwhile the field had been gone over with a grubbing machine, and the chances of the recovery of the discarded envelope were thereby greatly lessened. The ploughman's son was set to work, however, to make a search, and after toiling a whole day, he found the envelope. On examination, it was seen that the postage-stamp affixed was still undefaced, and the envelope bore nothing to show that it had ever been in the Post-office. The whole circumstances left no doubt that the letter had either got into the waste-paper basket of the senders, or had been dropped on the way to the Post-office, and that it had been carried ten miles into the country amongst street rubbish, with which, as manure, the farm in question was supplied from the town of Leith.

A registered letter posted at Newcastle, and addressed to a banker in Edinburgh, not having reached the addressee's hands, a telegram was forwarded to the sender intimating the fact, and requesting explanation of the failure. The banker supposed that the letter had been lost or purloined in the Post-office; but it was afterwards proved to have been duly delivered to the bank porter, who, having locked it up in his desk, had quite forgotten it.

A lady residing in Jersey applied to the Post-office respecting a letter which had been sent by her to a clergyman at Oxford. Inquiry was made for it at all the offices through which it would pass, but unsuccessfully, no trace whatever of it being found. Subsequently the clergyman informed the secretary of the Post-office that he had found the letter between the cushions of his own arm-chair, where it had been placed, no doubt, at the time of delivery.

"A person complained of delay in the receipt of a letter which appeared to have passed through the Post-office twice. It transpired that the letter had, in the first instance, been duly delivered at a shop, where it was to remain till called for, but that it had accidentally been taken away with some music by a customer, who had afterwards dropped it in the street. Subsequently the letter must have been picked up and again posted, and hence its double passage through the Post-office."

"A barrister complained of the non-delivery of a letter containing the halves of two £10 Bank of England notes, stating that he had posted the letter himself; but he shortly afterwards wrote to say that the letter had reached its destination. It appeared that instead of putting it into the letter-box, he had dropped the letter in the street, where, fortunately, it was picked up by some honest person, who posted it."

A business firm having frequently failed to receive letters which had been addressed to them, made complaint on the subject from time to time; but the inquiries which were instituted resulted in nothing. After much trouble, however, it was at length discovered that a defect existed in the letter-box in the firm's office-door, and fifteen letters were found lodged between the box and the door, some of which had been in that situation more than nine years.

A letter said to contain a cheque for £12, 4s., addressed to a London firm, not having reached its destination, inquiries were made with respect to it.

At the end of three months it turned up at a *papier-mâché* factory, whither it had, no doubt, been carried among waste-paper from the office at which it had been delivered.

In 1883, a registered letter sent from Dunkeld on a given date was duly received in Edinburgh, and delivered at its address, which was a bank, the postman obtaining a signature to the receipt-form in the usual way. Some little time afterwards complaint was made by the manager of the bank that the letter had not been received; but the Post-office was able to prove the contrary by the receipt, the signature to which, on being submitted to the manager, was acknowledged to be that of the wife of the housekeeper of the establishment. Yet this person could give no account of the letter, nor had any one else seen it; and as the letter was stated to have contained four £1 notes and a bank deposit-book, the fact of its disappearance gave rise to a state of things which can be better imagined than described. The Post-office, in the circumstances, offered the suggestion that the bank's waste-paper should be carefully examined. As it happened, however, a quantity of this material had just been cleared out, having been purchased by a waste-paper dealer; and the fact made the chances of recovery in that direction all the more remote. Yet the housekeeper was set to work: he traced the bags first to the store of the dealer, then to the premises of a waste-paper merchant in another part of the city. With assistance he carefully examined the contents of the bags filled at the bank, and his efforts were rewarded by the discovery of the registered letter, which was in precisely the same state as when delivered, never having been opened. It had very likely fallen from a desk in the bank on to the floor, and by a careless person been brushed aside with used envelopes and scraps of paper, thus finding its way into the waste-paper basket.

In April 1873, a letter was posted in a certain village in Ayrshire, addressed by a wife to her husband, who was in command of a vessel bound for New York. The letter was properly directed to the captain by name, it bore the name of his ship, and was addressed to the care of the British Consul, New York. The captain never received the letter, and this circumstance gave rise, upon his return from sea, to what is described as a "feud" between him and his wife,—he, reposing perhaps greater faith in the Post-office than in the dutiful attentions of his wife, believing that his better-half had not written to him, since he failed to receive the letter on application at its place of address in New York. Time, with its incessant changes, hopes, fears, joys, and disappointments, winged its hurried flight for a period of eleven years ere the matter which had caused the feud came to be fully understood. At the end of that time the same letter was returned to the writer through the Dead-letter Office, having (according to the stamp upon it) been unclaimed at New York. It was stated that the return of the letter had "put all to rights" between the couple concerned, though it is to be hoped that the healing hand of Time had already done much in this direction, and that the return of the long-lost letter did nothing more than put the finishing touch to restored confidence. In connection with this matter, it was afterwards ascertained that the letter was one of over 4000 similar letters returned to the New York Post-office from the offices of the British Consul in that city, upon a new appointment being made to the Consulate,—the "new broom," as one of his first acts, having made a clean sweep of this accumulation of letters, some of which had been lying there no less than seventeen years. How far the failure of these letters to reach the persons addressed was due to their not having been called for, or to the negligence of clerks at the Consulate, is not known, nor will it ever be ascertained what heart-burnings and misery may have been occasioned by this wholesale miscarriage of correspondence.

In March 1880, a letter plainly addressed to an individual by name, and bearing the name and number of a street in a certain district of London, reached the Dead-letter Office, whither it had been sent by the postman of the district, owing to the person to whom it was directed not being known at the address given. When opened, with a view to its return to the writer, the letter was discovered to contain a Bank of England note for £100, together with a short memorandum suggesting the return of the note to some person, but in such vague and general terms that no one who had not had previous information on the subject could have fully understood the purport of the message.

The memorandum was, moreover, without head or tail—it had no superscription to indicate whence it had come, nor had it a signature to show by whom it had been written. The circumstance being one of an exceptional character, special steps were taken with a view to trace the owner, and an advertisement was inserted in several of the metropolitan newspapers—bringing up, it is true, a responsive crop of claimants for lost notes, but without eliciting any such claims as would warrant the surrender of the note in question. From the terms of the memorandum in the letter, and the fact that it was anonymous, the suggestion readily arose that whoever had had the note last had not come by it in the regular way of business; and this idea was strengthened by the discovery that the note had been paid over by a bank about eight years previously to a person whose name and address were endorsed upon it; and from that period the note had evidently not been in circulation. It was thought probable that the endorser had lost the note in some way shortly after receiving it, and that coming into the hands of some individual who feared to put it in circulation, it had been kept up during these eight years. Meanwhile the right to receive the note not having been established by any one, the amount was paid in to the Revenue.

In the Postmaster-General's report for 1881, further mention was made of the finding of the note in the Dead-letter Office, and several claims again reached headquarters, one of which proved to be so far good, that, when the facts had been fully investigated, the amount was paid over to the claimant.

It appeared that the person whose name was endorsed on the note received it in part payment of a cheque cashed by him in 1872, when he was bought out of the business in which he had till then been a partner. Two years afterwards—viz., in 1874—he died, and his widow was unaware at the time that the note had been lost. From circumstances which this lady was able to prove, however, there seemed to be every reason to believe that her husband (whose practice it was to endorse notes when he received them) had by some means lost the note, or that it had been carelessly left by him in some old book or other papers which were sold as waste-paper after her husband's death; and thus the Post-office was made the means of restoring a considerable sum of money to the rightful owner, while the person who had without title possessed it in the interval dared not claim it.

"A letter said to have been posted by a person at Fochabers, enclosing a letter of credit for £50, was supposed to have been appropriated by an officer of the Post-office; but on inquiry, it was ascertained that, instead of posting the letter himself, as he asserted, the writer had intrusted it to a servant, who had destroyed the letter, and had attempted to negotiate the order."

"A person complained repeatedly of letters addressed to him having been intercepted and tampered with, and of drafts having been stolen from them and negotiated. There being ground to suspect that the thief was in the complainant's own office, he reluctantly consented to test the honesty of his clerks; and the result showed that one of them was the guilty party, the man being subsequently tried and convicted. The thefts had been committed by means of a duplicate key, which gave the clerk access to the letter-box."

"Several complaints were made of the non-delivery of letters addressed to the editor of a newspaper; but this gentleman afterwards intimated that he had discovered that the delinquent was his own errand-boy, who confessed to having pilfered his letter-box."

"A similar case occurred at Romsey, where, on an investigation by the surveyor, it was discovered that the applicant's errand-boy had abstracted the letters from his private bag, which it was found could be done even when the bag was locked."

"Application was made respecting a letter containing a cheque for £79, 12s. 11d., which had been presented and cashed. The letter had not been registered, and no trace of it could be discovered. The applicants, however, ultimately withdrew their complaint against the Post-office, stating their belief that the missing letter had not been posted, but had been stolen by one of their clerks, who had absconded."

"A merchant sent his errand-boy to post a letter,

and to purchase a stamp to put upon it. The letter contained negotiable bills amounting to £1200; and as the merchant did not receive an acknowledgment from his correspondent, he cast the blame on the Post-office. An inquiry followed, which resulted in showing that the errand-boy had met another boy on a similar mission, who undertook to post the letter in question. On further reflection, however, the latter resolved to convert the penny intended for a postage-stamp into sweetmeats, which he did, and then destroyed the letter with its contents, carrying the fragments into a field near the Post-office, where they were found hidden."

A sailor applied for a missing letter containing a money-order for 30s., which he said had been sent, but had not reached him; but when he found that the matter was under strict investigation, he confessed that the money had been paid to him, and that he had denied having received it, in order to excuse himself from not paying a debt to the person with whom he lodged.

"A person having applied for a missing letter, said to contain two £10 and one £5 Bank of England notes, and which he stated had been sent to him by his father, it appeared on inquiry that no such letter had been written; and he afterwards confessed that his object in asking for the letter was a device to keep in abeyance a pecuniary demand upon him by his landlady."

Some years ago a person complained that twelve sovereigns had been abstracted from a letter received by him while it was in transit through the post, but he was told in reply that the envelope bore evidence that it had not contained coin to that amount. This person then communicated with the sender of the letter, who persisted in declaring that she had put therein the amount stated. At this stage of the inquiry an officer was despatched to investigate the matter; and upon his requiring the woman who had sent the envelope to accompany him before a magistrate to attest the truth of her statement upon oath, she confessed that the statement was false, and explained her conduct by saying that she had promised to lend the person to whom the envelope had been addressed £12, but that she had been unwilling to do so, as she felt sure that she should never get her money back again; and that she determined, therefore, to keep her money, and throw the blame on the Post-office.

"A bank in Glasgow some years ago complained that a letter had been delivered there without its contents—halves of bank-notes for £75; and on a strict investigation, it appeared that the letter had been intrusted to a boy to post, who confessed that, being aware the letter contained money, and finding that the wafer with which it was fastened was wet, he had been tempted to steal the contents, which at the time he believed to be whole notes; but who added that when, on afterwards examining them, he found them to be halves only, he enclosed them in an unfastened sheet of paper, which he directed according, as he believed, to the address of the letter from which he had taken them. The halves of the notes and sheet of paper were subsequently discovered in the Glasgow Post-office, the address on the paper being, however, very different from that of the letter in which the notes had been enclosed."

"Complaint was made that a letter containing the halves of Bank of England notes for £65, sent to a firm in Liverpool, had failed to reach its destination. On inquiry, it appeared that the letter had been duly delivered, and subsequently stolen by a well-known thief, who had the audacity to go and claim the corresponding half-notes from another firm in Liverpool, to whose care the stolen letter showed they had been sent by the same post; and in this object the scoundrel succeeded."

An unregistered letter containing a £10 Bank of England note, posted at Macclesfield and addressed to Manchester, was stated not to have reached its destination. Full inquiry was made, but the letter could not be found. Subsequently, however, the note was presented at the Bank of England, and on being traced, it was discovered that the letter had been stolen after its delivery.

"A letter containing two £5 Bank of England notes was stated to have been posted at Leeds, addressed to a lady at Leamington, without reaching its destination; but the inquiry that was instituted by the Post-office caused the sender to withdraw his complaint, and to prefer against the clerk whom he had intrusted with the letter, a charge of having purloined it before it reached the Post-office."

"The secretary of a charitable institution in London gave directions for posting a large number of 'election papers,' and supposed that these directions had been duly acted upon. Shortly, however, he received complaints of the non-receipt of many of the papers, and in other cases of delay. He at once made a complaint at the Post-office; but, on examination, circumstances soon came to light which cast suspicion on the person employed to post the notices, although this man had been many years in the service of the society, and was supposed to be of strict integrity. Ultimately, the man confessed that he had embezzled the postage, amounting to £3, 15s. 6d., and had endeavoured to deliver the election papers himself."

"Complaint having been made by a dealer in foreign postage-stamps that several letters containing such stamps had not reached him, a careful investigation was made, but for some time without any result. The letters should have been dropped by the letter-carrier into the addressee's letter-box; but to this box no one, the dealer asserted, had access but himself. Some time afterwards, however, a cover addressed to the complainant was picked up in the street, and on inquiry being made whether the letter to which it belonged had been delivered, the complainant stated that it had not. But it so happened that the letter-carrier had a clear recollection of dropping this letter into the letter-box, and, moreover, remembered to have observed a young girl who was at the window move, as he thought, towards the box. This led to the girl being closely questioned, when she admitted the theft, confessing also that she had committed other similar thefts previously. Thus, by a mere chance, a suspicion which had been cast on the Post-office was dispelled."

"The publisher of one of the London papers complained of the repeated loss in the Post-office of copies of his journal addressed to persons abroad. An investigation showed that the abstraction was made by the publisher's clerk, his object apparently being to appropriate the stamps required to defray the foreign postage. In another case a general complaint having arisen as to the loss of newspapers sent to the chief office in St Martin's-le-Grand, inquiry led to the discovery of a regular mart held near the office, and supplied with newspapers by the private messengers employed to convey them to the post. On another occasion a man was detected in the act of robbing a news-vendor's cart, by volunteering on its arrival at the General Post-office to assist the driver in posting the newspapers: instead of doing so, he walked through the hall with those intrusted to him, and, upon his being stopped, three quires of a weekly paper were found in his possession."

In the spring of 1855, a young lady, fifteen years of age, whose parents resided in a small English town, which shall be nameless, was sent to a boarding-school at some distance therefrom to pursue her education. The mother of the young lady was in a delicate state of health, and, as was most proper in the circumstances, letters were written from time to time and forwarded to the daughter at school, giving particulars of her mother's progress. So far this is all plain and straightforward. The young lady, however, one day declared that though on a particular date mentioned by her she had written home to inquire how her mother was, that letter had not been delivered; and, that on the second day thereafter a brown-paper parcel was placed in a very mysterious manner in the hall of the house where she was at school. In this parcel was found a letter for the young lady intimating her mother's death, and explaining that the parcel had been brought by a friend—thus accounting for the absence from it of all post-marks. Other circumstances were related by the girl—that she had seen a man galloping along the road, and that he had left the parcel in question. Two days after this event, a letter was posted from her parents' residence to inform the young lady that her mother was much better; but when the letter arrived and was opened, she produced another letter requiring her immediate return, in order to attend her mother's funeral. The case was very puzzling, and naturally excited great interest,—the more so, as some suspicion arose that a conspiracy existed to carry off the young lady, in which some person in the Post-office was aiding and abetting. The matter formed the subject of two separate investigations, ending in failure, and the mystery still remained. It was only after a third attempt at elucidation—when an officer specially skilled in prosecuting inquiries of a difficult kind had visited the school—that the truth began to appear. This officer reported that, in his opinion, the whole proceedings were but a plot of a schoolgirl to get home; and the young lady afterwards confessed this to be the case.

T

It is not probable that the petty fraud of again using stamps which have already passed through the post is perpetrated with any great frequency upon the Post-office. Still, cases no doubt do occur, and may at any time lead to criminal proceedings, like those which took place at Hull some years ago. A person in that town having posted a letter with an old stamp affixed, the stamper who had to deface the stamp in the usual way, detected the irregularity, and brought the matter under notice. Proceedings were taken against the offender, and the case being established against him, and the fact being stated that this person had previously been warned by the Post-office against committing like frauds, he was mulcted in a fine of £5 and costs, with the alternative punishment of three months' imprisonment.

The accidents and misfortunes which are the lot of letters in this country, seem also to attend post-letters in their progress through the Post-offices of other countries. A curious case was noticed some years ago in the French capital. Some alterations were being carried out in the General Post-office in Paris, when there was found, in a panel situated near a letter-box, a letter which had been posted just fifty years before. There it had remained concealed half a century. The letter was forwarded to the person whose address it bore, and who, strange to say, was still alive; but the writer, it transpired, had been dead many years.

On one occasion notice was given to the Post-office by a clergyman residing in a country town in the south of England, that a packet sent by him containing a watch had been tampered with in the post, the packet having reached the person addressed, not with the watch that had been despatched, but containing a stone, which, it was alleged, must have been substituted in course of transit. As is usual in cases of this kind, very particular inquiries were necessary to establish whether the Post-office was really in fault, because experience has shown that very often obloquy is laid upon the Department which ought to rest elsewhere; and accordingly, a shrewd and practised officer in such matters was sent to the town in question to make investigations. Arrived at the clergyman's residence, the officer found that that gentleman was from home; but introducing himself to the sender's wife, he explained his mission, and in a general way learned from her what she was able to communicate with regard to the violated packet. While the interview was thus proceeding, the officer, with professional habit, made the best use of his eyes, which, lighting upon a rough causeway of small stones somewhere on the premises, afforded him a hint, if not as yet a suspicion, as to the locality of the fraud. In fact, he remarked a striking resemblance between the stone which had been received in the packet and the stones forming the causeway. In the most delicate way he insinuated the inquiry whether the lady might not possibly entertain some shadow of a suspicion of her own servants.

"Oh dear, no," was the reply; "they are all most respectable, and have the highest characters."

The lady had the utmost confidence in them, and to admit such a thought was to do them grave injustice. The officer was not to be satisfied with such an assurance, however, and by using tact and patience he brought the lady to see that, if there was no dishonesty with her own servants, they would come safely out of the inquiry, and it might be well to allow him to question them. It was further permitted, after some objection on the lady's part and persuasion on that of the officer, that the latter should ask each of the servants separately whether they would allow their boxes to be examined. If they had nothing to conceal, the ordeal could not, of course, hurt them. The female servants were called up one by one and closely questioned, and on the proposed examination of the boxes being suggested, the girls at once assented.

This was so far satisfactory, but there was still the butler to deal with. In due turn the presence of this household ornament was summoned to the room, when, up to a certain point, everything went well; but it being put to him to have his boxes searched, injured virtue cried out, and indignation and scorn were vented upon the obtrusive inquirer. The officer had, however, gained a point, for he was now in a position to say that if the butler continued to object, the suspicion would arise that he might possibly be the culprit, and it might even be concluded that he and not the Post-office ought to account for the watch. At length the man-servant gave way, and he and the officer proceeded to the butler's quarters. Upon the trunk being opened, the first thing to attract notice was three bottles of wine.

"Holloa!" says the officer, "what have we here? A strange wine-cellar this!"

"Oh," observed the butler, "these are three bottles of ginger-wine which were given me by my father, a grocer in the town."

"Indeed!" says the officer, who had meanwhile been noting the colour as he held a bottle between himself and the light; "it looks a queer colour for ginger-wine. You won't mind letting me taste your wine, will you?"

Overborne by the assurance of the officer perhaps,

or thinking him quite chatty and chummy, a cork was withdrawn, and the officer was sipping capital old crusted port. The wine was pronounced very good, but the missing watch was not forthcoming.

The scene of inquiry was now changed. The officer proceeded to the shop of the grocer, made some trifling purchase, put on his most affable ways, and he soon had the grocer talking, first on general topics, then on personal matters, and at last on the theme of his own family.

"How many have you?" says the officer.

"So-and-so," responds the grocer.

"All doing for themselves by this time, I suppose?" continues the officer.

This flung the door open for a full statement of the position of the family, which was given without reserve, as if to an old friend, until the butler with the clergyman was mentioned, when the officer interrupted him with the remark—

"Ah, to be sure; I know something of him. That was capital ginger-wine you gave him lately."

"Ginger-wine!" quoth the grocer; "I never had wine in my house in my life, and I certainly never gave my son any."

This was enough for the officer, who remarked that there might be a mistake; and soon thereafter he found means to bring the conversation to a close.

Returning immediately to the clergyman's house, he again saw the lady, and told her what had occurred. He made bold to say, moreover, that her butler was a thief, that he was stealing her husband's wine, that he in all probability had made away with the watch, and that she ought to give him into custody, and to prosecute him. At this point the butler was called in, and in presence of his mistress plainly taxed with the theft of the wine. Finding it useless to stand out, he confessed that he had taken it, but protested that he had not stolen the watch.

The lady, however, had no longer any doubt in the matter; and deeply distressed at finding how greatly she had been deceived in her estimate of his character for integrity, exclaimed—" Oh John! to think that after all the pains your master and I have taken to make you a good man, you should have done this wicked thing! Oh John, John!"

The officer saw that in the lady's view all suspicion was removed from the Post-office, and prepared to leave; but feeling anxious about the lady in the absence of her husband, said he should go to the police station and fetch a couple of constables to attend to the matter. On this hint the butler became greatly excited and alarmed, and earnestly begged that only one policeman might be sent.

"Oh no," said the officer, "you are a big man,

and we must have two;" and beckoning Mrs —— to leave the room, he turned the key in the door, and went for the police.

During his absence, the household was in a state of wild excitement, the lady of the house being in a high state of nervousness, while below-stairs the servants were in no better condition. Meanwhile one of the females, either through sympathy for the idol of the kitchen, or in pursuance of womanly curiosity, which is not less likely, sought the vantage-ground of a water-butt at the rear of the premises, in order to make a reconnaissance through the window, and ascertain how the butler was comporting himself in the new and extraordinary situation where he was. But one glance into the room was enough; she sprang to the ground, and ran to her mistress screaming that John was cutting his throat. Sure enough he had been engaged in this operation, using a pocket-knife for the purpose; and the officers of justice, on opening the door, found him streaming with blood from the self-inflicted wound.

At this juncture the Post-office official left the matter to be dealt with by the clergyman as he might see fit. He felt sufficient interest in the case, however, to make inquiry subsequently as to the fate of the culprit, and learnt that he had recovered from his injury; that his kind master and mistress had forgiven him; and although they did not receive him back into their service, they helped him in other ways, and were assiduous in their endeavours to keep him in the paths of rectitude and honesty.

The following anecdote, borrowed from a French source,[1] will illustrate how serious the consequences may be when letters are not clearly and intelligibly addressed, and by what slight accidents such missives sometimes go far from their right course.

About the year 1837 there was garrisoned at a small town in the Department of the Pas-de-Calais an honest soldier named Goraud, who had served with the colours a term of seven years. Though he had conducted himself well, and was favourably thought of by his superiors, he had never been able to rise above the grade of full private. He liked his profession, but being unable either to read or write, the avenues to promotion remained closed against him.

Goraud came from an obscure village in Provence, where his poor old mother, a woman of over sixty, lived, and where also resided a married brother, younger than himself, who was surrounded by a rising family of children. The soldier received from time to time letters from his mother, which, on being read to him, affected him deeply,

[1] La Poste Anecdotique et Pittoresque. Par Pierre Zaccone.

sometimes even to tears. There were, besides, other friends in his native place of whom he entertained kindly recollections, and with whom he kept up intercourse through his family; especially a young woman towards whom he had formerly had very tender feelings, which, though not now so strong, time and distance had not as yet effaced.

Becoming home-sick, and having no bright prospect before him in the army, Goraud yearned to be set free, so that he might spend the rest of his days "in the midst of those he so much loved," as is expressed on the tomb of the great Napoleon. He had already, as has been before stated, served seven years; he had been of good conduct; and now he had but to demand his discharge in order to accomplish his fondest wish.

But just as he was about to make the necessary request, and to realise the dream which he had been cherishing, a letter from his brother changed all his plans. His joy was turned to sorrow. This letter informed him that his mother was seriously ill, and, moreover, that some distemper had assailed his brother's stock, carrying many of them off; in fact, misery stared in the face those among whom he had hoped to live happily, and to eke out the remainder of his days in comfort. The poor fellow was sadly cast down; the phantom of pleasure had passed from his view; he shed bitter tears of disappointment, and was at his wits' end. Dejection and irresolution did not, however, last. He soon regained command of himself, and filial affection suggested to him the course which he should pursue.

Next day he proceeded to the office of an agent whose business it was to procure substitutes for individuals desirous of avoiding service in the army; and in a few days thereafter he engaged to serve his country for seven years more, receiving in return a payment down of 1500 francs. It may be guessed what was the next step taken by the worthy soldier. He remitted the 1500 francs to his mother, in a letter directed to the care of his brother; and at the same time he intimated that he was to start at once for Algeria, there to join the new regiment to which he had been posted.

Three months passed, and as yet no acknowledgment for the money came to hand. This to Goraud, after the sacrifice he had made, was sadly disappointing; but he did not at first feel alarmed. The idea occurred to him that his mother might be a trifle worse, or that something might have delayed the reply. He decided to write again. He related what he had done, explained the cause he had for uneasiness, and begged that an early answer might be sent to him. This was not long in coming. It stated that the old mother was again well, that the brother had had a hard struggle, and that though he hoped to pull through, it might prove necessary for him to quit the place. In regard to the alleged remittance, it was briefly added that no money had been received.

This latter statement created a most painful impression upon the soldier. His brother's letter appeared to breathe a tone which was not usual; he imagined that, under the guise of calculated frigidity, was to be perceived an insinuation that no money had been sent: and, smarting under the sting of such reflections, the blush of offended virtue rose to his cheek. His feelings ran over the whole gamut of wounded sentiment. He saw himself an injured man, and felt deeply hurt; his money had gone unacknowledged, and he became roused to anger; and then, revolving the whole circumstances in his mind, suspicion took possession of him. Recollecting that the money-letter had been sent as an ordinary letter by post, and that the reply had not seemed quite right, he now suspected that his brother had received the remittance, appropriated it to his own use, and denied the receipt of his letter. In this frame of mind, he had a communication penned to his brother full of denunciations and reproaches, and couched in such terms of violence, that he would not allow the epistle when written to be read over to him. Next day he started with a distant expedition on active service.

Gloomy, cast down, and above all irate, he was ready to fight with the wind or his own shadow. In the first brush with the enemy he threw himself into their midst with fury, and fought desperately for several hours, as if to provoke the end which he now longed for. Instead of meeting his death, however, he gained the hero's prize—the cross of honour. One month previously he would have hailed this distinction with delight; now everything was dull and indifferent to him—even glory!

About a year after this event Goraud accompanied his regiment to Paris. As he was leaving the barracks one day a voice hailed him with the question, "Is not your name Goraud?" "Yes, major," was the soldier's reply. "Very good," says the other, "here is a letter for you. There are several Gorauds in the regiment, and the letter has already been opened. I see you are wanted at the Dead-letter Office of the Post-office about some business which concerns you."

He took the letter, and at once hastened to the Post-office. There an explanation awaited him of the miscarriage of his remittance, and the mystery which had clouded his spirits and embittered his life for a whole year. The same letter that he had despatched lay before him with its contents intact. It had been written and addressed for him by a comrade in the regiment, the superscription, turned into English, being something in this form—

" To M. Jacques Goraud,
for Widow Goraud,
at La Bastide,
CANTON
of Marseilles."

As it happened, the obliging comrade was a poor scribe, and was without any great experience in letter-writing, or in the art of addressing letters. The only word in the direction which had been plainly written, and stood out in a way to catch the eye, was the word " Canton." This was the key to the mystery; the letter had been sent to China!

At the period in question the sailing-ships conveying the mails took about six months to reach that distant country, and the same time for the return voyage. The soldier's letter had made the double journey; and the blunder being discovered when the letter came back to France, it was sent to the village in Provence to which it was really addressed. But alas! adversity had overtaken the family in the old home. They had left the place, and gone no one knew whither; and, so far as the Post-office was concerned, it only remained to return the letter to the writer through the Dead-letter Office.

The moral of this anecdote is, that letters ought to be plainly addressed. Some examples of the rambling style in which addresses are often written are given in another chapter. It would be a useful work were the school boards to give some instruction in this matter to the children under their care. The copy-books might be headed with specimen addresses for the purpose, and the teachers could point out how desirable it is, in addition to plain writing, that the addresses should be well arranged —the name of the person occupying one line, the street and number another, and the name of the town a conspicuous place to the right, in a line by itself. In this particular "they do things better in France," for in that country instruction of the kind in question was introduced into the primary schools more than twenty years ago.

CHAPTER XVIII.

ODD COMPLAINTS.

THE Post-office, in its extensive correspondence with the public, has often great difficulty in satisfying what are deemed to be the reasonable claims and representations of reasonable people; but it has also to endeavour to satisfy and persuade persons who, as shown by the demands made by them, are not altogether within the category above mentioned. What would be thought of the following appeals made to the Secretary on the subject of the injury supposed to be done by electricity thrown off from telegraph wires?—

"SIR,—I have been rejoicing in the hope that when the last telegraph wire was removed I should be at peace; but alas for human hopes! Last Sunday and Saturday nights, I suppose all the wires must have been working simultaneously, for about 2.0 A.M. I was awakened by the most intense pains in my eyes, and for the two nights I do not think I had more than six hours sleep—that is, none after 2.0 in the morning. Since then I have slept from home, and must continue to do so until either the wires are removed or I leave the house, which I shall be obliged to do, even though it remain unoccupied. The wires are carried in a tube to a pole about 30 yards from my house on the angle, and I imagine that when they are all working, and emerge from the tube, that the electrical matter thrown off must be very great. Pipes have now been run up —— Road, where a pillar or pole might very easily be fixed, and the present one might be removed 100 yards further off, where it would electrify nothing but fields. — With many apologies for troubling you again, for, I hope, the last time, and with many thanks for your kindness hitherto, I am," &c.

" SIR,—I am sorry to be obliged to trouble you again respecting the wires opposite my house at ——. You promised in your favour of —— that the wires should be removed within a month from that date, a great amount of labour having to be gone through. I was not surprised that six months were required for their removal instead of one, and therefore bore patiently with the delay, although my eyesight, and indeed every one's in the house, suffered most severely; but why, when at last eight were removed, should one be allowed to remain? Since the eight have gone, I have been able to sit in my own house without being in as excruciating pain as formerly; but still I am pained, and particularly between the hours of four and seven in the morning. If one wire affects me so much, imagine my sufferings when nine were working! Such being the case, will you kindly cause the remaining wire either to be removed or encased in the vulcanised tube, so as to contract the current.—Thanking you for your kindness hitherto, and hoping you will add this favour to the rest, I am," &c.

There are some persons who suffer from the delusion that their landladies and the sorters in the Post-office habitually conspire to keep up, or rob them of, their letters—letters generally which they look for to bring them money or the right to property. These people are always giving trouble, and are difficult to shake off. On one occasion a lady, who was possessed of a set idea of this kind, called at the General Post-office in London to state her grievance, which she did in most fluent terms. Her complaint was noted for inquiry, and then she went away. An hour or two after, she returned to ascertain whether she had left a packet of papers which she had meanwhile missed; but they could not be found. This circumstance, she stated, convinced her that she had been robbed; and an incident that happened when she quitted the building in the morning confirmed her, she stated, in her idea. A man came up to her and asked if he could show her the way to the Dead-letter Office. "No, thank you," was the reply; "I can find the way myself." She said she knew him to be a magistrate or a judge: "He had a thick neck and flat nose, and the bull-dog type of countenance, and was altogether repulsive-looking." She felt assured he was watching her, &c.

An aged couple in the south of England moved about from place to place in order to escape from persons who were supposed by them to open their letters. Persecuted, as they imagined, in one town, they would take lodgings in another town, and very soon they would suspect the servants of the house and the officers of the Post-office of obtaining a knowledge of the nature of their correspondence. Then they would wait on the postmaster, and generally go through their chronic grievance. The postmaster, in turn, would assure them that their letters were fairly dealt with; but this did not satisfy them, and very soon they were off to another town, in the hope of evading their tormentors, but in reality to go through the same course as before.

Mr Anthony Trollope has left us, in the account of his life, a capital specimen of the frivolous and groundless complaints with which the Post-office has frequently to deal. His account is as follows : " A gentleman in county Cavan had complained most bitterly of the injury done to him by some arrangement of the Post-office. The nature of his grievance has no present significance; but it was so unendurable that he had written many letters, couched in the strongest language. He was most irate, and indulged himself in that scorn which is so easy to an angry mind. The place was not in my district; but I was borrowed, being young and strong, that I might remember the edge of his personal wrath. It was mid-winter, and I drove up to his house, a squire's country seat, in the middle of a snowstorm, just as it was becoming dark. I was on an open jaunting-car, and was on my way from one little town to another, the cause of his complaint having reference to some mail-conveyance between the two. I was certainly very cold, and very wet, and very uncomfortable when I entered his house. I was admitted by a butler, but the gentleman himself hurried into the hall. I at once began to explain my business. 'God bless me!' he said, 'you are wet through. John, get Mr Trollope some brandy-and-water,—very hot.' I was beginning my story about the post again, when he himself took off my greatcoat, and suggested that I should go up to my bedroom before I troubled myself with business. 'Bedroom!' I exclaimed. Then he assured me that he would not turn a dog out on such a night as that, and into a bedroom I was shown, having first drank the brandy-and-water standing at the drawing-room fire. When I came down I was introduced to his daughter, and the three of us went in to dinner. I shall never forget his righteous indignation when I again brought up the postal question, on the departure of the young lady. Was I such a Goth as to contaminate wine with business? So I drank my wine, and then heard the young lady sing, while her father slept in his armchair. I spent a very pleasant evening, but my host was too sleepy to hear anything about the Post-office that night. It was absolutely necessary that I should go away the next morning after breakfast, and I explained that the matter must be discussed then. He shook his head and wrung his hands in unmistakable disgust,—almost in despair. 'But what am I to say in my report?' I asked. 'Anything you please,' he said. 'Don't spare me, if you want an excuse for yourself. Here I sit all the day, —with nothing to do; and I like writing letters.' I did report that Mr —— was now quite satisfied with the postal arrangement of his district; and I felt a soft regret that I should have robbed my friend of his occupation. Perhaps he was able to take up the Poor-law Board, or to attack the Excise. At the Post-office nothing more was heard from him."

The Department not only takes much trouble to investigate cases of irregularity of which definite particulars can be given, but it has frequently to enter into correspondence with persons who seem to have no clear idea of the grounds upon which they make their complaints. A person having stated that his newspapers were not delivered regularly, was requested to answer certain questions on the subject, and the following is the result:—

Questions.	Answers.
Title and date of newspaper? . .	Don't know.
Whether posted within eight days from date of publication?	Don't know.
How many papers were there in the packet?	One.
Was each newspaper under 4 oz. in weight?	Don't know.
Where posted, when, and at what hour? .	Don't know.
By whom posted?	Don't know.
Amount of postage paid, and in what manner paid?	Don't know.

The want of information on the part of the public in regard to postal matters of the most ordinary kind cannot at times but give rise to wonder. A person in a fair position of life, residing in one of the eastern counties of England, having obtained a money-order from his postmaster, payable at a neighbouring town, called again a few days afterwards and complained that his correspondent could not obtain payment in consequence of some irregularity in the advice. Thereupon a second advice was sent; but a few days later the sender called again, stating that the payee was still unable to obtain payment. The sender added that he was quite sure that he had sent the money, as he had the receipt in his pocket. On being asked to show it, he produced the original order, which should, of course, have been forwarded to the payee, and without which the money could not be obtained.

A similar instance of ignorance of the method of business as carried on by the Post-office was exhibited by a poor Irishman in London, and is thus described in the 'Life of Sir Rowland Hill':

"The belief has more than once been manifested at a money-order-office window that the mere payment of the commission would be sufficient to procure an order for £5,—the form of paying in the £5 being deemed purely optional. An Irish gentleman (who had left his hod at the door) recently applied in Aldersgate Street for an order for £5 on a Tipperary post-office, for which he tendered (probably congratulating himself on having hit upon so good an investment) sixpence. It required a lengthened argument to prove to him that he would have to pay the £5 into the office before his friend could receive that small amount in Tipperary; and he went away, after all, evidently convinced that his not having this order was one of the personal wrongs of Ireland, and one of the particular injustices done to hereditary bondsmen only."

CHAPTER XIX.

CURIOUS LETTERS ADDRESSED TO THE POST-OFFICE.

THE fountain-head of the Post-office establishment of this country, whose personal embodiment is the Postmaster-General, possesses very ample means for the collection of information of various kinds through its willing and trusty agents, to be found in every corner of the empire; and this idea seems to be entertained as well by individuals abroad as by our neighbours at home, who, when they fail to ascertain what they want by other means, frequently fall back upon the Postmaster-General for assistance and guidance—the Post-office being pre-eminently a people's institution, whose head even no poor man need fear to approach—at any rate by letter. It is a common expression to say that a thing cannot be done for love or money; but while the Postmaster-General is addressed by inquirers on every variety of subject, it will be found that love and money are at the bottom of many of the communications addressed to him not strictly upon the business of his Department. In the following paragraphs will be found specimens of such letters— some entreating him to render assistance in tracing missing relatives, some asking help in the recovery of fortunes supposed to have been left to the writers, others begging him to obtain situations for them, and the like; but the letters generally explain themselves.

The Dead-letter Office must occasionally be supposed to be a repository for the human dead, as inquiries for deceased persons are sometimes addressed to the "Dead Office." Thus:—

"We heard in the paper about 12 or 14 months back Mary Ann —— the servant girl at London was dead. Please send it to the Printer's office by return of post whether their was a small fortune left for ——."

"i Beg of you to let me if you do no something about a young sailor. his name Hugh ——. he is away now since 4 or 5 years. i hope gentlemen you will let me no if he is dead or alive as i am anxious to no as it is a deal of trouble on my mind as he is a Boy that i have reared up without father an mother an he a deal of trouble on my mind. he has a dark eyes an Brown hair, looking pael. please gentlemen to let me no if you can by return."

"i rite a Line two see if you hard Enny thing of my husband —— that was left at —— ill. pleese will you rite back by return of post as we are in great trobble."

"I have just been hearing of 3 men that was drowned about 9 months ago. i hear there was one of the men went under the name of John ——. Could the manager of the office give any particulars about that man,—what he was like, or if there was such a name, or if he had any friend. He just went amissing about that time. I here enclose a stamp, and address to ——" &c.

Again, the Post-office is asked to hunt up missing relatives :—

"I write to ask you for some information about finding out persons who are missing. I want to find out my mother and sisters who are in Melbourne in Australia i believe—if you would find them out for me please let me know by return of post and also your charge at the lowest."

"i right to you and request of you sinsearly for to help me to find out my husband. i ham quite a stranger in London, only two months left Ireland. i can find know trace of my husband. Your the only gentleman that I know that can help me to find him. thears is letters goes to him to —— in his name and thears is letters comes to him to the —— Post-office for him. Sir you may be sure that i ham low in spirit in a strange contry without a friend. I hope you will be so kind as not to forget me. Sir, I would never find —— for i would go astray, besides I have no money."

" I right these fue lines to you to ask you if you would be so kind as to teel me if there his such a person living in england. She was living at Birmingham last Rtimmas — this his mi sister and brother-in-law—they hant in Birmingham now—let this letter go to every general post office there is."

Then come requests for information about property that may be supposed to have been left by relatives in this country to persons abroad—generally in America—in which the Postmaster-General is usually treated to an insight, more or less deep, into the family affairs or history of the writers, the rich relatives being as a rule faithfully remembered by the poor, while the recollections in the opposite direction would seem to exhibit features of a less enduring nature. Here are a few specimens :—

"KANSAS.

" My grandfather Mr John —— made a will on

or about 22 Oct. 18— dated at —— leaving to his son, my father, £1000, the interest to be paid to him half yearly, the prinsaple to be divided among his children at his death. My father died on the —— last leaving myself and one brother who wishes you to look up and collect the money for us."

"CALIFORNIA.

"I take the plesure in writing a few lines to you wishing you to ask some old friend of yours to find my father wether he is ded or gone to some other place. his trade was when I left a artist and a panter. I left London when I was four years old. I came to California, my mother and him had some fuss. the street where we lived is on oxford street. You will find my name on the regester in the blumsbery church. My father is german and my mother she is french. I wish you would try and find him for me i woud be so glad if you find him. I will pay you for your truble.

"I was born in 18—. if you go to that —— church you will find my age if the church is there or the book. pleas let me know as soon as you can."

"MISSOURI.

"You must excuse me for writing to you for I dont know any one in England. I know the names of no lawyers, and thought I would write to you. We have seen it in our paper several times of money being left to the —— heirs, and heard that a Lawyer of London made a flying visit to St Louis to find the heirs, but failed. My father was born and raised in —— England. His name was —— the oldest son of three. My parents died shortly after we came to America, and I was quite small. I know but little about any of them. I remember hearing my Father say that he had rich relatives who intended to make him their heir. I am very poor; lost everything during the war. If you know of some lawyer who will see to it without money as I have none to invest. Please answer to tell me what you think you can do for me."

"As I have no correspondent in London at present I adopt this plan of procuring one that I can transact business through—the matter I wish to call your attention to is this—To the estate of —— and the heirs. The papers were sent here once but have been lost. —— died in London about 45 years ago and left a large estate of which my client's interest would be about seventy-five thousand dollars at the time of his death—Will you please inform me what it is necessary for us to do in the matter in full."

"UNITED STATES.

"Will you do me the kind favour, as you are the Postmaster and able to know, as I judge of. It is this, give to me the full name and address of any 'Mac———' that you know of in England, or in Scotland, or Ireland, or Wales, or in India, or at or in any other country that you may know of, with their full names and correct address, so that I can write to them myself.

"If you have any list, or book, or pamphlet, with the names of parties who have died, and left money or land to their heirs at law, as I want such information," &c.

A farmer in the country wants a postmaster to act as go-between in a little business matter, and pens him a few lines to the following effect:—

"John ——— acting as Farmer here would be very much obliged to the postmaster if he would be so good as to name a suitable party at ——— to whom he might sell a 30 stone pig of good quality well—for he understands it is the best place to sell. The pig is now quite ready for killing."

A sharp fellow in Tennessee, anxious to become rich by a short cut, wants an instrument to hunt gold and silver, and forthwith applies to the Post-office:—

"I want you to do me a kines, to hand this (letter) to some good watch maker and tell him to see if I can by a instrument to tell where gold or silver is in the ground or if there is a instrument maid to find mettel—gold or silver—that are in the ground. If it will attrack it. A instrument for that perpos. I understand there are sutch a thing made. If so, be pleas tell me where I can by one and what it will cost me. It can be sent to New York to —— where I can get it. I want to get a instrument to hunt gold & silver. You will pleas write to me as I think if there are sutch a thing maid I could get one in your country. I send you a stamp."

A stranger in the country expresses his readiness to reward the Postmaster-General with some partridges if he will get some one to send him a parcel of mithridate mustard:—

"Will you do me the favour of dropping me a line to say if you know of an herbalist or greengrocer that could send me a parcel of Mithridate Mustard. It grows at Hatfield by the river side, and in the streets of Peckham on the Surrey side. As I am a stranger, if you will kindly see if you can get any one to send it me I will send a Post-office order or stamps for what it will cost before they start it by train; or if you will get it I will send it to you. I will send you some partridges for your trouble if you will kindly let me know. It dont grow in any part of ——shire that I am aware of. We have the common hedge mustard growing here, but that wont do what the gentleman wants it for."

A Massachusetts owner of an old clock begs for antiquarian search into the history of an ancient timepiece which has come into his possession:—

"I have tuke the liberty to address you, wishing to know if I could ask the favour by paying you for the trouble I ask to know.

"I have an old clock in my collection made by Henton Brown, London, in the first part of 1700. I would like to know where he was in business and when he died, if it could be ascertained. Please inform me if you could find out by any record in London. I would pay you for all trouble.

"This darling —— is one of the loveliest places in Massachusetts."

Now a brother, being doubtful of a love business in which his sister is concerned, claims the help of the Post-office in clearing matters up:—

"Will you, if you please, let me know if there is such a gentleman as Mr —— in ——. i beleave he is a Chirch Clurdgman. There is a young man in —— who has been engaged to my sister, and he says Mrs —— at —— is his sister. i should very much like to know, if you will oblige me by sending. i thought if Mrs —— was his sister i would rite and ask for his charetar, because he is a stranger to us all."

A Frenchman, with hat in hand, and all ready to propose, merely wants to know, as a preliminary, whether the lady he has in view is still alive!—

" À Monsieur le
   " Directeur de la Poste de Londres.

" J'ai cinquinte trois ans. Veuillez être assez bon de me faire réponse pour me donner des résultats sur l'existence de Madame —— ? Si parfois elle était toujours veuve je voudrais lui faire la proposition de lui demander sa main d'après que j'en aurais des nouvelles. En attendant, Monsieur, votre réponse."

A couple, having got over the proposal and acceptance stage, write for a special licence to get married forthwith :—

" Will you please oblige Susannah —— and Walter —— with the particulars of an aspecial licence to get married—is it possible for you to forward one to us without either of us coming to you — if you enclose the charge and have it returned, would we get one before next Monday week to get married at ———— If you will kindly send by return to the address enclosed the particulars, we should feel greatly obliged."

And matters being advanced one stage further in another case, the following inquiry is sent to the Postal headquarters :—

"Will you please inform me if there is to be a baby show this year at Woolwich; if so, where it is to be holden, and what day."

Nor is the purely social element lost sight of in the letters reaching St Martin's-le-Grand, unconnected with Post-office business, as the two specimens hereafter show :—

"UNITED STATES.

"I have always had a great desire to visit your country, but as I probly never shall, I thought I would write.

"I am a young lady attending the High School at ————, a pictorest town bordering on the ———— river. Our country seat is four miles and a half west of ————. My father is a rich gentleman farmer.

"We have four horses, 30 or 35 head of cattle, 15 or 20 pigs, and a large henery. We have about

250 acres of land, so of course we have to keep a house full of servants.

"We are quite well off in worldly goods, but should be better off if you could inform me about that fortune I expect from a great-uncle, great-aunt, or somebody. It is about half a million either on my father's or mother's side. If you would be so kind as to write and inform me, I would be a thousand times obliged. If you would assist me in getting it I will reward you handsomely. Their name is ———. They used to be very fond of me when I was a crowing infant in my mother's arms. It is a very pretty country out hear, wide rolling prairies enter spersed with fine forests. There is a stream of water running through our land, a stream so softly and peasfully wild that it looks as if nature had onely just made it and laid down her pencil and smiled.

"The schoolroom is just a little ways from ———, the name of our farm. It is the schoolroom where I learnt my A B, abs, but I probly never shall go there to school again. It is vacation now and I have come out on to the farm to stay till school commences again. It seems so nice to be where I can have new milk to drink and nice fresh eggs again. I intend to enjoy myself till school commences again. Father has sold off most all of our horses, but he saved my riding horse, so I intend to have rides and drives without number.

"Well, as I have said as much as you will care to read, I will stop. I hope you will excuse all mistakes as I am not a very old young lady—only 13 years old."

"INDIANA, U.S.

"Enclosed you will please find a letter which I would like for you to give some young lady or gent —lady preferred—who you think would like a correspondent in this country. Will correspond on topics of general interest. For further particulars glance at enclosed letter as it is not sealed.

"To the person in whose hands this message may fall, I would like a correspondent in your city which I think would be of interest to each of us in the way of information.

"My house is in the central part of the United States, my age is 18. I am a partner in the manufacturing of ———. We are also dealers in ——— work. I have travelled all over the United States and Canada. I can give you any information you may desire in reference to this country—this must necessarily be brief. Would like to discuss the habits and nature of our people. To-day is Thanksgiving Day set apart by our president as a day of thanksgiving for our prosperity, &c.; it is observed annually all over the U.S. It is principally observed by giving receptions, dinners, &c. It is snowing to-day; it is the first day of winter we have had. The thermometer is ten above zero. All business is suspended to-day. Please state what day you receive this, as I would like to know how long a letter is on the road—if you do not wish to answer this, please give to some of your friends who will—my address you will find on the enclosed card."

An individual who had apparently, like Rip Van Winkle, been asleep for a number of years, suddenly starts up, and imagines that he has committed a petty fraud upon the Post-office, and so, to ease his conscience, pens the following confession :—

"I enclose you 7 sixpenny stamps, and ask you to credit 2 shillings to revenue as conscience money, as I consider that I owe your Department that amount, having enclosed some weeks ago 3 letters to India within a cover to a friend. At the time of my doing so I thought I was doing no wrong, as the three letters enclosed were merely messages which I did not like to trouble my friend with; but lately I have thought differently, and to quiet my conscience I send you the enclosed stamps, and beg of you to be good enough to acknowledge the receipt of 2s. in the columns of the 'Daily Telegraph' as conscience money from ———. I send 1s. 6d. extra as cost of insertion of the acknowledgment."

The question even of "who shall be the hangman" is thought to be a fit subject for elucidation at the Post-office.

"I hope you will pardon me for asking of you the favour of satisfying a curiosity which cannot, without distortion, be called a morbid one. The question I am about to put is prompted by the statement in the London papers that Marwood is to be the executioner of Peace.

"Now, being fully cognizant, from my readings of journals more than 50 years back, that York has always retained its own executioners (Askern having succeeded Howard), I am sceptical as to the correctness of the above statement. But, assuming it to be correct, I should like to be informed why Peace's particular case should cause a deviation from the old bylaws of your county (York), which gives name to an archiepiscopal province.—Hoping to be pardoned for thus troubling you, I am," &c.

And again, the Postmaster-General is begged to step in and prevent people being called hard names.

"I humbly beg your consideration if there is no

law to stop persons from calling all manner of bad names day after day as it is annoying me very much in my calling as a Gardener and Seedsman; as I have applyed to the office at —— for a summons for a little protection and they tell not, so i think it rather too hard for me as i have done all the good I have had the means to do with to the Hospitals and Institutions and all charityable purposes both in —— and elsewhere if needed; but i suffer from lameness with a ulcerated leg not being able for laborious hard work, although i wish to do as i would be done by. Please to answer this at your leisure."

The next specimens are from persons out of employment:—

"I am taking the liberty of writeing you those few lines, as I am given to understand that you do want men in New South Wales, and I am a Smith by Trade, a single man. My age is 24 next birthday. I shood be verry thankfull if you wood be so kind and send all the particulars by return."

"Having lost my parents, I am desirous of taking a housekeeper's situation where a domestic is kept. Must be a dissenting family, Baptist preferred. Thinking that such a case might come under your notice, I have therefore taken the liberty of sending to you."

"ILLINOIS, U.S.

"Mr Postmaster if you would be so kind as to seek for us work as we are two colored young men of —— Illinois, and would like to come to England and get work as Coachmen or race horse trainers, as we have been experance for twelve years practicesing training—if any further information about it we can be reckemend to any one that wish to hire us, pleas to advertise it in the papers for us."

The two letters of inquiry for situations which follow, are rather amusing owing to their mode of expression, being written by foreigners not having a command of the English idiom; and they will mirror to our own countrymen what sort of figures they must sometimes cut in the eyes of our neighbours across the Channel, when airing their "dictionary French" in the metropolis of fashion :—

"SIR,—I have the honour of coming to solicit of your goodwill of telling me if I could not to pass into the English Telegraphic Administration, and, in the affirmative, what I would must make for that. I have undergone here all the examens demanded by the French Administration; I am now surnumerary, and in a few months I shall be named clerck. I know completely the two Breguet's and Morse machines, and I have begun the 'Hughes.' But, as I am now in a little office where that last is not employed, I cannot improve me actually. I have also some knowledge of the English language. I have kept the last year the post of —— during several months.

"As for my family, my father died from two years, was advocate and sus-prefect —— during thirty years. Myself, at Paris, I have had for scholl-fellow, several young gentlemen, among others, Master ——, the son of the great English perfumery, and others notable manufacturers of London, where I should desire ardently to be clerck, if, by effect of your good-will, you give satisfaction to my claim. I am old of twenty five years, and I have satisfied to the military law.

"I dare to hope, Master the Director, that, be it as it may, you will make to me the honour of answering what I must expect of your resolution, and in the same time yours conditions.

"I am, Master, in expecting, with the most profound respect, your very humble servant."

"SWITZERLAND.

"You will excuse me of the liberty which I take to write to you, but as I know nobody in your town, I have not found an other way for find relations with some body honourable. I will ask you if you can procure me a place in the English Colonies or plantations as teacher in an institution or tutor in a good family. I am old of 22 years. I have gone a good course of study in the college and gymnasium in ——, and I have held during a 1½ year in the pensionnat —— an place as teacher of French language and Mathematics. I can give you some good Certificates; I speak French, German, and a little English. I should wish for be entirely defrayed of the charges of lodging, nourishment, &c., to have a good salary and the voyage paid. These are my conditions; perhaps will you found something for satisfy them. I will give you a commission proportionably to the importance of the place. I hope Sir a favorible answer, and it is in this expectation that I am," &c.

The next letter is of another kind, and is not a bad effort for a schoolboy:—

"Not having received the live bullfinch mentioned by you as having arrived at the Returned-letter Office two days ago, having been posted as a letter contrary to the regulations of the postal system, I now write to ask you to have the bird fed and forwarded at once to ——; and to apply for all fines and expenses to ——. If this is not done and I do not receive the bird before the end of the week, I shall write to the Postmaster-General, who is a very intimate friend of my father's, and ask him to see that measures are taken against you for neglect. This is not an idle threat, so you will oblige by following the above instructions."

In the rules laid down by the Post-office for the guidance of its officers and the information of the public, an endeavour is made to use plain language; but in any case of doubtful meaning, the Post-office, having framed the rules, claims the right of interpreting them. At one time an element in the definition of a newspaper, under the newspaper post, was that it should consist of a sheet or sheets *unstitched*. A newspaper having been taxed a penny, owing to the sheets being tied together with thread, the person who sent the newspaper made the following sharp remonstrance:—

"SIR,—I had hoped that the utterly indefensible regulation in reference to which I send a wrapper had been silently abolished. The public is quite unable to understand why stitching is made the *differentia* of a newspaper and a pamphlet, and I can hardly suppose that the occasional penalty of 1d. can be the motive. If in the printed regulations you would assign a sufficient motive, no one would of course object. Allow me to ask, if a piece of string is passed through two holes and the ends not tied in a knot, if that is considered stitching? According to Johnson's definition of stitching my newspaper was not stitched, but tied, *for I used no needle.*"

Again, a person having suffered the loss of a letter, containing something of value perhaps, launched a bolt from Scripture at the Department:—

"I got no redress before, but I trust I shall on this occasion; or else there must be something rotten in the State of Denmark. Judas Iscariot was a thief, and carried the bag, and it will be a pity and a great scandal if he has found a successor in some branch of the Post-office."

A fond parent, finding that some white mice sent by his little boy were detained in the Post-office, owing to the transmission of live animals being contrary to regulations, writes very indignantly to the Department, overlooking its impersonal nature, and singles out the officer whose performance of duty provoked him for such castigation as his pen was capable of inflicting. Here is his letter, and it is mild compared with some of the comminatory effusions which occasionally reach the Post-office:—

"SIR,—Tuesday last week my little son sent

three white mice to a friend at ——, in a wooden revolving cage, done up strongly in brown paper, with such sufficient biscuit to serve them for the day; but to-day we have heard that your officious manager at our district office delayed sending it, and wrote instead to ask the address of the sender, and called to-day to say he would not forward the cage. Now allow me to ask by what law has he dared to delay the delivery, and by that means no doubt killed the little animals? They were in a wooden cage, carefully packed, and could not in any way have been an annoyance; they were not explosive, they were not loose; and I know of no notice in your regulations whereby he dare to delay the delivery and starve the little creatures to death. I would also ask by what law did he open the package? The full postage was on the parcel, and no doubt the stamp (4d.) has been obliterated, which he will of course have to refund, as also the cost of the white mice; he cannot, of course, pay the disappointment. Why did the office at —— take it if wrong? But it is not, because he has sent several such little creatures to others, and they have always reached safely. He likewise had the impudence to say I was to send to the office for the cage, &c. I feel assured you will be equally astonished with me at his assurance. The package was booked from here over eight days ago, and it was his duty to have delivered it. Please see to it; the address on the parcel was ———."[1]

A young man, conceiving that he had a call to the ministry, quitted the Post-office service to qualify for that vocation. After a time the following letter, which fully explains its own purpose, reached headquarters :—

"Enclosed is from a young man in my parish, whose sister is a permanent invalid, and his father a retired Church officer, so that he must have a *dry* crust.

"I suppose his *style* does not take amongst the Independent congregations wanting pastors, so he is sent back to business (a great mistake, I told him, he ever left it).

"He says something about being over twenty-four years of age; but I think it hard he should go to college for three years, and then be sent adrift without a plank. Is it possible to reinstate him at the Post-office? He goes to chapel in my parish, and his family are all deserving and needy. Excuse this effort to help a respectable though needy fellow."

[1] The mice were duly fed during their detention, and were eventually sent for by the applicant.

CHAPTER XX.

SINGULAR COINCIDENCES.

EXTRAORDINARY coincidences have been chronicled in connection with almost every situation in life, some fortunate and attended with profit to those involved, others unfortunate or disastrous; and the Post-office is no exception to the rule as being a field for the observation of such occurrences. The peculiar nature of the coincidences to be observed in the following examples may be worthy of note, or at any rate the cases may repay their perusal with some small degree of interest :—

"Among the workmen employed in some alterations at a nobleman's country seat were two bearing exactly the same Christian name and surname, but unconnected and unacquainted with each other, one being a joiner, the other a mason. The joiner, who was a depositor in the Post-office Savings Bank, having received no acknowledgment of a deposit of

£3, obtained a duplicate. The mason, who was not a depositor, became insane and was removed to a lunatic asylum about the same time; and the original acknowledgment, intended for the joiner, having fallen into the hands of the mason's mother, she concluded that the account was his, and made a claim for the money towards defraying the expenses of his maintenance, and was with difficulty undeceived."

A registered packet containing a valuable gold seal was sent to a firm of fancy stationers in Newcastle-on-Tyne, and delivered at its address in due course. Complaint was shortly afterwards made, however, that the young person who opened the packet found the seal was not enclosed, and inquiries were at once set on foot in the Post-office to discover how and where it could have been abstracted. A week or two after, and while these inquiries were still proceeding, the firm in question reported that a tradesman in town had presented to them the identical seal, with the view of ascertaining its value! This information served as a clue to the elucidation of the matter, and the loss of the seal was shown to have occurred in the following fashion: In the process of opening the packet, the young person concerned had carelessly allowed the seal to fall, unobserved by her; it got mixed up with waste-paper, which formed part of some waste shortly thereafter removed to the premises of a marine-store dealer, where it underwent a course of sortation. An old woman engaged in this work found the seal, appropriated it, and without more ado pawned it. The person with whom it was pledged was he who presented it at the address where it had dropped from the letter. The coincidence is not only a curious one, but the case illustrates how, but for the coincidence, the blame of the loss would have rested on the Post-office.

A traveller in the north of Europe became sadly puzzled with letters which followed him about, although not intended for him, and the difficulties in his case are described in a letter written by him, of which the following is a transcript :—

"I am sorry you have had so much trouble respecting the registered letter supposed to have been lost in transmission from my wife to me in ——. But I assure you the letter was most carefully and punctually delivered, not having been even a post behind its due time, and I think your case can hardly have referred to me at all. There was another Rev. J—— D—— (the same name) travelling in Norway at the same time, whose letters kept crossing my path everywhere; and when I read them, I was almost in doubt whether I was myself or him, for his wife had the same name as mine, and his baby the same name as mine, and just the same age ; but who he can be I cannot make out, only he is not I. Perhaps the registered letter which has given you such trouble may have been for him. It may satisfy you, however, to know that mine was all right."

The following incident occurred about twenty years ago. A gentleman of the uncommon name of Onions was travelling in Scotland, and was expected by his friends to call at a certain post-office for letters on a particular day. The day prior to this, a telegram reached this post-office from his home in the south of England, requesting that he might be told to return at once, owing to the serious illness of his brother. The telegram upon its receipt was duly placed in the proper box by the clerk in charge of the *poste restante* at the time, and who of course, the telegram being open, was aware of its contents. Next day, when the same clerk was upon duty, a Mr Onions presented himself, asking for letters ; but the clerk, on going to the box to get the aforesaid telegram, was unable to find it, nor could any one in the office at the time say anything about it. Mr Onions was, however, informed of its import, whereupon he said he had no brother, but as his father had been ailing when he left, he supposed a mistake of "brother" for "father" had been made in transmission, and that the message was no doubt intended for him. He then left the office. A few days later the postmaster received a letter from this gentleman, then in the south of England, stating that he had been made the victim of a cruel hoax (he having found on reaching home that no telegram had been sent to him), and he was the more convinced of this because his visit to Scotland was in pursuance of his honeymoon. The matter being investigated, it transpired that on the morning of the day on which Mr Onions called for letters, another Mr Onions, for whom the message was meant, had called and received the telegram from a clerk who shortly thereafter went off duty. The confusion had thus arisen through two persons of the same uncommon name calling at the same post-office on the same day for letters, and, as it happened, applying for their letters at hours when two different clerks were in attendance.

In the following case the names are fictitious, but in their similarity they will adequately illustrate the narrative :—

The sudden expansion of telegraph business upon the transfer of the telegraphs to the State in 1870, necessitated the employment of a large number of inexperienced operators, and some awkward blunders were the consequence. In the year mentioned, a Liverpool man named Parlane went to London; but before parting with his wife, it was arranged that on a certain day he would telegraph whether she should join him in London or he would return to Liverpool. On the appointed day the promised telegram was sent asking his wife to come to London, the message being directed (we shall say) to Mrs Parlane, 24 Menzies Street, Toxteth Park, Liverpool. By some accidental failure of current, or imperfect signalling, the word "Menzies"[1] reached Liverpool as "Meins,"[1] and there being no Meins Street in Liverpool, the messenger was directed to take the message for trial to Main Street, for which it was thought it might be intended. The messenger found at 24 Main Street[1] a Mrs M'Farlane, and to this person the message was presented. The names being similar, Mrs M'Farlane opened the telegram, and her husband also being in London, she had no doubt whatever that the command which it contained to repair to London, though altogether unexpected, was intended for herself. That evening she accordingly started for the metropolis.

Meanwhile Mrs Parlane had been suffering intense anxiety at not receiving the promised telegram, and

[1] The names are given from memory.

being unable longer to endure the suspense in which she found herself, she likewise started for London the same evening. Strange as it may appear, both Mrs Parlane and Mrs M'Farlane travelled to London not only by the same train, but in the same compartment; and it was by a comparison of notes that the telegram intended for the one was discovered to have got into the hands of the other. The string of coincidences in this matter is exceedingly singular— viz., that two persons of similar names should reside at the same number in neighbouring streets; that the husbands of both should be in London at the same time; that the two wives should travel to London in the same train; and that they should find themselves companions in the same compartment.

Identity in names and addresses in all particulars sometimes gives rise to trouble and inconvenience. Through the misdelivery of a savings-bank acknowledgment, it was brought to light that in a suburban district of London, where there were two terraces bearing exactly the same designation, there were residing, at the same number in each, two persons having not only the same surname, but the same Christian name.

But even more curious are the following facts in the matter of similar names and addresses, though in this instance nothing of ill-consequence has yet arisen beyond the occasional misdelivery of a letter. In Edinburgh at the present time (1885), there resides at 5 St Andrew's Terrace a Mr James Gibson, and, immediately opposite, at 5 St Andrew's Place, another Mr James Gibson. It happens, also, that a Mr John Gibson is to be found at 5 St Andrew Square. Hence we have this very singular series of almost identical addresses, the persons concerned being all different, and, so far as we are aware, unacquainted with each other :—

   (1) Mr J. Gibson,
     5 St Andrew's Terrace.

   (2) Mr J. Gibson,
     5 St Andrew's Place.

   (3) Mr J. Gibson,
     5 St Andrew Square.

In consequence of the misdelivery of a post-packet, the following case of almost identical addresses in two different towns was brought under notice :—

  Mr Andrew Thom,
   Boot Maker,
    8 South Bridge Street,
      Airdrie.

And
>   Mr Andrew Thom,
>   Boot Top Manufacturer,
>   86 South Bridge,
>   Edinburgh.

Not very long ago, two letters directed to Mrs R—— at her residence in Edinburgh were duly delivered there; but as the lady was at the time living at the Grand Hotel in London, they were placed under a fresh cover by one of her family and forwarded thither. Some days thereafter the Postmaster of Glasgow received a communication from a Mrs R—— (the same name), residing at the Grand Hotel, expressing great astonishment that the two letters, which she now returned, had been sent to her, since her permanent address was not in Edinburgh, but Glasgow. The matter was afterwards explained, on the fact becoming known that two ladies of the same name, one hailing from Glasgow, the other from Edinburgh, had been living at the same time in the same hotel, and that the waiter had delivered the letters to the wrong person.

CHAPTER XXI.

SAVINGS-BANK CURIOSITIES.

WITH persons who deposit their hard-earned savings in the Post-office Savings Bank, there is sometimes observed a disposition, not to be wondered at in their case, to use more than ordinary care in keeping their savings secret,—which care, however, does not always secure the aim which they have in view, but results in quite a different fashion.

A domestic servant who had invested in a Trustee Savings Bank about £100, entered the holy bonds of matrimony in 1826, when it might have been expected she would be ready to admit the man of her choice to a knowledge of her monetary worth; but instead of doing so, she concealed this matter from him, and he remained ignorant of it throughout the remainder of his life. The sum at her credit in the Trustee Savings Bank was afterwards transferred to the Post-office Savings Bank, and by dint of saving she added to that amount nearly £50 more. At length, in 1862, after thirty-six years of married life, she died, leaving her husband with three children, but without revealing what she had so jealously guarded, in the interest, no doubt, of her children. Not many months thereafter the man married again. The second wife seems by some means to have come to a knowledge of her predecessor's savings, and in order to pave the way to future possession, prevailed upon the old man to make a will in her favour, which he consented to do, not knowing that he was worth anything, and thus gratified a whim, as he might suppose, at small cost. The effect of this was, that, when the old man died, the second wife obtained the whole amount of the account, while the poor children, whose mother had kept her secret so many years in their interest, derived no benefit whatever from the savings which she had hoped to leave them.

An Irishman who had managed to get some savings together in the savings bank was exercised as to the safe-keeping of his deposit-book, and he adopted the following plan to give himself peace of mind on this score. First of all, he placed his book inside a box, which he then locked. This box he placed inside a second box, which he locked likewise. Continuing the series of operations, he locked the second box inside a third box; and then, to crown the business, hung up all the keys in a place where they were accessible to many persons. In a short time the book disappeared, and by forging the signature of the rightful owner, the thief succeeded in obtaining payment of the poor Irishman's deposits to the amount of about £100. This unfortunate depositor is a type of a considerable class of persons, who show themselves capable of carrying out plans to a certain stage, but fail in some one particular to give them the completeness necessary to success.

Another individual who had some misgivings as to the safety of his deposit-book, suggested a plan for his identification, furnishing the necessary data, which were his age, and a statement that he had a scar under his left arm, known to himself alone. He desired that no one should be allowed to withdraw money from his account unless upon satisfactory information being given on these points.

In another instance a depositor proposed to send his likeness, with a view to his identification, lest some other person might get possession of his book, and so withdraw his savings. He then proceeded in his letter to touch upon another matter as follows: "There are some little articles I would like to get from London, and one of them is some natural leaf-tobacco, which I would be glad if you sent me an ounce of, and charge me for it—it is only to be bought in the largest tobacco-stores." Not receiving the tobacco, he expressed surprise in a subsequent letter that his request had not been complied with, observing, by way of reproach perhaps, that "the commonest person in America (my country) can speak to General Grant, and there is nothing said wrong about it."

A good deal of trouble has to be taken in sifting claims for moneys in the Post-office Savings Bank—especially in cases where the persons concerned are of a poor and illiterate class. The following may be taken as a case in point:—

"An account had been opened in a manufacturing town in Yorkshire in 1868 by a girl who was described as a minor over seven years of age. Only one deposit was made; and nothing further was heard of the account until 1872, when a labourer wrote from Northumberland claiming the money as having been deposited by his wife, who had recently died. On a marriage certificate being forwarded, it was found that the marriage took place in 1851, and that the wife was thirty-five years of age at that time. The applicant also stated that he could swear to his wife's handwriting, whereas the depositor could not write. He was informed of these discrepancies, but still insisted that the money was deposited by his wife, and employed a lawyer to urge his claim."

Sometimes depositors mislay their deposit-books, or lose them altogether, and in course of time forget that they have anything lying at their credit. This is an instance of such a case: A depositor, upon being reminded that he had not sent up his book for a periodical examination—the time for which was already past—replied that his book was lost, but that if there was any balance due to him, he would be glad to have the particulars. The amount due to him was upwards of £10; but as, when a depositor has lost his book, it is usual to test his knowledge of the account, this course was followed, when, from the answers received, it was made clear that he was entirely ignorant of the sum standing to his credit — and, indeed, that he believed his account to be closed. But for the notice sent to him in regard to his deposit-book, he would never have made any claim.

As might readily be supposed, strange communications are often received on savings-bank business —some quaint and curious, though written quite seriously, while others are evidently written with the intention of making fun; yet another class deriving their peculiarities from a too common cause —want of education. A few of such specimens are given as follows:—

A depositor being asked to furnish particulars

of his account, the reply received from some one who had opened the letter on his behalf was to this effect: "He is a tall man, deeply marked with smallpox, has one eye, wears a billycock, and keeps a pea-booth at Lincoln Fair,"—a description ample enough, and one that would rejoice the heart of a detective.

The envelopes supplied to depositors, in which they send their books to headquarters, have within the flap a space provided to receive the depositor's address, and the request is printed underneath— "State here whether the above address is permanent." This request has called forth such rejoinders as these—"Here we have no continuing city," "This is not our rest," "Heaven is our home," "Yes, *D.V.*" In one case the reply was "No, *D.V.*, for the place is beastly damp and unhealthy;" while another depositor, being floored by the wording of the inquiry, wrote—"Doant know what permanent is"!

When deposit-books are lost or destroyed, some explanation is usually forthcoming as to how the circumstance occurred, and some of these statements are of a very curious kind. Thus a person employed in a travelling circus accounted for the loss of his book in these terms: "Last night, when I was sleeping in the tent, one of our elephants broke loose and tore up my coat, in the pocket of which was my bank-book, and eat part of it. I enclose the fragments." In another case the statement furnished was: "I think the children has taken it out of doors and lost it, as they are in the habbit of playing shutal cock with the backs of books." Another depositor said that his book was "supposed to have been taken from the house by our tame monkey." While in a further case the explanation vouchsafed was as follows: "I was in a yard feeding my pigs. I took off my coat and left it down on a barrell; while engaged doing so, a goat in the yard pulled it down. The book falling out, the goat was chewing it when I caught her." A sergeant in the army lost his book "whilst in the act of measuring a recruit for the army,"—a circumstance which is, perhaps, not creditable to the recruit. A needy depositor pledged his coat, forgetting, however, to withdraw his deposit-book, which was in one of the pockets. On applying to redeem his property, he found that the coat had been mislaid by the pawnbroker, and that his book was thus lost. In a somewhat similar way another depositor accounted for his loss "through putting the book in an old coat-pocket, and selling the coat without taking out the book again." It was suggested that he should apply to the person who purchased the coat, when he replied that he had been "to the rag merchant," but could find no trace of his book. On another occasion a depositor explained that his book had been mutilated by a cat. Another book, which was kept in a strong box in a pigsty, had been destroyed by the tenant—a pig. While in yet another case the depositor explained that "his little puppy of a dog got hold of it and tore it all to pieces—not leaving so much as the number." A coast-guardsman employed on the Sussex coast, writing shortly after the occurrence of some severe storms, explained that his book had been washed away with the whole of his household effects. In a case of mutilation of a book, the following account of the circumstance was given by the owner: "In the early part of last year I was taken seriously ill away from home; and having my bank-book with me, I wrote in the margin in red ink what was to be done with the balance in case of a fatal result, and as a precaution against its being wrongfully claimed on my recovery, I cut this out."

These are some of the more curious instances of the loss of books—the loss being ordinarily ascribed either to change of residence, to the book being dropped in the street, or to its being burnt with waste-paper.

CHAPTER XXII.

REPLIES TO MEDICAL INQUIRIES.

FOR many years past it has been incumbent upon all candidates seeking employment in the Post-office, as in other public departments, to undergo medical examination, with the view of securing healthy persons for the service; and in the course of such examinations the medical officer requires to make inquiry into the state of health of the candidates' parents, brothers, sisters, &c., the information being elicited in forms to be filled up by the candidates. Though it is not to be expected that persons entering as postmen, messengers, and so on, should exhibit perfection in their orthography, still, in referring to the more common troubles that afflict the human frame, some approach to an intelligible description of diseases might be hoped for. Dr Lewis, who held the post of medical officer in the General Post-office, London, for many years, recorded the following examples of answers received to his questions:—

"Father had sunstroke, and I caught it of him." "My little brother died of some funny name." "A great white cat drawed my sister's breath, and she died of it." A parent died of "Apperplexity"; another died of "Parasles." One "caught Tiber fever in the Hackney Road"; another had had "goarnders"; a third "burralger in the head." Some of the other complaints were described as "rummitanic pains," "carracatic fever," "indigestion of the lungs," "toncertina in the throat," "pistoles on the back." One candidate stated that "his sister was consumpted, now she's quite well again"; while the sister of another was stated to have "died of compulsion."

It is to be hoped that the work of the school boards will be seen in the absence of such answers from the medical officers' schedules of the future.

CHAPTER XXIII.

VARIOUS.

Superstition.

SUPERSTITION rarely stands in the way of the extension of postal accommodation or convenience; but a case of the kind occurred some time ago in the west of Ireland. Application was made for the erection of a wall letter-box, and authority had been granted for setting it up; but when arrangements came to be made for providing for the collection of letters, no one could be found to undertake the duty, in consequence of a general belief among the poorer people in the neighbourhood that, at that particular spot, "a ghost went out nightly on parade." The ghost was stated to be a large white turkey without a head.

Curious Names.

Everything that departs from the usual mode or fashion of things is regarded as curious, and the term may be applied also to the incidence of names and professions, either in regard to their relative fitness of relationship, or to an opposite quality. As the sight of two or three individuals with wooden legs walking in company would be sure to claim our attention, if it did not excite our mirth, so the coming together of persons having similar names under the same roof by mere chance, would not fail to attract notice, and be thought a peculiar circumstance. Of the first class the following cases may be noted,—namely, that at Torquay, Devonshire, there used to be a butcher called Bovine; in the east of London there is a James Bull, a cowkeeper; and at Birnam, Perthshire, a gardener and strawberry-grower called John Rake. There is further, we are informed, at Cork a person carrying on the pawnbroking business whose name is Uncle, than which there could be nothing more appropriate. Of the second class the following is an instance, persons of the names given having been employed together in a single office of the General Post-office some years ago :—

A Lacroix.	A Parsons.	A Partridge.
A Laforêt.	An Archer.	A Peacock,
A Deforge.	A Fisher.	and
A Defraine.	A Hunter.	One Berdmore.
A Clark.		

Letter-box, St Martin's-le-Grand.

So much has it become the custom in these later times for the Post-office to afford facilities to the public in whatever will tend to increase the business of the Department, that in all large towns pillar-boxes or branch offices are dotted about everywhere at short distances, thus altering the conditions which formerly obtained, when the chief office was the great central point where correspondence had to be deposited for despatch. London is no exception to this general plan of accommodation, and there may be some lingering regrets that the stirring scenes which used to attend the closing of the letter-box at St Martin's-le-Grand (when the great hall led right through the building) no longer exist, at least as things worthy of note. Lewins, who wrote the History of the Post-office (Her Majesty's Mails), thus describes what nightly took place at the closing of the box at six o'clock :—

"The newspaper window, ever yawning for more, is presently surrounded and besieged by an array of boys of all ages and costumes, together with children of a larger growth, who are all alike pushing, heaving, and surging in one great mass. The window, with tremendous gape, is assaulted with showers of papers, which fly thicker and faster than the driven snow. Now it is, that small boys of eleven and twelve years of age, panting Sinbad-like under the weight of huge bundles of newspapers, manage somehow to dart about and make rapid sorties into other ranks of boys, utterly disregarding the cries of the official policemen, who vainly endeavour to reduce the tumult into something like post-office order. If the lads cannot quietly and easily disembogue, they will whizz their missiles of intelligence over other people's heads, now and then sweeping off hats and caps with the force of shot. The gathering every moment increases in number, and intensifies in purpose; arms, legs, sacks, baskets, heads, bundles, and woollen comforters—for who ever saw a veritable newspaper boy without that appendage?—seem to be getting into a state of confusion and disagreeable communism, and yet 'the cry is still, they come.' Heaps of papers of widely opposed political views are thrown in together—no longer placed carefully in the openings; they are now sent in in sackfuls and basketfuls, while over the heads of the surging crowd were flying back the empty sacks, thrown out of the office by the porters inside. Semi-official legends, with a very strong smack of probability about them, tell of sundry boys being thrown in, seized, emptied, and thrown out again void. As six o'clock approaches still nearer and nearer, the turmoil increases more perceptibly, for the intelligent British public is fully alive to the awful truth that the Post-office officials never allow a minute of grace, and that 'Newspaper Fair' must be over when the last stroke of six is heard. One —in rush files of laggard boys, who have purposely loitered in the hope of a little pleasurable excitement; two—and grown men hurry in with the last sacks; three — the struggle resembles nothing so much as a pantomimic *mêlée;* four — a babel of tongues vociferating desperately; five — final and furious showers of papers, sacks, and bags; and six — when all the windows fall like so many swords of Damocles, and the slits close with such a sudden and simultaneous snap, that we naturally suppose it to be a part of the Post-office operations that attempts should be made to guillotine a score of hands; and then all is over, so far as the outsiders are concerned."

Though the tradition referred to of boys being thrown into the letter-box may not have a very sure foundation in fact, it is the case at any rate that a live dog was posted at Lombard Street, and falling into the bag attached to the letter-box, it was not discovered till the contents of the bag were emptied out on a table in the General Post-office.

Curious Explanations.

In the considerable army of servants who carry on the work of the Post-office, embracing all grades from the Postmaster-General to the rural postman, are to be found individuals of every temperament, character of mind, and disposition—the candid, the simple, the astute, the wary; and the peculiarities of the individuals assert themselves in their official dealings as surely as they would do in the ordinary connections of life.

The following "explanations" furnished by postmasters who had failed to send up their accounts at the proper time, will illustrate the procedure of the candid or simple when in trouble, who seem quite unnecessarily to give every detail of their shortcomings, instead of doing, as most men would do in the circumstances — make a general excuse :—

"My daily accounts would have reached you in time; but on Saturday morning, whilst purchasing American cheeses and sampling them, I tasted some of them, which brought on a bilious complaint, so that I was obliged to suspend work on Monday. Being now somewhat better, I trust all will go on right."

"I regret the daily accounts should have been delayed so long; but having some friends to see me, the accounts were forgotten."

"The Postmistress of ——, Cambridge, is very sorry that she has not sent her accounts before this; she will be sure to do so to-morrow. The delay is on account of her having three little motherless grandchildren staying with her for a few days."

The following will bear company with the three foregoing specimens. It is a pathetic appeal from a letter-receiver, who, mistaking the purpose for which a certain credit of official money was allowed him, spent it, and was unexpectedly called upon to account for the balance due by him to the head office:—

"Mr ——, Superintendent of the Money-order Department, called upon me yesterday, and dispelled a very mistaken notion of mine—viz., that as I had given a guarantee of £200, I was perfectly 'justifiable' in making use of a portion of the money received for my own business. I am now very sorry indeed that the idea had gained such an ascendancy over me as it had done. The letter I received from you a few days ago aroused me from that delusive lethargy into which I was sinking; and if you would have the kindness to compare the amount now with what it was then, you will perceive that an effort has been made to retrieve my folly.

"My object in writing this to you is an earnest appeal not to degrade me in the position I have struggled so hard to maintain through such distress as we have had, by suspending the business of the office. I beg and earnestly entreat of you to give me time to recover myself; and I assure you that under such a stimulation a vigorous effort will be made to place myself in that honourable position which it has been my desire to hold. Therefore, hoping that you will take a favourable view of the case, I subscribe myself, your contrite and obedient servant."

Prisoners of War.

The following incident, though not directly bearing upon Post-office matters, has a relation to letters. It forms the subject of a pathetic story, and brings into contrast the possible isolation of poor fellows who may be taken in war, with the rapid and constant intercourse kept up between the peoples of enlightened countries during times of peace by the intermediary of the Post-office. The facts are here quoted from a notice of the circumstance published in a local newspaper :—

"The extensive works for the manufacture of paper belonging to Alex. Cowan & Sons at Valleyfield, near Edinburgh, were in 1811, owing to the dulness of trade, sold to Government, and converted into a prison for the French soldiers and sailors, of whom over 6000 were kept from 1811 to 1814, when peace was happily established between Britain and France. During these three years 309 died, whose remains rest in a quiet spot near the mills. Of these, a list of the names, ages, and place of capture is preserved by Messrs Cowan. The mills were reacquired from Government about 1818, and are carried on as among the largest paper-mills of Britain by the same firm. In some repairs lately carried out at these works (1881) an old floor was lifted, and underneath was found a letter written by a prisoner, but which he was never able to despatch. A copy of this letter is annexed, as possibly some of the writer's relatives may see it and be interested by a perusal."

The French is not very good; but here it is:—

"PRISON, VALLEYFIEL,
16 *Mars, année* 1812.

"MON CHER PERRE ET MA CHER MÈRE,—D'après plusieur lettre que je vous ecrives, étant en Angleterre, sans en avoir pu en recevoir aucune réponse.

Je ne sais à quoi attribuer cette interuption, et depuis on va arrivez en Ecosse, je me suis toujours empressez pour vous donner de mes nouvelles, et qui a été bien impossible, à moins jusqu'à presens, d'en recevoir. Je désirai ardement d'en recevoir des votres, ainsi mon cherre père et ma cherre mère, je vous prie trêes umblement de prendre des procotions pour me donné de vos nouvellé, est des changement du pays, est dans ce qui est égale à mon égard, de la famille, seullement pour à l'égard de ma santé, elle a toujours etté bonne depuis mon de part. Je désire que la présente vous soient pareille, ainsi que mes frerre et seurre, paran, et ami, rien autre chose que je puis vous marqué pour le ———. Je soussignez Jean François Noel de Sariget, la Commune de Saint Leonard, Canton de Fraize, arrondissement de Saint Dies, Departemeant Voges. Monsieur Perigord Lafeste, Banquier à Paris, dans la Rue de Mont No. 9. Je soussignez Jean Nicolas Demange de Saint Leonard, Canton de Franche."

A handsome monument was erected in 1830 over the last resting-place of the poor prisoners who died during their period of captivity, and it bears the following inscription:—

"Près de ce lieu réposent les cendres de 309 prisonniers de guerre morts dans ce voisinage entre le 21 Mars 1811 et le 26 Juillet 1814.

"Nés pour bénir les vœux de vieillissantes mères,
Par le sort appelés
A devenir amants aimés, epoux, et pères,
Ils sont morts exilés !

"Plusieurs habitans de cette Paroisse aimant à croire que tous les hommes sont frères, firent élever ce monument l'an 1830."

Explosion in a Pillar-box.

A singular accident, though one not altogether unique in its character, befell one of the pillar letter-boxes in Montrose some years ago. A street had been opened up for the purpose of effecting repairs on the gas-pipes, and while the examination and repairs were in progress, some gas, escaping from the pipes, found its way into the letter-box. The night watchman, intending to light his pipe, struck a match on the box close to the aperture, when a violent explosion immediately followed, blowing out the door, and otherwise doing damage; but, luckily, neither the watchman nor the letters sustained any injury.

The Mulready Envelope.

The failure of the Mulready envelope to establish itself in public favour is surely a monument to the caprice of the national taste, if it be not an evidence of how readily the tide of thoughtless opposition may set in to reject that which is new or unusual, without serious grounds for dislike. A facsimile of the design is here given, the envelopes for sale being printed in two colours—black and blue.

It was introduced to the notice of the public at the time of the establishment of the penny postage, being intended to supply a desideratum in this respect, that the cover should serve the combined purposes of an envelope and a postage-stamp, the envelopes being good for a postage of one penny or twopence, according as they were printed in black or blue.

Mulready, a member of the Royal Academy, was the artist, and the design had the approval of the Royal Academicians, so that it did not go forth without substantial recommendations. If the subjects be examined, it will be found that they are accurately drawn, ingeniously worked together, and apposite in their references to the beneficent work of the Post-office Department. Britannia sending forth her messengers to every quarter of the globe, ships upon the sea with sails unfurled ready to obey her instant behests, the reindeer as the emblem of speed in the regions of snow, intercourse with the nations of the East and of the West, and the blessings of cheap postage in its social aspects, are all suitably depicted. Yet the whole thing fell flat; the envelope drew down upon itself scorn and ridicule, and it had to be quickly withdrawn. In the end, it was necessary to provide special machinery to destroy the immense quantities of the envelope which had been prepared for issue.

It is amusing, however, to read the contemptuous and very funny criticisms which were showered upon the artist and Mr Rowland Hill by the newspapers of the day, in one of which the following remarks appear:—

"The envelopes and half-sheets have an engraved surface, extremely fantastic, and not less grotesque. In the centre, at the top, sits Britannia, throwing out her arms, as if in a tempest of fury, at four winged urchins, intended to represent postboys, letter-carriers, or Mercuries, but who, instead of making use of their wings and flying, appear in the act of striking out or swimming, which would have been natural enough if they had been furnished with fins instead of wings. On the right of Britannia there are a brace of elephants, all backed and ready to start, when some Hindoo, Chinese, Arabic, or Turkish merchants, standing quietly by, have closed their bargains and correspondence. The elephants are symbolic of the lightness and rapidity with which Mr Rowland Hill's penny postage is to be carried on, and perhaps, also, of the power requisite for transporting the £1500 a-year to his quarters, which is all he obtains for strutting about the Post-office with his hands in his pockets, and nothing to do, like a fish out of water. On the left of Britannia, who looks herself very much like a termagant, there is an agglomeration of native Indians, missionaries, Yankees, and casks of tobacco, with a sprinkling of foliage, and the rotten stem of a tree, not forgetting a little terrier dog inquisitively gliding between the legs of the mysterious conclave to see the row. Below, on the left, a couple of heads of the damsel tribe are curiously peering over a valentine just received (scene, Valentine's Day), whilst a little girl is pressing the elders for a sight of Cupid, and the heart transfixed with a score of arrows. On the right, again, stands a dutiful boy, reading to his anxious mamma an account of her husband's hapless shipwreck, who, with hands clasped, is blessing Rowland Hill for the cheap rate at which she gets the disastrous intelligence. With very great propriety the name of the artist is conspicuously placed in one corner, so that the public and posterity may know who is the worthy Oliver of the genius of a Rowland on this important occasion. As may well be imagined, it is no common man, for the mighty effort has taxed the powers of the Royal Academy itself, if the engraved announcement of W. Mulready, R.A., in the corner, may be credited. Considering the infinite drollery of the whole, the curious assortment of figures and faces; the harmonious *mélange* of elephants, mandarins' tails, Yankee beavers, naked Indians squatted with their hindquarters in front, Cherokee chiefs with feathered tufts shaking missionaries by the hand; casks of Virginia threatening the heads of young ladies devouring their loveletters; and the old woman in the corner, with hands uplifted, blessing Lord Lichfield and Sir Rowland for the saving grace of 11d. out of the shilling, and valuing her absent husband's calamity or death as nothing in comparison with such an economy,—altogether, it may be said that this is a wondrous combination of pictorial genius, after which Phiz and Cruikshank must hide their diminished heads, for they can hardly be deemed worthy now of the inferior grade of associates and aspirants for Academic honours."

All this is excessively funny, and enables us to smile; but if the grounds of condemnation were of no more solid kind, we might venture the suggestion that the envelopes had hardly a fair trial at the bar of serious public judgment.

Lines on the Penny Postage.

The following lines were popular about the year 1840, when Sir Rowland Hill introduced the uniform penny rate of postage. The scheme was not looked upon hopefully in all quarters, and some persons predicted an early failure for it, while others only saw in the new departure grounds for ridicule or jest. These lines, which are certainly amusing, are said to be the production of Mr James Beaton :—

Something I want to write upon, to scare away each vapour—
The " Penny Postage " shall I try ? Why, yes, I'll write on paper.
Thy great invention, Rowland Hill, each person loudly hails;
The females they are full of it, and so are all the mails.
This may be called the " Penny Age," and those who are not
    mulish,
Are daily growing " penny wise," though not, I hope, pound
    foolish.

We've penny blacking, penny plays, penny mags. for information,
And now a "Penny Post," which proves we've lots of penetration.
Their love-sick thoughts by this new act may Lucy, Jane, or Mary,
Array in airy-diction from Johnson's dictionary.
Each maid will for the postman watch the keyhole like a cat,
And spring towards the door whene'er there comes a big rat-tat.
And lots of paper will be used by every scribbling elf,
That each should be a paper manufacturer himself.
To serve all with ink enough they must have different plans;
They must start an "Ink walk" just like milk, and serve it round in cans.
The letters in St Valentine so vastly will amount,
Postmen may judge them by the lot, they won't have time to count;
They must bring round spades and measures, to poor love-sick souls
Deliver them by bushels, the same as they do coals.
As billet-doux will so augment, the mails will be too small,
So omnibuses they must use, or they can't carry all;
And ladies pleasure will evince, instead of any fuss,
To have their lovers' letters all delivered with a 'bus!
Mail-coachmen are improving much in knowledge of the head,
For like the letter which they take, they're themselves all over red.
Postmen are "men of letters" too; each one's a learned talker,
And 'cause he reads the diction'ry, the people call him "Walker."
Handwriting now of every sort the connoisseur may meet;
Though a running hand, I think, does most give postmen running feet.

They who can't write will make their mark when they a line
   are dropping,
And where orthography is lame, of course it will "come
   hopping."
Invention is progressing so, and soon it will be seen,
That conveyance will be quicker done than it has ever been;
A plan's in agitation—as nought can genius fetter—
To let us have the answer back, before they get the letter.

At the Stamp-counter.

A man who can stand at the stamp-counter and serve the public without fear and without reproach, must needs be possessed of a highly sweetened temper. What with the impatient demands of some, the unreasonable demurs of others, the tiresome iteration of questions propounded by the eccentric, and the attention required to be given to the Mrs Browns of society, not to mention the irritating remarks at times of the inconsiderate, the position behind the counter is one which calls for self-control and a large share of good-nature.

The sort of thing that has to be endured at the hands of

      "Perfect woman, nobly planned,
      To warn, to comfort, and command,"

when she chooses to lay siege to the stamp-window, is thus described by an American writer, and the description is not to any great extent an exaggeration (if it be so at all) of experiences which are had in our own country in this particular direction :—

"Just about eleven o'clock yesterday forenoon there were thirteen men and one woman at the stamp-window of the Post-office. Most of the men had letters to post on the eastern trains. The woman had something tied up in a blue match-box. She got there first, and she held her position with her head in the window and both elbows on the shelf.

"'Is there such a place in this country as Cleveland?' she began.

"'Oh yes.'

"'Do you send mail there?'

"'Yes.'

"'Well, a woman living next door asked me to mail this box for her. I guess it's directed all right. She said it ought to go for a cent.'

"'Takes two cents,' said the clerk, after weighing it. 'If there is writing inside, it will be twelve cents.'

"'Mercy on me, but how you do charge!'

"Here the thirteen men began to push up and bustle around, and talk about the old match-box delaying two dozen business letters; but the woman had lots of time.

"'Then it will be two cents, eh?'

"'If there is no writing inside,' observed the clerk.

"'Well, there may be; I know she is a great hand to write. She's sending some flower-seed to her sister, and I suppose she has told her how to plant 'em——'

"'Two threes,' called out one of the crowd, as he tried to get at the window.

"'Hurry up!' cried another.

"'There ought to be a separate window here for women,' growled a third.

"'Then it will take twelve cents?' she calmly queried, as she fumbled around for her purse.

"'Yes.'

"'Well, I'd better pay it, I guess.'

"From one pocket she took two coppers, from her reticule she took a three-cent piece, from her purse she fished out a nickel; and it was only after a hunt of eighty seconds that she got the twelve cents together. She then consumed four minutes in licking on the stamps, asking where to post the box, and wondering if there was really any writing inside.

"But woman proposes and man disposes. Twenty thousand dollars worth of business was being detained by a twelve-cent woman, and a tidal wave suddenly took her away from the window. In sixty seconds the thirteen men had been waited on and gone their ways, and the woman returned to the window, handed in the box, and said, 'Them stamps are licked on crooked; it won't make any difference, will it?'"

CHAPTER XXIV.

ABOUT POSTMASTERS.

THE description furnished by Scott in the 'Antiquary' of the internal management of a country Post-office, as existing towards the close of last century, is extremely amusing and piquant; but the probability is that, while so much of what is said might be true to circumstances, the picture was heightened in colour for the purpose of literary effect. No doubt a certain amount of gossip emerged from such country offices, derived from the outsides and occasionally from the insides of letters; yet it is hardly likely that a group of curious women should have gathered together in the postmaster's room to make a general overhaul of the contents of the mail-bag, as is described in the case of the Post-office at Fairport. In small country towns in the present day, it is no uncommon thing to attribute the spread of " secrets " about the place to a breach of confidence at the Post-office, while the real fact is that things told by the persons concerned in strictest secrecy to their most intimate friends are by these communicated again to other kind friends, and so the ripple of information rolls on till there is no longer any secret at all, and the poor official at the Post-office is assumed to be the only possible offender. The smaller the place the greater is the thirst for neighbourly gossip, the more quickly does it spread when out, and the more ready are those whose secrets ooze forth to point the finger of suspicion at the Post-office.

Every one knows what a small country Post-office is nowadays. When we seek change of air and relaxation in the holiday season, choice is made maybe of some little country village or seaside resort whereat to spend the few weeks at our disposal. If the place be a *place* at all, there we shall find a Post-office; but possibly there is no house-to-house delivery, and letters must be called for at the Post-office itself. As the post-hour approaches, groups of visitors take up positions near the office door, or squat themselves down on any patch of sward that may be conveniently near. Young ladies waited upon by their admirers, mothers with their children, a bachelor group or two from the inn, and here and there a native of the place, some expecting letters, others indulging a feeble hope in that direction, attend as assistants at what is one of the excitements of the day. Presently the post-runner, with his wallet slung upon his back and a rustic walking-stick in his hand, appears in the distance, jogging along with that steady swinging stride which is so characteristic of his class. The visitors begin to close up around the Post-office; in a few minutes the runner steps into it; he throws down his wallet of treasures on the counter, removes his faded and dusty hat, and with his coloured cotton handkerchief wipes the sweat from his soiled and heated face. Meanwhile the attention of the postmistress is given to the contents of the bag; and as the expectant receivers of letters crowd in at or around the door, a few who have been unable to approach sufficiently near derive what consolation they can from eyeing the operations through the shop window, or .by vainly endeavouring to catch an early glimpse of some well-known superscription as the letters pass one by one through the hands of the postmistress.

The division of the letters, which can hardly be called a system of sorting, is a proceeding worthy of study. Some letters are placed up on end against sweetie-bottles in the window, others are laid down on shelves, others again are spread out on drawers or tables, quite in an arbitrary fashion. The postmistress has no difficulty in reading the addresses, as a rule, but the name of a new-comer seems to demand a little study: the letter is looked at back and front, and then laid down hesitatingly in a place by itself, as if it were an uncanny thing. The address of a letter for any young lady supposed to be engaged in correspondence of a tender kind seems also to require scrutiny; and should she happen to be well in at the door, it is immediately handed to her, those who are in the secret and those who are not forming different ideas as to the reason for this special mark of favour. While this is being done, an undefined sensation is produced in the small crowd, and the recipient retires in confusion to peruse the letter in peace and quiet elsewhere. At length the whole treasures are ready, and the distribution to the eager callers is a matter of a very few minutes, to be renewed again at the same hour next day.

Something like this is the routine observed when the delivery is being effected at small rural Post-offices in our own days—the keeper of the post being a shopkeeper, generally a grocer.

In the earlier history of the post, and up till the time of mail-coaches, the Post-office was very generally to be found established at the inn of the place. There was an evident convenience in this, owing to the innkeeper being the postmaster in the other and original sense of the provider of horses to ride post, when it was common to send on expresses, by means of these agents, from stage to stage. But the innkeepers, being often farmers besides, had business more important than that of the post to look after, and consequently the work was delegated to others. The duty of receiving and despatching the mails was frequently left to waiters or chambermaids, with the undesirable but inevitable result that the work was badly done. Often there was no separate place set apart for Post-office business; letters were sorted in the bar or in one of the public rooms, where any one could see them, thereby excluding all possibility of secrecy in dealing with the correspondence. Referring to the middle of last century, a surveyor expressed himself to the effect that "the head ostler was often the postmaster's prime minister in matters relating to the mails."

The interest taken by Boniface in the Post-office does not seem to have been very great; for an English surveyor, writing in 1792, thus expresses himself: "Persons who keep horses for other uses, and particularly innkeepers, may assuredly more conveniently and at less expense work the mails than those who keep horses for that business only. But, on the other hand, it may be observed that innkeepers, so far from paying Government service the compliment of employing in it their best horses, too often send their worst with the mails; and as to their riders, they are, in general, the dregs of the stable-yard, and by no means to be compared to those employed by postmasters in private stations."

Lack of interest in the mails did not, however, stand in the way of their turning the post to account in favour of their visitors; for in another official report the following observation is made on the subject of franking: "The Post-office is not of the consequence or recommendation to an inn which it used to be before the restriction in franking took place; and a traveller, now finding that my host at the public office is deprived of that privilege, moves over to the Red Lyon."

When mail-coaches came to be put upon the road, the necessity for having postmasters other than innkeepers forced itself upon the authorities, so that there should be an independent check upon the contractors, and a better regulation of the arrival and departure of the mails, with less chance of excuse for delays; and thus a change was brought about in the status of country postmasters.

But postmasters in the old days do not seem to have been uniformly happy in their posts. The following from a surveyor's report of December

1792, relating to the postmaster of Wetherby, in Yorkshire, shows this, and no doubt describes the case accurately. The Wetherby office had been made more important by some rearrangement of posts, with the result which the surveyor thus pathetically brings under notice: "The Postmaster-General's humanity, I humbly apprehend, would be very much affected if they knew exactly the situation of this poor deputy. He has now experienced the difference between his former snug duty and the very great fatigue of a large centre office, and labour throughout almost the whole of every night since the 10th October 1791. Also the very heavy expenses incurred thereby for assistance, coal, candles, paper, wax, &c., without any addition to his salary. To add to his distresses—for he is not rich" (who ever heard of a rich postmaster?)—"he has been so closely pressed from the Bye-letter Office for his balance due there as to have been compelled to borrow money to discharge them, at the very time that he could not obtain any account from the General Office, nor warrants for payment of as large sums due to him."

It is not difficult to picture this poor postmaster of Wetherby, tied to duty all night long arranging his mails by the light of a guttering candle, and smarting under financial difficulties; the Head Office squeezing him for revenue with one hand, and holding back what was due to him for his services with the other.

Sometimes country Post-offices would be the scene of small gatherings late at night, waiting the arrival of the mail, as was the case at Dumfries in 1799, when some few of the inhabitants would wait up till ten, eleven, or twelve o'clock to receive the English newspapers, so eager were they to peruse them. Then again, when a mail was passing through a town between stages in the middle of the night, the postmaster, awoke by the post-boy's horn, would present himself at an upper window and take in his bag by means of a hook and line, his body shivering the while in the cold night blast.

These postmasters required looking after occasionally, however, for they sometimes did wrong. In 1668 the postmaster of Edinburgh got into trouble by levying charges of 1d., 2d., or 3d. upon letters over and above the proper rates, and he was peremptorily ordered to discontinue the practice.

They also, it would appear, exercised some sort of surveillance over private correspondence. Chambers, in his 'Domestic Annals of Scotland,' to which valuable work we are again indebted, gives a case in point: "In July 1701, two letters from Brussels, *having the cross upon the back of them*, had come with proper addresses under cover to the Edinburgh postmaster. He *was surprised with them*, and brought them to the Lord Advocate, who, however, on opening them, found they were of no value, being only on private business; wherefore he ordered them to be delivered by the postmaster to the persons to whom they were directed." Yet zeal for the King's interest did not always have an acceptable reward, as is shown by the Scotch Privy Council record of **1679.** The keeper of the Edinburgh letter-office was accused of "sending up a *bye-letter* with the flying packet upon the twenty-two day of June last, giving ane account to the postmaster of England of the defeat of the rebels in the west, which was by the said postmaster communicated to the King before it could have been done by his Majesty's Secretary for Scotland, and which letter contains several untruths in matter of fact." For having forestalled his Majesty's Secretary, probably, rather than for the inaccuracy as to facts, the keeper of the post was sent to the Tolbooth, there to meditate upon the unprofitableness of official zeal, during the Council's pleasure.

It does not seem to have been thought prudent to intrust the date-stamping of letters to postmasters generally until some time in the present century. Down to the close of last century, at any rate, according to a Survey report of the year 1800, this was allowed only at the more important offices. The report is as follows: "In regard to having the Dumbarton letters stamped with the day of the month, as now done at Glasgow, the subject has often been considered, and although it has been approved of with some large commercial towns in England, and Edinburgh and Glasgow in Scotland, it has been much doubted how far it would be proper or necessary to establish it generally with less towns, where the practice might be more subject to irregularity or abuses, besides the very great expense such a supply of stamps would occasion to the revenue."

The smallness of the salaries allowed to the postmasters of former times is referred to in another chapter, and this may, no doubt, have contributed to the lack of interest taken in the work by some of these officials.

Traditions of hard work and long hours linger still in the Post-office, though nowadays the periods of duty are generally reduced to moderate limits. Some idea of the service required to be rendered formerly by Post-office servants may be gathered from the following order, dating about 1780 or 1790. It refers to the Secretary to the Post-office in Dublin, but we ought perhaps to put a very free interpretation upon it:—" The duty of the Secretary is to carry on the general correspondence, and, under the direction of the Postmaster-General, to superintend the whole business of the office; to attend the Board, and give directions for carrying into execution the orders of the Postmaster-General. His attendance is constant, and at all hours by day and by night —generally from 7 until 10, from 12 until 5, and from 9 until 11 o'clock each day."

The Postmasters of the United Kingdom are a very large class, numbering many thousands, and comprising every variety of individual from the honest country shopkeeper to the highly intelligent men who are placed in charge of the offices in our principal towns. The former have enough to do in mastering the various codes of rules under which the many branches of business are carried on; while the latter, in exercising discipline over their forces, carrying out changes of administration, and endeavouring to meet the wishes of a public ever wakeful to their interests and privileges, are something in their way like petty sovereigns, of whom it might not inaptly be said, "Uneasy is the head that wears a crown," though the material emblem itself be wanting.

CHAPTER XXV.

RED TAPE.

THE Post-office is no stranger to the taunt that it is swathed from head to foot in red tape; or, at any rate, that its operations are so trammelled with routine that no inquiry into irregularities can be made with anything like due expedition. Such accusations as these often come from unreflecting persons, or from those whose business operations are of a small kind, and who have no idea of the methods necessary for carrying on a huge administration.

An ordinary shopkeeper, for example, has under his own eye the whole sphere of his daily business; he has a personal knowledge of all purchases from the wholesale houses, and knows exactly the particulars of his daily sales; he has, moreover, the behaviour of his servants constantly under observation with a view to discipline; in fact, he is ever present in his own business world, the whole scope of which is within his individual purview. If a person of this class were asked a question in regard to his affairs, it would probably be in his power to afford an answer at once; and when he addresses an inquiry to the Post-office he expects a reply with like rapidity. Not receiving an answer with the looked-for despatch, as might very likely happen, the cause would be assumed to be ·needless routine—otherwise red tape!

Now it is proper here to observe, that between business or trade in the ordinary sense, and the administration of a department like the Post-office, there exists a gulf which forbids all comparison, and establishes a contrast of the most striking kind. A stranger, were he taken through the Secretariat of the Post-office at St Martin's-le-Grand, the brain of the whole Department, could not fail to be struck by the method which reigns throughout, and the way in which various subjects coming up for consideration are disposed of in different branches. In one quarter he would find inquiry going on into the characters and antecedents of candidates for appointments throughout the country, and preparations being made for their examination by the Civil Service Commissioners. In another room would be found officers exercising judicial functions in regard to cases of misbehaviour reported from the country—meting out arrest of pay or dismissal in accordance with the gravity of the offence in each instance. Then in other rooms questions as to new buildings, their fittings and furniture, and the increase of staff when demanded by provincial offices, are undergoing close examination. Inquiries for missing letters take up attention in one branch; various other kinds of irregularities are dealt with in another. The foreign mails branch, the home mails and parcel-post branch, the telegraph branch, with all their subdivisions of work, occupy separate rooms, and claim the attention of officers specially trained to their several duties.

And how does all the correspondence for the Secretary at headquarters find its way to its proper quarter for treatment? There is a branch called the Registry, in which every letter or communication of any importance is registered on receipt—that is, it receives a number, the name of the writer is indexed, and the subject of his letter recorded. The number of officers employed in the Registry is 73; and the original papers passing through the branch in the way stated exceed 320,000 annually. From this branch every morning the papers for treatment are distributed over the Secretariat, each officer receiving the papers proper to his duty. Nor does the business of the Registry end here, for every *case*— each separate set of papers on a subject is called a *case*—is recorded again whenever sent elsewhere, so that its destination can be traced. Were this not done, laggard postmasters, or persons acting from base or interested motives, might find it convenient not to return the papers, and so by silence *end them*. Sometimes a single case will go backwards and forwards thirty or forty times, yet its whole history of travel is recorded. This is the routine which some people call *red tape*.

In dealing in this way with large masses of correspondence, each atom of which has to receive its due share of brain-attention, there is necessarily some degree of retardation; and it may be remarked that, between this process and the law in mechanics, under which, other things being equal, a gain of power is accompanied by a loss of speed, there exists a strong analogy. But by this classification and division of labour it is possible to bring about results which could not be achieved by a much larger staff under any plan of desultory working.

We will mention one thing which, perhaps more than any other, excites the public to use the taunt of *red tape*. It is a printed reply to a complaint, commonly spoken of as the "stereotyped reply." The public do not know how carefully and conscientiously delays and reported losses of letters are investigated in the Post-office. Inquiries are made in every office through which the letters would pass in transit, and records made, lest an explanation should afterwards be forthcoming; but after all, in the eyes of some persons, the printed reply spoils all. These persons forget, however, that the printed letter conveys all that is to be said on the subject, and that it is used in the interests of economy.

It may be admitted of the Post-office, that of all its characteristics, the most prominent is that of its method, routine, or red-tapeism, in the limited sense of what is necessary for the furtherance of the public service; but there is, perhaps, no concern of like magnitude in the world in which there is less of the musty fusty red tape of antiquity that has outlived its time, and no longer serves any useful purpose.

CATALOGUE

OF

MESSRS BLACKWOOD & SONS'

PUBLICATIONS.

PHILOSOPHICAL CLASSICS FOR ENGLISH READERS.
EDITED BY WILLIAM KNIGHT, LL.D.,
Professor of Moral Philosophy in the University of St Andrews.
In crown 8vo Volumes, with Portraits, price 3s. 6d.

Now ready—

1. **Descartes.** By Professor MAHAFFY, Dublin.
2. **Butler.** By Rev. W. LUCAS COLLINS, M.A.
3. **Berkeley.** By Professor FRASER, Edinburgh.
4. **Fichte.** By Professor ADAMSON, Owens College, Manchester.
5. **Kant.** By Professor WALLACE, Oxford.
6. **Hamilton.** By Professor VEITCH, Glasgow.
7. **Hegel.** By Professor EDWARD CAIRD, Glasgow.
8. **Leibniz.** By J. THEODORE MERZ.
9. **Vico.** By Professor FLINT, Edinburgh.

The Volumes in preparation are—

HOBBES. By Professor Croom Robertson, London.
HUME. By the Editor.
BACON. By Professor Nichol, Glasgow.
SPINOZA. By the Very Rev. Principal Caird, Glasgow.

IN COURSE OF PUBLICATION.

FOREIGN CLASSICS FOR ENGLISH READERS.
EDITED BY MRS OLIPHANT.
In Crown 8vo, 2s. 6d.

The Volumes published are—

DANTE. By the Editor.
VOLTAIRE. By Major-General Sir E. B. Hamley, K.C.M.G.
PASCAL. By Principal Tulloch.
PETRARCH. By Henry Reeve, C.B.
GOETHE. By A. Hayward, Q.C.
MOLIÈRE. By the Editor and F. Tarver, M.A.
MONTAIGNE. By Rev. W. L. Collins, M.A.
RABELAIS. By Walter Besant, M.A.
CALDERON. By E. J. Hasell.
SAINT SIMON. By Clifton W. Collins, M.A.
CERVANTES. By the Editor.
CORNEILLE AND RACINE. By Henry M. Trollope.
MADAME DE SÉVIGNÉ. By Miss Thackeray.
LA FONTAINE, AND OTHER FRENCH FABULISTS. By Rev. W. Lucas Collins, M.A.
SCHILLER. By James Sime, M.A., Author of 'Lessing: his Life and Writings.'
TASSO. By E. J. Hasell.
ROUSSEAU. By Henry Grey Graham.

*In preparation—*LEOPARDI, by the Editor.

NOW COMPLETE.

ANCIENT CLASSICS FOR ENGLISH READERS.
EDITED BY THE REV. W. LUCAS COLLINS, M.A.

Complete in 28 Vols. crown 8vo, cloth, price 2s. 6d. each. And may also be had in 14 Volumes, strongly and neatly bound, with calf or vellum back, £3, 10s.

Saturday Review.—"It is difficult to estimate too highly the value of such a series as this in giving 'English readers' an insight, exact as far as it goes, into those olden times which are so remote and yet to many of us so close."

CATALOGUE

OF

MESSRS BLACKWOOD & SONS'
PUBLICATIONS.

ALISON. History of Europe. By Sir ARCHIBALD ALISON, Bart., D.C.L.
1. From the Commencement of the French Revolution to the Battle of Waterloo.
   LIBRARY EDITION, 14 vols., with Portraits. Demy 8vo, £10, 10s.
   ANOTHER EDITION, in 20 vols. crown 8vo, £6.
   PEOPLE'S EDITION, 13 vols. crown 8vo, £2, 11s.
2. Continuation to the Accession of Louis Napoleon.
   LIBRARY EDITION, 8 vols. 8vo, £6, 7s. 6d.
   PEOPLE'S EDITION, 8 vols. crown 8vo, 34s.
3. Epitome of Alison's History of Europe. Twenty-ninth Thousand, 7s. 6d.
4. Atlas to Alison's History of Europe. By A. Keith Johnston.
   LIBRARY EDITION, demy 4to, £3, 3s.
   PEOPLE'S EDITION, 31s. 6d.

—— Life of John Duke of Marlborough. With some Account of his Contemporaries, and of the War of the Succession. Third Edition, 2 vols. 8vo. Portraits and Maps, 30s.

—— Essays: Historical, Political, and Miscellaneous. 3 vols. demy 8vo, 45s.

—— Lives of Lord Castlereagh and Sir Charles Stewart, Second and Third Marquesses of Londonderry. From the Original Papers of the Family. 3 vols. 8vo, £2, 2s.

ADAMS. Great Campaigns. A Succinct Account of the Principal Military Operations which have taken place in Europe from 1796 to 1870. By Major C. ADAMS, Professor of Military History at the Staff College. Edited by Captain C. COOPER KING, R.M. Artillery, Instructor of Tactics, Royal Military College. 8vo, with Maps. 16s.

AIRD. Poetical Works of Thomas Aird. Fifth Edition, with Memoir of the Author by the Rev. JARDINE WALLACE, and Portrait. Crown 8vo, 7s. 6d.

ALFORD. The Romance of Coombehurst. By E. M. ALFORD. Author of 'Honor,' 'Netherton-on-Sea,' 'The Fair Maid of Taunton,' &c. In 2 vols. post 8vo. 17s.

ALLARDYCE. The City of Sunshine. By ALEXANDER ALLARDYCE. Three vols. post 8vo, £1, 5s. 6d.

—— Memoir of the Honourable George Keith Elphinstone, K.B., Viscount Keith of Stonehaven Marischal, Admiral of the Red. One vol. 8vo, with Portrait, Illustrations, and Maps. 21s.

LIST OF BOOKS PUBLISHED BY

ANCIENT CLASSICS FOR ENGLISH READERS. Edited by Rev. W. LUCAS COLLINS, M.A. Complete in 28 vols., cloth, 2s. 6d. each; or in 14 vols., tastefully bound, with calf or vellum back, £3, 10s.

Contents of the Series.

HOMER: THE ILIAD. By the Editor.
HOMER: THE ODYSSEY. By the Editor.
HERODOTUS. By George C. Swayne, M.A.
XENOPHON. By Sir Alexander Grant, Bart., LL.D.
EURIPIDES. By W. B. Donne.
ARISTOPHANES. By the Editor.
PLATO. By Clifton W. Collins, M.A.
LUCIAN. By the Editor.
ÆSCHYLUS. By the Right Rev. the Bishop of Colombo.
SOPHOCLES. By Clifton W. Collins, M.A.
HESIOD AND THEOGNIS. By the Rev. J. Davies, M.A.
GREEK ANTHOLOGY. By Lord Neaves.
VIRGIL. By the Editor.
HORACE. By Sir Theodore Martin, K.C.B.
JUVENAL. By Edward Walford, M.A.
PLAUTUS AND TERENCE. By the Editor.
THE COMMENTARIES OF CÆSAR. By Anthony Trollope.
TACITUS. By W. B. Donne.
CICERO. By the Editor.
PLINY'S LETTERS. By the Rev. Alfred Church, M.A., and the Rev. W. J. Brodribb, M.A.
LIVY. By the Editor.
OVID. By the Rev. A. Church, M.A.
CATULLUS, TIBULLUS, AND PROPERTIUS. By the Rev. Jas. Davies, M.A.
DEMOSTHENES. By the Rev. W. J. Brodribb, M.A.
ARISTOTLE. By Sir Alexander Grant, Bart., LL.D.
THUCYDIDES. By the Editor.
LUCRETIUS. By W. H. Mallock, M.A.
PINDAR. By the Rev. F. D. Morice, M.A.

AYLWARD. The Transvaal of To-day: War, Witchcraft, Sports, and Spoils in South Africa. By ALFRED AYLWARD, Commandant, Transvaal Republic; Captain (late) Lydenberg Volunteer Corps. Second Edition. Crown 8vo, with a Map, 6s.

AYTOUN. Lays of the Scottish Cavaliers, and other Poems. By W. EDMONDSTOUNE AYTOUN, D.C.L., Professor of Rhetoric and Belles-Lettres in the University of Edinburgh. Twenty-ninth Edition. Fcap. 8vo, 7s. 6d.

—— An Illustrated Edition of the Lays of the Scottish Cavaliers. From designs by Sir NOEL PATON. Small 4to, 21s., in gilt cloth.

—— Bothwell: a Poem. Third Edition. Fcap., 7s. 6d.

—— Firmilian; or, The Student of Badajoz. A Spasmodic Tragedy. Fcap., 5s.

—— Poems and Ballads of Goethe. Translated by Professor AYTOUN and Sir THEODORE MARTIN, K.C.B. Third Edition. Fcap., 6s.

—— Bon Gaultier's Book of Ballads. By the SAME. Fourteenth and Cheaper Edition. With Illustrations by Doyle, Leech, and Crowquill. Fcap. 8vo, 5s.

—— The Ballads of Scotland. Edited by Professor AYTOUN. Fourth Edition. 2 vols. fcap. 8vo, 12s.

—— Memoir of William E. Aytoun, D.C.L. By Sir THEODORE MARTIN, K.C.B. With Portrait. Post 8vo, 12s.

BACH. On Musical Education and Vocal Culture. By ALBERT B. BACH. Fourth Edition. 8vo, 7s. 6d.

BAGOT. The Art of Poetry of Horace. Free and Explanatory Translations in Prose and Verse. By the Very Rev. DANIEL BAGOT, D.D. Third Edition, Revised, printed on *papier vergé*, square 8vo, 5s.

BATTLE OF DORKING. Reminiscences of a Volunteer. From 'Blackwood's Magazine.' Second Hundredth Thousand. 6d.

BY THE SAME AUTHOR.

The Dilemma. Cheap Edition. Crown 8vo, 6s.

BEDFORD. The Regulations of the Old Hospital of the Knights of St John at Valetta. From a Copy Printed at Rome, and preserved in the Archives of Malta; with a Translation, Introduction, and Notes Explanatory of the Hospital Work of the Order By the Rev. W. K. R. BEDFORD, one of the Chaplains of the Order of St John in England. Royal 8vo, with Frontispiece, Plans, &c., 7s. 6d.

BELLAIRS. The Transvaal War, 1880-81. Edited by Lady BEL-
LAIRS. With a Frontispiece and Map. 8vo, 15s.
ESANT. The Revolt of Man. By WALTER BESANT, M.A.
Seventh Edition. Crown 8vo, 3s. 6d.
—— Readings in Rabelais. Crown 8vo, 7s. 6d.
BLACKIE. Lays and Legends of Ancient Greece. By JOHN
STUART BLACKIE, Emeritus Professor of Greek in the University of Edinburgh. Second Edition. Fcap. 8vo. 5s.
—— The Wisdom of Goethe. Fcap. 8vo. Cloth, extra gilt, 6s.
BLACKWOOD'S MAGAZINE, from Commencement in 1817 to
December 1883. Nos. 1 to 818, forming 134 Volumes.
—— Index to Blackwood's Magazine. Vols. 1 to 50. 8vo, 15s.
—— Tales from Blackwood. Forming Twelve Volumes of
Interesting and Amusing Railway Reading. Price One Shilling each in Paper Cover. Sold separately at all Railway Bookstalls.
They may also be had bound in cloth, 18s., and in half calf, richly gilt, 30s. or 12 volumes in 6, Roxburghe, 21s., and half red morocco, 28s.
—— Tales from Blackwood. New Series. Complete in Twenty-
four Shilling Parts. Handsomely bound in 12 vols., cloth, 30s. In leather back, Roxburghe style, 37s. 6d. In half calf, gilt, 52s. 6d. In half morocco, 55s.
—— Standard Novels. Uniform in size and legibly Printed.
Each Novel complete in one volume.

Florin Series, Illustrated Boards.

TOM CRINGLE'S LOG. By Michael Scott.
THE CRUISE OF THE MIDGE. By the Same.
CYRIL THORNTON. By Captain Hamilton.
ANNALS OF THE PARISH. By John Galt.
THE PROVOST, &c. By John Galt.
SIR ANDREW WYLIE. By John Galt.
THE ENTAIL. By John Galt.
MISS MOLLY. By Beatrice May Butt.
REGINALD DALTON. By J. G. Lockhart.

PEN OWEN. By Dean Hook.
ADAM BLAIR. By J. G. Lockhart.
LADY LEE'S WIDOWHOOD. By General
Sir E. B. Hamley.
SALEM CHAPEL. By Mrs Oliphant.
THE PERPETUAL CURATE. By Mrs Oliphant.
MISS MARJORIBANKS. By Mrs Oliphant.
JOHN: A Love Story. By Mrs Oliphant.

Or in Cloth Boards, 2s. 6d.

Shilling Series, Illustrated Cover.

THE RECTOR, and THE DOCTOR'S FAMILY.
By Mrs Oliphant.
THE LIFE OF MANSIE WAUCH. By D. M. Moir.
PENINSULAR SCENES AND SKETCHES. By F. Hardman.

SIR FRIZZLE PUMPKIN, NIGHTS AT MESS, &c.
THE SUBALTERN.
LIFE IN THE FAR WEST. By G. F. Ruxton.
VALERIUS: A Roman Story. By J. G. Lockhart.

Or in Cloth Boards, 1s. 6d.

BLACKMORE. The Maid of Sker. By R. D. BLACKMORE, Author
of 'Lorna Doone,' &c. Tenth Edition. Crown 8vo, 7s. 6d.
BOSCOBEL TRACTS. Relating to the Escape of Charles the
Second after the Battle of Worcester, and his subsequent Adventures. Edited by J. HUGHES, Esq., A.M. A New Edition, with additional Notes and Illustrations, including Communications from the Rev. R. H. BARHAM, Author of the 'Ingoldsby Legends.' 8vo, with Engravings, 16s.
BRACKENBURY. A Narrative of the Ashanti War. Prepared
from the official documents, by permission of Major-General Sir Garnet Wolseley, K.C.B., K.C.M.G. By Major H. BRACKENBURY, R.A., Assistant Military Secretary to Sir Garnet Wolseley. With Maps from the latest Surveys made by the Staff of the Expedition. 2 vols. 8vo, 25s.
BROADLEY. Tunis, Past and Present. With a Narrative of the
French Conquest of the Regency. By A. M. BROADLEY. With numerous Illustrations and Maps. 2 vols. post 8vo. 25s.

BROOKE, Life of Sir James, Rajah of Sarāwak. From his Personal Papers and Correspondence. By SPENSER ST JOHN, H.M.'s Minister-Resident and Consul-General Peruvian Republic; formerly Secretary to the Rajah. With Portrait and a Map. Post 8vo, 12s. 6d.

BROUGHAM. Memoirs of the Life and Times of Henry Lord Brougham. Written by HIMSELF. 3 vols. 8vo, £2, 8s. The Volumes are sold separately, price 16s. each.

BROWN. The Forester: A Practical Treatise on the Planting, Rearing, and General Management of Forest-trees. By JAMES BROWN, LL.D., Inspector of and Reporter on Woods and Forests, Benmore House, Port Elgin, Ontario. Fifth Edition, revised and enlarged. Royal 8vo, with Engravings. 36s.

BROWN. The Ethics of George Eliot's Works. By JOHN CROMBIE BROWN. Fourth Edition. Crown 8vo, 2s. 6d.

BROWN. A Manual of Botany, Anatomical and Physiological. For the Use of Students. By ROBERT BROWN, M.A., Ph.D. Crown 8vo, with numerous Illustrations, 12s. 6d.

BUCHAN. Introductory Text-Book of Meteorology. By ALEXANDER BUCHAN, M.A., F.R.S.E., Secretary of the Scottish Meteorological Society, &c. Crown 8vo, with 8 Coloured Charts and other Engravings, pp. 218. 4s. 6d.

BURBIDGE. Domestic Floriculture, Window Gardening, and Floral Decorations. Being practical directions for the Propagation, Culture, and Arrangement of Plants and Flowers as Domestic Ornaments. By F. W. BURBIDGE. Second Edition. Crown 8vo, with numerous Illustrations, 7s. 6d.

—— Cultivated Plants: Their Propagation and Improvement. Including Natural and Artificial Hybridisation, Raising from Seed, Cuttings, and Layers, Grafting and Budding, as applied to the Families and Genera in Cultivation. Crown 8vo, with numerous Illustrations, 12s. 6d.

BURTON. The History of Scotland: From Agricola's Invasion to the Extinction of the last Jacobite Insurrection. By JOHN HILL BURTON, D.C.L., Historiographer-Royal for Scotland. New and Enlarged Edition, 8 vols., and Index. Crown 8vo, £3, 3s.

—— History of the British Empire during the Reign of Queen Anne. In 3 vols. 8vo. 36s.

—— The Scot Abroad. New Edition. Complete in One volume. Crown 8vo, 10s. 6d.

—— The Book-Hunter. New Edition. Uniform with 'History of Scotland.' Crown 8vo, 7s. 6d.

BUTE. The Roman Breviary: Reformed by Order of the Holy Œcumenical Council of Trent; Published by Order of Pope St Pius V.; and Revised by Clement VIII. and Urban VIII.; together with the Offices since granted. Translated out of Latin into English by JOHN, Marquess of Bute, K.T. In 2 vols. crown 8vo, cloth boards, edges uncut. £2, 2s.

—— The Altus of St Columba. With a Prose Paraphrase and Notes. In paper cover, 2s. 6d.

BUTT. Miss Molly. By BEATRICE MAY BUTT. Cheap Edition, 2s.

—— Geraldine Hawthorne: A Sketch. By the Author of 'Miss Molly.' Crown 8vo, 7s. 6d.

—— Alison. By the Author of 'Miss Molly.' 3 vols. crown 8vo, 25s. 6d.

CAIRD. Sermons. By JOHN CAIRD, D.D., Principal of the University of Glasgow. Sixteenth Thousand. Fcap. 8vo, 5s.

—— Religion in Common Life. A Sermon preached in Crathie Church, October 14, 1855, before Her Majesty the Queen and Prince Albert. Published by Her Majesty's Command. Cheap Edition, 3d.

CAMERON. **Gaelic Names of Plants (Scottish and Irish).** Collected and Arranged in Scientific Order, with Notes on their Etymology, their Uses, Plant Superstitions, &c., among the Celts, with copious Gaelic, English, and Scientific Indices. By JOHN CAMERON, Sunderland. 8vo, 7s. 6d.

CAMPBELL. **Sermons Preached before the Queen at Balmoral.** By the Rev. A. A. CAMPBELL, Minister of Crathie. Published by Command of Her Majesty. Crown 8vo, 4s. 6d.

CARLYLE. **Autobiography of the Rev. Dr Alexander Carlyle,** Minister of Inveresk. Containing Memorials of the Men and Events of his Time. Edited by JOHN HILL BURTON. 8vo. Third Edition, with Portrait, 14s.

CARRICK. **Koumiss; or, Fermented Mare's Milk: and its Uses** in the Treatment and Cure of Pulmonary Consumption, and other Wasting Diseases. With an Appendix on the best Methods of Fermenting Cow's Milk. By GEORGE L. CARRICK, M.D., L.R.C.S.E. and L.R.C.P.E., Physician to the British Embassy, St Petersburg, &c. Crown 8vo, 10s. 6d.

CAUVIN. **A Treasury of the English and German Languages.** Compiled from the best Authors and Lexicographers in both Languages. Adapted to the Use of Schools, Students, Travellers, and Men of Business; and forming a Companion to all German-English Dictionaries. By JOSEPH CAUVIN, LL.D. & Ph.D., of the University of Göttingen, &c. Crown 8vo, 7s. 6d.

CAVE-BROWN. **Lambeth Palace and its Associations.** By J. CAVE-BROWN, M.A., Vicar of Detling, Kent, and for many years Curate of Lambeth Parish Church. With an Introduction by the Archbishop of Canterbury. Second Edition, containing an additional Chapter on Medieval Life in the Old Palaces. 8vo, with Illustrations, 21s.

CHARTERIS. **Canonicity; or, Early Testimonies to the Existence** and Use of the Books of the New Testament. Based on Kirchhoffer's 'Quellensammlung.' Edited by A. H. CHARTERIS, D.D., Professor of Biblical Criticism in the University of Edinburgh. 8vo, 18s.

CHEVELEY NOVELS, THE.
 I. A MODERN MINISTER. 2 vols. bound in cloth, with Twenty-six Illustrations. 17s.
 II. SAUL WEIR. 2 vols. bound in cloth. With Twelve Illustrations by F. Barnard. 16s.

CHIROL. **'Twixt Greek and Turk.** By M. VALENTINE CHIROL. Post 8vo. With Frontispiece and Map, 10s. 6d.

CHURCH SERVICE SOCIETY. **A Book on Common Order:** Being Forms of Worship issued by the Church Service Society. Fourth Edition, 6s.

COCHRAN. **A Handy Text-Book of Military Law.** Compiled chiefly to assist Officers preparing for Examination; also for all Officers of the Regular and Auxiliary Forces. Specially arranged according to the Syllabus of Subjects of Examination for Promotion, Queen's Regulations, 1883. Comprising also a Synopsis of part of the Army Act. By MAJOR F. COCHRAN, Hampshire Regiment, Garrison Instructor, North British District. Crown 8vo, 7s. 6d.

COLQUHOUN. **The Moor and the Loch.** Containing Minute Instructions in all Highland Sports, with Wanderings over Crag and Corrie, Flood and Fell. By JOHN COLQUHOUN. Sixth Edition, greatly enlarged. With Illustrations. 2 vols. post 8vo, 26s.

COTTERILL. **The Genesis of the Church.** By the Right. Rev. HENRY COTTERILL, D.D., Bishop of Edinburgh. Demy 8vo, 16s.

CRANSTOUN. **The Elegies of Albius Tibullus.** Translated into English Verse, with Life of the Poet, and Illustrative Notes. By JAMES CRANSTOUN, LL.D., Author of a Translation of 'Catullus.' Crown 8vo, 6s. 6d.

CRANSTOUN. The Elegies of Sextus Propertius. Translated into English Verse, with Life of the Poet, and Illustrative Notes. Crown 8vo, 7s. 6d.

CRAWFORD. The Doctrine of Holy Scripture respecting the Atonement. By the late THOMAS J. CRAWFORD, D.D., Professor of Divinity in the University of Edinburgh. Third Edition. 8vo, 12s.

—— The Fatherhood of God, Considered in its General and Special Aspects, and particularly in relation to the Atonement, with a Review of Recent Speculations on the Subject. Third Edition, Revised and Enlarged. 8vo, 9s.

—— The Preaching of the Cross, and other Sermons. 8vo, 7s. 6d.

—— The Mysteries of Christianity. Being the Baird Lecture for 1874. Crown 8vo, 7s. 6d.

DAVIES. A Book of Thoughts for every Day in the Year. Selected from the Writings of the Rev. J. LLEWELLYN DAVIES, M.A. By Two CLERGYMEN. Fcap. 8vo, 3s. 6d.

DAVIES. Norfolk Broads and Rivers; or, The Waterways, Lagoons, and Decoys of East Anglia. By G. CHRISTOPHER DAVIES, Author of 'The Swan and her Crew.' Illustrated with Seven full-page Plates. New and Cheaper Edition. Crown 8vo, 6s.

DE AINSLIE. Life as I have Found It. By General DE AINSLIE. Post 8vo, 12s. 6d.

DESCARTES. The Method, Meditations, and Principles of Philosophy of Descartes. Translated from the Original French and Latin. With a New Introductory Essay, Historical and Critical, on the Cartesian Philosophy. By JOHN VEITCH, LL.D., Professor of Logic and Rhetoric in the University of Glasgow. A New Edition, being the Eighth. Price 6s. 6d.

DIDON. The Germans. By the Rev. Father DIDON, of the Order of Preaching Friars. Translated into English by RAPHAEL LEDOS DE BEAUFORT. Crown 8vo, 7s. 6d.

DU CANE. The Odyssey of Homer, Books I.-XII. Translated into English Verse. By Sir CHARLES DU CANE, K.C.M.G. 8vo, 10s. 6d.

DUDGEON. History of the Edinburgh or Queen's Regiment Light Infantry Militia, now 3rd Battalion The Royal Scots; with an Account of the Origin and Progress of the Militia, and a Brief Sketch of the old Royal Scots. By Major R. C. DUDGEON, Adjutant 3rd Battalion The Royal Scots. Post 8vo, with Illustrations, 10s. 6d.

DUPRÉ. Thoughts on Art, and Autobiographical Memoirs of Giovanni Dupré. Translated from the Italian by E. M. PERUZZI, with the permission of the Author. Crown 8vo, 10s. 6d.

ELIOT. George Eliot's Life, Related in her Letters and Journals. Arranged and Edited by her husband, J. W. CROSS. With Portrait and other Illustrations. Second Edition. 3 vols. post 8vo, 42s.

—— Essays. By GEORGE ELIOT. Revised by the Author for publication. Post 8vo, 10s. 6d.

—— Novels by GEORGE ELIOT. Cheap Edition. Adam Bede. Illustrated. 3s. 6d., cloth.—The Mill on the Floss. Illustrated. 3s. 6d., cloth.—Scenes of Clerical Life. Illustrated. 3s., cloth.—Silas Marner: The Weaver of Raveloe. Illustrated. 2s. 6d., cloth.—Felix Holt, the Radical. Illustrated. 3s. 6d., cloth.—Romola. With Vignette. 3s. 6d., cloth.

—— Middlemarch. Crown 8vo, 7s. 6d.

—— Daniel Deronda. Crown 8vo, 7s. 6d.

—— Works of George Eliot (Cabinet Edition). Complete and

WILLIAM BLACKWOOD AND SONS. 9

Uniform Edition, handsomely printed in a new type, 20 volumes, crown 8vo, price £5. The Volumes are also sold separately, price 5s. each, viz.:—
Romola. 2 vols.—Silas Marner, The Lifted Veil, Brother Jacob. 1 vol.—Adam Bede. 2 vols.—Scenes of Clerical Life. 2 vols.—The Mill on the Floss. 2 vols.—Felix Holt. 2 vols.—Middlemarch. 3 vols.—Daniel Deronda. 3 vols.—The Spanish Gypsy. 1 vol.—Jubal, and other Poems, Old and New. 1 vol.—Theophrastus Such. 1 vol.

ELIOT. The Spanish Gypsy. Crown 8vo, 5s.

——— The Legend of Jubal, and other Poems, Old and New. New Edition. Fcap. 8vo, 5s., cloth.

——— Impressions of Theophrastus Such. New Edition. Crown 8vo, 5s.

——— Wise, Witty, and Tender Sayings, in Prose and Verse. Selected from the Works of GEORGE ELIOT. Sixth Edition. Fcap. 8vo, 6s.

——— The George Eliot Birthday Book. Printed on fine paper, with red border, and handsomely bound in cloth, gilt. Fcap. 8vo, cloth, 3s. 6d. And in French morocco or Russia, 5s.

ESSAYS ON SOCIAL SUBJECTS. Originally published in the 'Saturday Review.' A New Edition. First and Second Series. 2 vols. crown 8vo, 6s. each.

EWALD. The Crown and its Advisers; or, Queen, Ministers, Lords, and Commons. By ALEXANDER CHARLES EWALD, F.S.A. Crown 8vo, 5s.

FAITHS OF THE WORLD, The. A Concise History of the Great Religious Systems of the World. By various Authors. Being the St Giles' Lectures—Second Series. Complete in one volume, crown 8vo, 5s.

FARRER. A Tour in Greece in 1880. By RICHARD RIDLEY FARRER. With Twenty-seven full-page Illustrations by LORD WINDSOR. Royal 8vo, with a Map, 21s.

FAUCIT. Some of Shakespeare's Female Characters. In a Series of Letters. By HELENA FAUCIT, LADY MARTIN. With Portraits engraved by the late F. Holl. Dedicated by Special Permission to Her Most Gracious Majesty the Queen. In one vol. 4to, printed on hand-made paper.
[In the press.

FERRIER. Philosophical Works of the late James F. Ferrier, B.A. Oxon., Professor of Moral Philosophy and Political Economy, St Andrews. New Edition. Edited by Sir ALEX. GRANT, Bart., D.C.L., and Professor LUSHINGTON. 3 vols. crown 8vo, 34s. 6d.

——— Institutes of Metaphysic. Third Edition. 10s. 6d.

——— Lectures on the Early Greek Philosophy. Third Edition, 10s. 6d.

——— Philosophical Remains, including the Lectures on Early Greek Philosophy. 2 vols., 24s.

FISH AND FISHERIES. A Selection from the Prize Essays of the International Fisheries Exhibition, Edinburgh, 1882. Edited by DAVID HERBERT, M.A. With Maps and Illustrations. 8vo, 7s. 6d.

FLETCHER. Lectures on the Opening Clauses of the Litany delivered in St Paul's Church, Edinburgh. By JOHN B. FLETCHER, M.A. Crown 8vo, 4s.

FLINT. The Philosophy of History in Europe. Vol. I., containing the History of that Philosophy in France and Germany. By ROBERT FLINT, D.D., LL.D., Professor of Divinity, University of Edinburgh. 8vo, 15s.

——— Theism. Being the Baird Lecture for 1876. Fourth Edition. Crown 8vo, 7s. 6d.

——— Anti-Theistic Theories. Being the Baird Lecture for 1877. Second Edition. Crown 8vo, 10s. 6d.

FORBES. The Campaign of Garibaldi in the Two Sicilies: A Personal Narrative. By CHARLES STUART FORBES, Commander, R.N. Post 8vo, with Portraits, 12s.

FOREIGN CLASSICS FOR ENGLISH READERS. Edited by Mrs OLIPHANT. Price 2s. 6d.

Now published:—
DANTE, by the Editor.—VOLTAIRE, by Major-General Sir E. B. Hamley, K.C.M.G.—PASCAL, by Principal Tulloch.—PETRARCH, by Henry Reeve, C.B.—GOETHE, by A. Hayward, Q.C.—MOLIÈRE, by the Editor and F. Tarver, M.A.—MONTAIGNE, by Rev. W. L. Collins, M.A.—RABELAIS. by Walter Besant, M.A.—CALDERON, by E. J. Hasell.—SAINT SIMON, by Clifton W. Collins, M.A.—CERVANTES, by the Editor.—CORNEILLE AND RACINE, by Henry M. Trollope.—MADAME DE SÉVIGNÉ, by Miss Thackeray.—LA FONTAINE, AND OTHER FRENCH FABULISTS, by Rev. W. L. Collins, M.A.—SCHILLER, by James Sime, M.A., Author of 'Lessing: his Life and Writings.'—TASSO, by E. J. Hasell.—ROUSSEAU, by Henry Grey Graham.
In preparation—LEOPARDI, by the Editor.

FRANZOS. The Jews of Barnow. Stories by KARL EMIL FRANZOS. Translated by M. W. MACDOWALL. Crown 8vo, 6s.

GALT. Annals of the Parish. By JOHN GALT. Fcap. 8vo, 2s.

——— The Provost. Fcap. 8vo, 2s.

——— Sir Andrew Wylie. Fcap. 8vo, 2s.

——— The Entail; or, The Laird of Grippy. Fcap. 8vo, 2s.

GENERAL ASSEMBLY OF THE CHURCH OF SCOTLAND.
——— Family Prayers. Authorised by the General Assembly of the Church of Scotland. A New Edition, crown 8vo, in large type, 4s. 6d. Another Edition, crown 8vo, 2s.

——— Prayers for Social and Family Worship. For the Use of Soldiers, Sailors, Colonists, and Sojourners in India, and other Persons, at home and abroad, who are deprived of the ordinary services of a Christian Ministry. Cheap Edition, 1s. 6d.

——— The Scottish Hymnal. Hymns for Public Worship. Published for Use in Churches by Authority of the General Assembly. Various sizes—viz.: 1. Large type, for Pulpit use, cloth, 3s. 6d. 2. Longprimer type, cloth, red edges, 1s. 6d.; French morocco, 2s. 6d.; calf, 6s. 3. Bourgeois type, cloth, red edges, 1s.; French morocco, 2s. 4. Minion type, limp cloth, 6d.; French morocco, 1s. 6d. 5. School Edition, in paper cover, 2d. 6. Children's Hymnal, paper cover, 1d. No. 2, bound with the Psalms and Paraphrases, cloth, 3s.; French morocco, 4s. 6d.; calf, 7s. 6d. No. 3, bound with the Psalms and Paraphrases, cloth, 2s.; French morocco, 3s.

——— The Scottish Hymnal, with Music. Selected by the Committees on Hymns and on Psalmody. The harmonies arranged by W. H. Monk. Cloth, 1s. 6d.; French morocco, 3s. 6d. The same in the Tonic Sol-fa Notation, 1s. 6d. and 3s. 6d.

——— The Scottish Hymnal, with Fixed Tune for each Hymn. Longprimer type, 3s. 6d.

——— The Scottish Hymnal Appendix. 1. Longprimer type, 1s. 2. Nonpareil type, cloth limp, 4d.; paper cover, 2d.

——— Scottish Hymnal with Appendix Incorporated. Bourgeois type, limp cloth, 1s.

GERARD. Reata: What's in a Name. By E. D. GERARD. New Edition. In one volume, crown 8vo, 6s.

——— Beggar my Neighbour. A Novel. New Edition, complete in one volume, crown 8vo, 6s.

GOETHE'S FAUST. Translated into English Verse by Sir THEODORE MARTIN, K.C.B. Second Edition, post 8vo, 6s. Cheap Edition, fcap., 3s. 6d.

GOETHE. Poems and Ballads of Goethe. Translated by Professor AYTOUN and Sir THEODORE MARTIN, K.C.B. Third Edition, fcap. 8vo, 6s.

WILLIAM BLACKWOOD AND SONS. 11

GORDON CUMMING. At Home in Fiji. By C. F. GORDON
CUMMING, Author of 'From the Hebrides to the Himalayas.' Fourth Edition,
complete in one volume post 8vo. With Illustrations and Map. 7s. 6d.

—— A Lady's Cruise in a French Man-of-War. New and
Cheaper Edition. In one volume, 8vo. With Illustrations and Map. 12s. 6d.

—— Fire-Fountains. The Kingdom of Hawaii: Its Volcanoes,
and the History of its Missions. With Map and numerous Illustrations. 2
vols. 8vo, 25s.

—— Granite Crags: The Yō-semité Region of California. Illustrated with 8 Engravings. One vol. 8vo, 16s.

GRANT. Bush-Life in Queensland. By A. C. GRANT. New
Edition. Crown 8vo, 6s.

HAMERTON. Wenderholme: A Story of Lancashire and Yorkshire Life. By PHILIP GILBERT HAMERTON, Author of 'A Painter's Camp.' A
New Edition. Crown 8vo, 6s.

HAMILTON. Lectures on Metaphysics. By Sir WILLIAM HAMILTON, Bart., Professor of Logic and Metaphysics in the University of Edinburgh.
Edited by the Rev. H. L. MANSEL, B.D., LL.D., Dean of St Paul's; and JOHN
VEITCH, M.A., Professor of Logic and Rhetoric, Glasgow. Sixth Edition. 2
vols. 8vo, 24s.

—— Lectures on Logic. Edited by the SAME. Third Edition.
2 vols., 24s.

—— Discussions on Philosophy and Literature, Education and
University Reform. Third Edition, 8vo, 21s.

—— Memoir of Sir William Hamilton, Bart., Professor of Logic
and Metaphysics in the University of Edinburgh. By Professor VEITCH of the
University of Glasgow. 8vo, with Portrait, 18s.

—— Sir William Hamilton: The Man and his Philosophy.
Two Lectures Delivered before the Edinburgh Philosophical Institution,
January and February 1883. By the SAME. Crown 8vo, 2s.

HAMILTON. Annals of the Peninsular Campaigns. By Captain
THOMAS HAMILTON. Edited by F. Hardman. 8vo, 16s. Atlas of Maps to
illustrate the Campaigns, 12s.

HAMILTON. Mr Montenello. A Romance of the Civil Service.
By W. A. BAILLIE HAMILTON. In 3 vols. post 8vo, 25s. 6d.

HAMLEY. The Operations of War Explained and Illustrated. By
Major-General Sir EDWARD BRUCE HAMLEY, K.C.M.G. Fourth Edition,
revised throughout. 4to, with numerous Illustrations, 30s.

—— Thomas Carlyle: An Essay. Second Edition. Crown
8vo. 2s. 6d.

—— The Story of the Campaign of Sebastopol. Written in the
Camp. With Illustrations drawn in Camp by the Author. 8vo, 21s.

—— On Outposts. Second Edition. 8vo, 2s.

—— Wellington's Career; A Military and Political Summary.
Crown 8vo, 2s.

—— Lady Lee's Widowhood. Crown 8vo, 2s. 6d.

—— Our Poor Relations. A Philozoic Essay. With Illustrations, chiefly by Ernest Griset. Crown 8vo, cloth gilt, 3s. 6d.

HAMLEY. Guilty, or Not Guilty? A Tale. By Major-General
W. G. HAMLEY, late of the Royal Engineers. New Edition. Crown 8vo, 3s. 6d.

—— The House of Lys: One Book of its History. A Tale.
Second Edition. 2 vols. crown 8vo. 17s.

—— Trascaden Hall. "When George the Third was King."
New and Cheaper Edition, crown 8vo, 6s.

LIST OF BOOKS PUBLISHED BY

HANDY HORSE-BOOK; or, Practical Instructions in Riding, Driving, and the General Care and Management of Horses. By 'MAGENTA.' Ninth Edition, with 6 Engravings, 4s. 6d.

BY THE SAME.

Our Domesticated Dogs: their Treatment in reference to Food, Diseases, Habits, Punishment, Accomplishments. Crown 8vo, 2s. 6d.

HARBORD. Definitions and Diagrams in Astronomy and Navigation. By the Rev. J. B. HARBORD, M.A., Assistant Director of Education, Admiralty. 1s.

—— Short Sermons for Hospitals and Sick Seamen. Fcap. 8vo, cloth, 4s. 6d.

HARDMAN. Scenes and Adventures in Central America. Edited by FREDERICK HARDMAN. Crown 8vo. 6s.

HARRISON. Oure Tounis Colledge. Sketches of the History of the Old College of Edinburgh, with an Appendix of Historical Documents. By JOHN HARRISON. Crown 8vo, 5s.

HASELL. Bible Partings. By E. J. HASELL. Crown 8vo, 6s.

—— Short Family Prayers. By Miss HASELL. Cloth, 1s.

HAY. The Works of the Right Rev. Dr George Hay, Bishop of Edinburgh. Edited under the Supervision of the Right Rev. Bishop STRAIN. With Memoir and Portrait of the Author. 5 vols. crown 8vo, bound in extra cloth, £1, 1s. Or, sold separately—viz.:

The Sincere Christian Instructed in the Faith of Christ from the Written Word. 2 vols., 8s.—The Devout Christian Instructed in the Law of Christ from the Written Word. 2 vols., 8s.—The Pious Christian Instructed in the Nature and Practice of the Principal Exercises of Piety. 1 vol., 4s.

HEATLEY. The Horse-Owner's Safeguard. A Handy Medical Guide for every Man who owns a Horse. By G. S. HEATLEY, M.R.C., V.S. Crown 8vo, 5s.

—— The Stock-Owner's Guide. A Handy Medical Treatise for every Man who owns an Ox or a Cow. Crown 8vo, 4s. 6d.

HEMANS. The Poetical Works of Mrs Hemans. Copyright Editions.—One Volume, royal 8vo, 5s.—The Same, with Illustrations engraved on Steel, bound in cloth, gilt edges, 7s. 6d.—Six Volumes in Three, fcap., 12s. 6d.

SELECT POEMS OF MRS HEMANS. Fcap., cloth, gilt edges, 3s.

HOLE. A Book about Roses: How to Grow and Show Them. By the Rev. Canon HOLE. Eighth and Cheaper Edition, revised. Crown 8vo, 3s. 6d.

HOME PRAYERS. By Ministers of the Church of Scotland and Members of the Church Service Society. Second Edition. Fcap. 8vo, 3s.

HOMER. The Odyssey. Translated into English Verse in the Spenserian Stanza. By PHILIP STANHOPE WORSLEY. Third Edition, 2 vols. fcap., 12s.

—— The Iliad. Translated by P. S. WORSLEY and Professor CONINGTON. 2 vols. crown 8vo, 21s.

HOSACK. Mary Queen of Scots and Her Accusers. Containing a Variety of Documents never before published. By JOHN HOSACK, Barrister-at-Law. A New and Enlarged Edition, with a Photograph from the Bust on the Tomb in Westminster Abbey. 2 vols. 8vo, £1, 1s.

HUNTER. Santo, Lucia, & Co. in Austria. By ELLA HUNTER, Author of 'A Lady's Drive from Florence to Cherbourg.' With Frontispiece and Map. Crown 8vo, 5s.

—— A Lady's Drive from Florence to Cherbourg. With a Frontispiece and Map. Crown 8vo, 5s.

HYDE. The Royal Mail; its Curiosities and Romance. By JAMES WILSON HYDE, Superintendent in the General Post Office, Edinburgh. Crown 8vo, with Illustrations, 8s. 6d.

INDEX GEOGRAPHICUS : Being a List, alphabetically arranged, of the Principal Places on the Globe, with the Countries and Subdivisions of the Countries in which they are situated, and their Latitudes and Longitudes. Applicable to all Modern Atlases and Maps. Imperial 8vo, pp. 676, 21s.

JEAN JAMBON. Our Trip to Blunderland ; or, Grand Excursion to Blundertown and Back. By JEAN JAMBON. With Sixty Illustrations designed by CHARLES DOYLE, engraved by DALZIEL. Fourth Thousand. Handsomely bound in cloth, gilt edges, 6s. 6d. Cheap Edition, cloth, 3s. 6d. In boards, 2s. 6d.

JOHNSON. The Scots Musical Museum. Consisting of upwards of Six Hundred Songs, with proper Basses for the Pianoforte. Originally published by JAMES JOHNSON; and now accompanied with Copious Notes and Illustrations of the Lyric Poetry and Music of Scotland, by the late WILLIAM STENHOUSE; with additional Notes and Illustrations, by DAVID LAING and C. K. SHARPE. 4 vols. 8vo, Roxburghe binding, £2, 12s. 6d.

JOHNSTON. The Chemistry of Common Life. By Professor J. F. W. JOHNSTON. New Edition, Revised, and brought down to date. By ARTHUR HERBERT CHURCH, M.A. Oxon.; Author of 'Food: its Sources, Constituents, and Uses;' 'The Laboratory Guide for Agricultural Students;' 'Plain Words about Water,' &c Illustrated with Maps and 102 Engravings on Wood. Complete in one volume, crown 8vo, pp. 618, 7s. 6d.

—— Elements of Agricultural Chemistry and Geology. Thirteenth Edition, Revised, and brought down to date. By CHARLES A. CAMERON, M.D, F.R.C.S.I., &c. Fcap. 8vo, 6s. 6d.

—— Catechism of Agricultural Chemistry and Geology. An entirely New Edition, revised and enlarged, by CHARLES A. CAMERON, M.D., F.R.C.S.I., &c. Eighty-first Thousand, with numerous Illustrations, 1s.

JOHNSTON. Patrick Hamilton : a Tragedy of the Reformation in Scotland, 1528. By T. P. JOHNSTON. Crown 8vo, with Two Etchings by the Author, 5s.

KENNEDY. Sport, Travel, and Adventures in Newfoundland and the West Indies. By Captain W. R. KENNEDY, R.N. With Illustrations by the Author. In one vol. 8vo. [*In the press.*

KING. The Metamorphoses of Ovid. Translated in English Blank Verse. By HENRY KING, M.A, Fellow of Wadham College, Oxford, and of the Inner Temple, Barrister-at-Law. Crown 8vo, 10s. 6d.

KINGLAKE. History of the Invasion of the Crimea. By A. W. KINGLAKE. Cabinet Edition. Seven Volumes, crown 8vo, at 6s. each. The Volumes respectively contain :—
  I. THE ORIGIN OF THE WAR between the Czar and the Sultan.
  II. RUSSIA MET AND INVADED. With 4 Maps and Plans.
  III. THE BATTLE OF THE ALMA. With 14 Maps and Plans.
  IV. SEBASTOPOL AT BAY. With 10 Maps and Plans.
  V. THE BATTLE OF BALACLAVA. With 10 Maps and Plans.
  VI. THE BATTLE OF INKERMAN. With 11 Maps and Plans.
  VII. WINTER TROUBLES. With Map.

—— History of the Invasion of the Crimea. Vol. VI. Winter Troubles. Demy 8vo, with a Map, 16s.

—— History of the Invasion of the Crimea. Vol. VII. Demy 8vo. [*In preparation.*

—— Eothen. A New Edition, uniform with the Cabinet Edition of the 'History of the Crimean War,' price 6s.

KNOLLYS. The Elements of Field-Artillery. Designed for the Use of Infantry and Cavalry Officers. By HENRY KNOLLYS, Captain Royal Artillery; Author of 'From Sedan to Saarbrück,' Editor of 'Incidents in the Sepoy War,' &c. With Engravings. Crown 8vo, 7s. 6d.

LAING. Select Remains of the Ancient Popular and Romance Poetry of Scotland. Originally collected and Edited by DAVID LAING, LL.D. Re-edited, with Memorial-Introduction, by JOHN SMALL, M.A. With a Portrait of Dr Laing. 4to, 25s. The Edition has been limited to 350 copies, and when one-half of the Edition is disposed of, the price will be increased.

LAVERGNE. The Rural Economy of England, Scotland, and Ireland. By LEONCE DE LAVERGNE. Translated from the French. With Notes by a Scottish Farmer. 8vo, 12s.

LEE. Lectures on the History of the Church of Scotland, from the Reformation to the Revolution Settlement. By the late Very Rev. JOHN LEE, D.D., LL.D., Principal of the University of Edinburgh. With Notes and Appendices from the Author's Papers. Edited by the Rev. WILLIAM LEE, D.D. 2 vols. 8vo, 21s.

LEE. Miss Brown: A Novel. By VERNON LEE. 3 vols. post 8vo, 25s. 6d.

LEE. Glimpses in the Twilight. Being various Notes, Records, and Examples of the Supernatural. By the Rev. GEORGE F. LEE, D.C.L. Crown 8vo. 8s. 6d.

LEE-HAMILTON. Poems and Transcripts. By EUGENE LEE-HAMILTON. Crown 8vo, 6s.

LEES. A Handbook of Sheriff Court Styles. By J. M. LEES, M.A., LL.B., Advocate, Sheriff-Substitute of Lanarkshire. 8vo, 16s.

——— A Handbook of the Sheriff and Justice of Peace Small Debt Courts. 8vo, 7s. 6d.

LETTERS FROM THE HIGHLANDS. Reprinted from 'The Times.' Fcap. 8vo, 4s. 6d.

LINDAU. The Philosopher's Pendulum and other Stories. By RUDOLPH LINDAU. Crown 8vo, 7s. 6d.

LITTLE. Madagascar: Its History and People. By the Rev. HENRY W. LITTLE, some years Missionary in East Madagascar. Post 8vo, 10s. 6d.

LOCKHART. Doubles and Quits. By LAURENCE W. M. LOCKHART. With Twelve Illustrations. Third Edition. Crown 8vo, 6s.

——— Fair to See: a Novel. Eighth Edition, crown 8vo, 6s.

——— Mine is Thine: a Novel. Seventh Edition, crown 8vo, 6s.

LORIMER. The Institutes of Law: A Treatise of the Principles of Jurisprudence as determined by Nature. By JAMES LORIMER, Regius Professor of Public Law and of the Law of Nature and Nations in the University of Edinburgh. New Edition, revised throughout, and much enlarged. 8vo, 18s.

——— The Institutes of the Law of Nations. A Treatise of the Jural Relation of Separate Political Communities. In 2 vols. 8vo. Volume I., price 16s. Volume II., price 20s.

M'COMBIE. Cattle and Cattle-Breeders. By WILLIAM M'COMBIE, Tillyfour. A New and Cheaper Edition, 2s. 6d., cloth.

MACRAE. A Handbook of Deer-Stalking. By ALEXANDER MACRAE, late Forester to Lord Henry Bentinck. With Introduction by HORATIO ROSS, Esq. Fcap. 8vo, with two Photographs from Life. 3s. 6d.

M'CRIE. Works of the Rev. Thomas M'Crie, D.D. Uniform Edition. Four vols. crown 8vo, 24s.

——— Life of John Knox. Containing Illustrations of the History of the Reformation in Scotland. Crown 8vo, 6s. Another Edition, 3s. 6d.

——— Life of Andrew Melville. Containing Illustrations of the Ecclesiastical and Literary History of Scotland in the Sixteenth and Seventeenth Centuries. Crown 8vo, 6s.

——— History of the Progress and Suppression of the Reformation in Italy in the Sixteenth Century. Crown 8vo, 4s.

——— History of the Progress and Suppression of the Reformation in Spain in the Sixteenth Century. Crown 8vo, 3s. 6d.

——— Sermons, and Review of the 'Tales of My Landlord.' Crown 8vo, 6s.

——— Lectures on the Book of Esther. Fcap. 8vo, 5s.

WILLIAM BLACKWOOD AND SONS. 15

M'INTOSH. The Book of the Garden. By CHARLES M'INTOSH, formerly Curator of the Royal Gardens of his Majesty the King of the Belgians, and lately of those of his Grace the Duke of Buccleuch, K.G., at Dalkeith Palace. Two large vols. royal 8vo, embellished with 1350 Engravings. £4, 7s. 6d.
Vol. I. On the Formation of Gardens and Construction of Garden Edifices. 776 pages, and 1073 Engravings, £2, 10s.
Vol. II. Practical Gardening. 868 pages, and 279 Engravings, £1, 17s. 6d.

MACKAY. A Manual of Modern Geography; Mathematical, Physical, and Political. By the Rev. ALEXANDER MACKAY, LL.D., F.R.G.S. New and Greatly Improved Edition. Crown 8vo, pp. 688. 7s. 6d.

—— Elements of Modern Geography. 51st Thousand, revised to the present time. Crown 8vo, pp. 300, 3s.

—— The Intermediate Geography. Intended as an Intermediate Book between the Author's 'Outlines of Geography' and 'Elements of Geography.' Ninth Edition, revised. Crown 8vo, pp. 224, 2s.

—— Outlines of Modern Geography. 160th Thousand, revised to the present time. 18mo, pp. 118, 1s.

—— First Steps in Geography. 82d Thousand. 18mo, pp. 56. Sewed, 4d.; cloth, 6d.

—— Elements of Physiography and Physical Geography. With Express Reference to the Instructions recently issued by the Science and Art Department. 25th Thousand, revised. Crown 8vo, 1s. 6d.

—— Facts and Dates; or, the Leading Events in Sacred and Profane History, and the Principal Facts in the various Physical Sciences. The Memory being aided throughout by a Simple and Natural Method. For Schools and Private Reference. New Edition, thoroughly Revised. Crown 8vo, 3s. 6d.

MACKAY. Mackay's Regiment: A Narrative of the Principal Services of the Regiment, from its Formation in 1626 to the Battle of Nordlingen in 1634; and of its subsequent Incorporation with the Corps now known as The Royal Scots, or First Regiment of Foot of the British Army. By JOHN MACKAY OF HERRIESDALE. Fcap. 8vo. [In the press.

MACKAY. The Founders of the American Republic. A History of Washington, Adams, Jefferson, Franklin, and Madison. With a Supplementary Chapter on the Inherent Causes of the Ultimate Failure of American Democracy. By CHARLES MACKAY, LL.D. In one vol. post 8vo.
[In the press.

MACKENZIE. Studies in Roman Law. With Comparative Views of the Laws of France, England, and Scotland. By LORD MACKENZIE, one of the Judges of the Court of Session in Scotland. Fifth Edition, Edited by JOHN KIRKPATRICK, Esq., M.A. Cantab.; Dr Jur. Heidelb.; LL.B., Edin.; Advocate. 8vo, 12s.

MAIN. Three Hundred English Sonnets. Chosen and Edited by DAVID M. MAIN. Fcap. 8vo, 6s.

MANNERS. Notes of an Irish Tour in 1846. By Lord JOHN MANNERS, M.P., G.C.B. New Edition. Crown 8vo, 2s. 6d.

MANNERS. Gems of German Poetry. Translated by Lady JOHN MANNERS. Small quarto, 3s. 6d.

—— Impressions of Bad-Homburg. Comprising a Short Account of the Women's Associations of Germany under the Red Cross. By Lady JOHN MANNERS. Crown 8vo, 1s. 6d

—— Some Personal Recollections of the Later Years of the Earl of Beaconsfield, K G. Fifth Edition, 6d.

—— Employment of Women in the Public Service. 6d.

—— Some of the Advantages of Easily Accessible Reading and Recreation Rooms, and Free Libraries. With Remarks on Starting and Maintaining Them. Reprinted from 'The Queen.' Dedicated by Special Permission to Her Majesty the Queen. Crown 8vo, 1s.

MARMORNE. The Story is told by ADOLPHUS SEGRAVE, the youngest of three Brothers. Third Edition. Crown 8vo, 6s.

LIST OF BOOKS PUBLISHED BY

MARSHALL. French Home Life. By FREDERIC MARSHALL. Second Edition. 5s.

MARSHMAN. History of India. From the Earliest Period to the Close of the India Company's Government; with an Epitome of Subsequent Events. By JOHN CLARK MARSHMAN, C.S.I. Abridged from the Author's larger work. Second Edition, revised. Crown 8vo, with Map, 6s. 6d.

MARTIN Goethe's Faust. Translated by Sir THEODORE MARTIN, K.C.B. Second Edition, crown 8vo, 6s. Cheap Edition, 3s. 6d.

—— The Works of Horace. Translated into English Verse, with Life and Notes. In 2 vols. crown 8vo, printed on hand-made paper, 21s.

—— Poems and Ballads of Heinrich Heine. Done into English Verse. Second Edition. Printed on *papier vergé*, crown 8vo, 8s.

—— Catullus. With Life and Notes. Second Edition, post 8vo, 7s. 6d.

——. The Vita Nuova of Dante. With an Introduction and Notes. Second Edition, crown 8vo, 5s.

—— Aladdin: A Dramatic Poem. By ADAM OEHLENSCHLAEGER. Fcap. 8vo, 5s.

—— Correggio: A Tragedy. By OEHLENSCHLAEGER. With Notes. Fcap. 8vo, 3s.

—— King Rene's Daughter: A Danish Lyrical Drama. By HENRIK HERTZ. Second Edition, fcap., 2s. 6d.

MARTIN. Some of Shakespeare's Female Characters. In a Series of Letters. By HELENA FAUCIT, LADY MARTIN. With Portraits engraved by the late F. Holl. Dedicated by Special Permission to Her Most Gracious Majesty the Queen. In one vol. 4to, printed on hand-made paper.
[*In the press.*

MATHESON. Can the Old Faith Live with the New? or the Problem of Evolution and Revelation. By the Rev. GEORGE MATHESON, D.D., Innellan. Crown 8vo, 7s. 6d.

MEIKLEJOHN. An Old Educational Reformer—Dr Bell. By J. M. D. MEIKLEJOHN, M.A., Professor of the Theory, History, and Practice of Education in the University of St Andrews. Crown 8vo, 3s. 6d.

MICHEL. A Critical Inquiry into the Scottish Language. With the view of Illustrating the Rise and Progress of Civilisation in Scotland. By FRANCISQUE-MICHEL, F.S.A. Lond. and Scot., Correspondant de l'Institut de France, &c. In One handsome Quarto Volume, printed on hand-made paper, and appropriately bound in Roxburghe style. Price 66s.

MICHIE. The Larch: Being a Practical Treatise on its Culture and General Management. By CHRISTOPHER YOUNG MICHIE, Forester, Cullen House. Crown 8vo, with Illustrations. 7s. 6d.

MILLIONAIRE, THE. By LOUIS J. JENNINGS, Author of 'Field Paths and Green Lanes,' 'Rambles among the Hills,' &c. Second Edition. 3 vols. crown 8vo, 25s. 6d.

MILNE. The Problem of the Churchless and Poor in our Large Towns. With special reference to the Home Mission Work of the Church of Scotland. By the Rev. ROBT. MILNE, M.A., Towie. Crown 8vo, 5s.

MINTO. A Manual of English Prose Literature, Biographical and Critical: designed mainly to show Characteristics of Style. By W. MINTO, M.A., Professor of Logic in the University of Aberdeen. Second Edition, revised. Crown 8vo, 7s. 6d.

—— Characteristics of English Poets, from Chaucer to Shirley. Crown 8vo, 9s.

MITCHELL. Biographies of Eminent Soldiers of the last Four Centuries. By Major-General JOHN MITCHELL, Author of 'Life of Wallenstein.' With a Memoir of the Author. 8vo, 9s.

MOIR. Life of Mansie Wauch, Tailor in Dalkeith. With 8 Illustrations on Steel, by the late GEORGE CRUIKSHANK. Crown 8vo, 3s. 6d. Another Edition, fcap. 8vo, 1s. 6d.

MOMERIE. Defects of Modern Christianity, and other Sermons.
By the Rev. A. W. MOMERIE, M.A., D.Sc., Professor of Logic and Metaphysics in King's College, London. New Edition. Crown 8vo, 5s.
—— The Basis of Religion. Being an Examination of Natural Religion. Crown 8vo. 2s. 6d.
—— The Origin of Evil, and other Sermons. Third Edition, enlarged. Crown 8vo, 5s.
—— Personality. The Beginning and End of Metaphysics, and a Necessary Assumption in all Positive Philosophy. Second Edition. Crown 8vo, 3s.
—— Agnosticism, and other Sermons. Crown 8vo, 6s.
MONTAGUE. Campaigning in South Africa. Reminiscences of an Officer in 1879. By Captain W. E. MONTAGUE, 94th Regiment, Author of 'Claude Meadowleigh,' &c. 8vo, 10s. 6d.
MONTALEMBERT. Memoir of Count de Montalembert. A Chapter of Recent French History. By Mrs OLIPHANT, Author of the 'Life of Edward Irving,' &c. 2 vols. crown 8vo, £1, 4s.
MURDOCH. Manual of the Law of Insolvency and Bankruptcy: Comprehending a Summary of the Law of Insolvency, Notour Bankruptcy, Composition-contracts, Trust-deeds, Cessios, and Sequestrations; and the Winding-up of Joint-Stock Companies in Scotland; with Annotations on the various Insolvency and Bankruptcy Statutes; and with Forms of Procedure applicable to these Subjects. By JAMES MURDOCH, Member of the Faculty of Procurators in Glasgow. Fourth Edition, Revised and Enlarged, 8vo, £1.
MY TRIVIAL LIFE AND MISFORTUNE: A Gossip with no Plot in Particular. By A PLAIN WOMAN. New Edition, crown 8vo, 6s.
NEAVES. Songs and Verses, Social and Scientific. By an Old Contributor to 'Maga.' By the Hon. Lord NEAVES. Fifth Edition, fcap. 8vo, 4s.
—— The Greek Anthology. Being Vol. XX. of 'Ancient Classics for English Readers.' Crown 8vo, 2s. 6d.
NEEDELL. Lucia, Hugh, and Another. By Mrs J. H. Needell. 3 vols. post 8vo, 25s. 6d.
NICHOLSON. A Manual of Zoology, for the Use of Students. With a General Introduction on the Principles of Zoology. By HENRY ALLEYNE NICHOLSON, M.D., D.Sc., F.L.S., F.G.S., Regius Professor of Natural History in the University of Aberdeen. Sixth Edition, revised and enlarged. Crown 8vo, pp. 816, with 394 Engravings on Wood, 14s.
—— Text-Book of Zoology, for the Use of Schools. Third Edition, enlarged. Crown 8vo, with 188 Engravings on Wood, 6s.
—— Introductory Text-Book of Zoology, for the Use of Junior Classes. Fifth Edition, revised and enlarged, with 156 Engravings, 3s.
—— Outlines of Natural History, for Beginners; being Descriptions of a Progressive Series of Zoological Types. Third Edition, with Engravings, 1s. 6d.
—— A Manual of Palæontology, for the Use of Students. With a General Introduction on the Principles of Palæontology. Second Edition. Revised and greatly enlarged. 2 vols. 8vo, with 722 Engravings, £2, 2s.
—— The Ancient Life-History of the Earth. An Outline of the Principles and Leading Facts of Palæontological Science. Crown 8vo, with numerous Engravings, 10s. 6d.
—— On the "Tabulate Corals" of the Palæozoic Period, with Critical Descriptions of Illustrative Species. Illustrated with 15 Lithograph Plates and numerous Engravings. Super-royal 8vo, 21s.
—— On the Structure and Affinities of the Genus Monticulipora and its Sub-Genera, with Critical Descriptions of Illustrative Species. Illustrated with numerous Engravings on wood and lithographed Plates. Super-royal 8vo, 18s.
—— Synopsis of the Classification of the Animal Kingdom. 8vo, with 106 Illustrations, 6s.

18 LIST OF BOOKS PUBLISHED BY

NICHOLSON. Communion with Heaven, and other Sermons. By the late MAXWELL NICHOLSON, D.D., Minister of St Stephen's, Edinburgh. Crown 8vo, 5s. 6d.
——— Rest in Jesus. Sixth Edition. Fcap. 8vo, 4s. 6d.
OLIPHANT. The Land of Gilead. With Excursions in the Lebanon. By LAURENCE OLIPHANT, Author of 'Lord Elgin's Mission to China and Japan,' &c. With Illustrations and Maps. Demy 8vo, 21s.
——— The Land of Khemi. Post 8vo, with Illustrations, 10s. 6d.
——— Sympneumata: or, Evolutionary Functions now Active in Man Post 8vo, 10s. 6d.
——— Altiora Peto. Seventh Edition, Illustrated. Crown 8vo, 6s.
——— Traits and Travesties; Social and Political. Post 8vo, 10s. 6d.
——— Piccadilly: A Fragment of Contemporary Biography. With Eight Illustrations by Richard Doyle. Fifth Edition, 4s. 6d. Cheap Edition, in paper cover, 2s. 6d.
OLIPHANT. The Ladies Lindores. By Mrs OLIPHANT. 3 vols., 25s. 6d.
——— The Story of Valentine; and his Brother. 5s., cloth.
——— Katie Stewart. 2s. 6d.
——— Salem Chapel. 2s. 6d., cloth.
——— The Perpetual Curate. 2s. 6d., cloth.
——— Miss Marjoribanks. 2s. 6d., cloth.
——— The Rector, and the Doctor's Family. 1s. 6d., cloth.
——— John: A Love Story. 2s. 6d., cloth.
OSBORN. Narratives of Voyage and Adventure. By Admiral SHERARD OSBORN, C.B. 3 vols. crown 8vo, 12s.
OSSIAN. The Poems of Ossian in the Original Gaelic. With a Literal Translation into English, and a Dissertation on the Authenticity of the Poems. By the Rev. ARCHIBALD CLERK. 2 vols. imperial 8vo, £1, 11s. 6d.
OSWALD. By Fell and Fjord; or, Scenes and Studies in Iceland. By E. J. OSWALD. Post 8vo, with Illustrations. 7s. 6d.
PAGE. Introductory Text-Book of Geology. By DAVID PAGE, LL.D., Professor of Geology in the Durham University of Physical Science, Newcastle. With Engravings on Wood and Glossarial Index. Eleventh Edition, 2s. 6d.
——— Advanced Text-Book of Geology, Descriptive and Industrial. With Engravings, and Glossary of Scientific Terms. Sixth Edition, revised and enlarged, 7s. 6d.
——— Geology for General Readers. A Series of Popular Sketches in Geology and Palæontology. Third Edition, enlarged, 6s.
——— Introductory Text-Book of Physical Geography. With Sketch-Maps and Illustrations. Edited by CHARLES LAPWORTH, F.G.S., &c., Professor of Geology and Mineralogy in the Mason Science College, Birmingham. 11th Edition. 2s. 6d.
——— Advanced Text-Book of Physical Geography. Third Edition, Revised and Enlarged by Professor LAPWORTH. With Engravings. 5s.
PATON. Spindrift. By Sir J. NOEL PATON. Fcap., cloth, 5s.
——— Poems by a Painter. Fcap., cloth, 5s.
PATTERSON. Essays in History and Art. By R. HOGARTH PATTERSON. 8vo, 12s.
——— The New Golden Age, and Influence of the Precious Metals upon the World. 2 vols. 8vo, 31s. 6d.
PAUL. History of the Royal Company of Archers, the Queen's Body-Guard for Scotland. By JAMES BALFOUR PAUL, Advocate of the Scottish Bar. Crown 4to, with Portraits and other Illustrations. £2, 2s.

WILLIAM BLACKWOOD AND SONS. 19

PAUL. Analysis and Critical Interpretation of the Hebrew Text of the Book of Genesis. Preceded by a Hebrew Grammar, and Dissertations on the Genuineness of the Pentateuch, and on the Structure of the Hebrew Language. By the Rev. WILLIAM PAUL, A.M. 8vo, 18s.

PETTIGREW. The Handy Book of Bees, and their Profitable Management. By A. PETTIGREW. Fourth Edition, Enlarged, with Engravings. Crown 8vo, 3s. 6d.

PHILOSOPHICAL CLASSICS FOR ENGLISH READERS. Companion Series to Ancient and Foreign Classics for English Readers. Edited by WILLIAM KNIGHT, LL.D., Professor of Moral Philosophy, University of St Andrews. In crown 8vo volumes, with portraits, price 3s. 6d.

1. DESCARTES. By Professor Mahaffy, Dublin.
2. BUTLER. By the Rev. W. Lucas Collins, M.A., Honorary Canon of Peterborough.
3. BERKELEY. By Professor A. Campbell Fraser, Edinburgh.
4. FICHTE. By Professor Adamson, Owens College, Manchester.
5. KANT. By Professor Wallace, Oxford.
6. HAMILTON. By Professor Veitch, Glasgow.
7. HEGEL. By Professor Edward Caird, Glasgow.
8. LEIBNIZ. By J. Theodore Merz.
9. VICO. By Professor Flint, Edinburgh.

POLLOK. The Course of Time: A Poem. By ROBERT POLLOK, A.M. Small fcap. 8vo, cloth gilt, 2s. 6d. The Cottage Edition, 32mo, sewed, 8d. The Same, cloth, gilt edges, 1s. 6d. Another Edition, with Illustrations by Birket Foster and others, fcap., gilt cloth, 3s. 6d., or with edges gilt, 4s.

PORT ROYAL LOGIC. Translated from the French: with Introduction, Notes, and Appendix. By THOMAS SPENCER BAYNES, LL.D., Professor in the University of St Andrews. Eighth Edition, 12mo, 4s.

POST-MORTEM. Third Edition, 1s.

BY THE SAME AUTHOR.

The Autobiography of Thomas Allen. 3 vols. post 8vo, 25s. 6d.

The Apparition. Crown 8vo, with Frontispiece, 5s.

Simiocracy: A Fragment from Future History. Crown 8vo. 1s. 6d.

POTTS AND DARNELL. Aditus Faciliores: An easy Latin Construing Book, with Complete Vocabulary. By A. W. POTTS, M.A., LL.D., Head-Master of the Fettes College, Edinburgh, and sometime Fellow of St John's College, Cambridge; and the Rev. C. DARNELL, M.A., Head-Master of Cargilfield Preparatory School, Edinburgh, and late Scholar of Pembroke and Downing Colleges, Cambridge. Eighth Edition, fcap. 8vo, 3s. 6d.

——— Aditus Faciliores Graeci. An easy Greek Construing Book, with Complete Vocabulary. Third Edition, fcap. 8vo, 3s.

PRINGLE. The Live-Stock of the Farm. By ROBERT O. PRINGLE. Third Edition, crown 8vo. [In the press.

PRINGLE. Towards the Mountains of the Moon. A Journey in East Africa. By Mrs Pringle of Whytbank, Yair. With a Map, 8vo, 12s. 6d.

PUBLIC GENERAL STATUTES AFFECTING SCOTLAND, from 1707 to 1847, with Chronological Table and Index. 3 vols. large 8vo, £3, 3s.

PUBLIC GENERAL STATUTES AFFECTING SCOTLAND, COLLECTION OF. Published Annually with General Index.

RAMSAY. Rough Recollections of Military Service and Society. By Lieut.-Col. BALCARRES D. WARDLAW RAMSAY. Two vols. post 8vo, 21s.

RANKINE. A Treatise on the Rights and Burdens incident to the Ownership of Lands and other Heritages in Scotland. By JOHN RANKINE, M.A., Advocate. Second Edition, Revised and Enlarged. In One large Volume, 8vo, 45s.

RECORDS OF THE TERCENTENARY FESTIVAL OF THE UNIVERSITY OF EDINBURGH. Celebrated in April 1884. Published under the Sanction of the Senatus Academicus. Large 4to, £2, 12s. 6d. Only 150 copies printed for sale to the public.

REID. A Handy Manual of German Literature. By M. F. REID.
For Schools, Civil Service Competitions, and University Local Examinations.
Fcap. 8vo. 3s.

RIMMER. The Early Homes of Prince Albert. By ALFRED
RIMMER, Author of 'Our Old Country Towns,' &c. Beautifully Illustrated
with Tinted Plates and numerous Engravings on Wood. 8vo, 21s.

ROBERTSON. Orellana, and other Poems. By J. LOGIE ROBERT-
SON. Fcap. 8vo. Printed on hand-made paper. 6s.

—— Our Holiday Among the Hills. By JAMES and JANET
LOGIE ROBERTSON. Fcap. 8vo, 3s. 6d.

ROSCOE. Rambles with a Fishing-rod. By E. S. ROSCOE. Crown
8vo, 4s. 6d.

ROSS. Old Scottish Regimental Colours. By ANDREW ROSS,
S.S.C., Hon. Secretary Old Scottish Regimental Colours Committee. Dedicated by Special Permission to Her Majesty the Queen. In one vol. folio,
handsomely bound in cloth, £2, 12s. 6d.

RUSSELL. The Haigs of Bemersyde. A Family History. By
JOHN RUSSELL. Large octavo, with Illustrations. 21s.

RUSTOW. The War for the Rhine Frontier, 1870 : Its Political
and Military History. By Col. W. RUSTOW. Translated from the German,
by JOHN LAYLAND NEEDHAM, Lieutenant R.M. Artillery. 3 vols. 8vo, with
Maps and Plans, £1, 11s. 6d.

SCHETKY. Ninety Years of Work and Play. Sketches from the
Public and Private Career of JOHN CHRISTIAN SCHETKY, late Marine Painter in
Ordinary to the Queen. By his DAUGHTER. Crown 8vo, 7s. 6d

SCOTCH LOCH FISHING. By "Black Palmer." Crown 8vo,
interleaved with blank pages, 4s.

SELLAR. Manual of the Education Acts for Scotland. By
ALEXANDER CRAIG SELLAR, Advocate. Seventh Edition. To which are pre-
fixed the New Acts and Recent Decisions. By J. EDWARD GRAHAM, Advocate.
8vo, 15s.

SELLER AND STEPHENS. Physiology at the Farm; in Aid of
Rearing and Feeding the Live Stock. By WILLIAM SELLER, M.D., F.R.S.E.,
Fellow of the Royal College of Physicians, Edinburgh, formerly Lecturer on
Materia Medica and Dietetics; and HENRY STEPHENS, F.R.S.E., Author of 'The
Book of the Farm,' &c. Post 8vo, with Engravings, 16s.

SETON. Memoir of Alexander Seton, Earl of Dunfermline, Seventh
President of the Court of Session, and Lord Chancellor of Scotland. By
GEORGE SETON, M.A. Oxon.; Author of the 'Law and Practice of Heraldry in
Scotland,' &c. Crown 4to, 21s.

SEYMOUR AND ROBERTSON. The Golden Pin ; or, A Week
of Madness. By HAMILTON SEYMOUR and KEITH ROBERTSON. Seventh
Thousand. Crown 8vo, 1s.

SHADWELL. The Life of Colin Campbell, Lord Clyde. Illustrated by Extracts from his Diary and Correspondence. By Lieutenant-
General SHADWELL, C.B. 2 vols. 8vo. With Portrait, Maps, and Plans.
36s.

SHAND. Letters from the West of Ireland. Reprinted from the
'Times.' By ALEXANDER INNES SHAND, Author of 'Letters from the West
Highlands.' Crown 8vo, 5s.

SIM. Margaret Sim's Cookery. With an Introduction by L. B.
WALFORD, Author of 'Mr Smith: A Part of His Life,' &c. Crown 8vo, 5s.

SIME. King Capital. By WILLIAM SIME. 2 vols. post 8vo, 17s.

SIMPSON. Dogs of other Days: Nelson and Puck. By EVE
BLANTYRE SIMPSON. Fcap. 8vo, with Illustrations. 2s. 6d.

SMITH. Italian Irrigation : A Report on the Agricultural Canals of Piedmont and Lombardy, addressed to the Hon. the Directors of the East India Company ; with an Appendix, containing a Sketch of the Irrigation System of Northern and Central India. By Lieut.-Col. R. BAIRD SMITH, F.G.S., Captain, Bengal Engineers. Second Edition. 2 vols. 8vo, with Atlas in folio, 30s.

SMITH. Thorndale ; or, The Conflict of Opinions. By WILLIAM SMITH, Author of 'A Discourse on Ethics,' &c. A New Edition. Crown 8vo, 10s. 6d.

—— Gravenhurst ; or, Thoughts on Good and Evil. Second Edition, with Memoir of the Author. Crown 8vo, 8s.

—— A Discourse on Ethics of the School of Paley. 8vo, 4s.

—— Dramas. 1. Sir William Crichton. 2. Athelwold. 3. Guidone. 24mo, boards, 3s.

SMITH. Greek Testament Lessons for Colleges, Schools, and Private Students, consisting chiefly of the Sermon on the Mount and the Parables of our Lord. With Notes and Essays. By the Rev. J. HUNTER SMITH, M.A., First Assistant Master at King Edward's School, Birmingham. Crown 8vo, 6s.

SMITH. Writings by the Way. By JOHN CAMPBELL SMITH, M.A., Advocate. Crown 8vo, 9s.

SOLTERA. A Lady's Ride Across Spanish Honduras. By MARIA SOLTERA. With Illustrations. Post 8vo, 12s. 6d.

SOUTHEY. The Birthday, and other Poems. Second Edition, 5s.

—— Chapters on Churchyards. Fcap., 2s. 6d.

SPEEDY. Sport in the Highlands and Lowlands of Scotland with Rod and Gun. By T. Speedy. 8vo, with Illustrations, 15s.

SPEKE. What led to the Discovery of the Nile Source. By JOHN HANNING SPEKE, Captain H.M. Indian Army. 8vo, with Maps, &c., 14s.

SPROTT. The Worship and Offices of the Church of Scotland ; or, the Celebration of Public Worship, the Administration of the Sacraments, and other Divine Offices, according to the Order of the Church of Scotland. By GEORGE W. SPROTT, D.D., Minister of North Berwick. Crown 8vo, 6s.

STARFORTH. Villa Residences and Farm Architecture : A Series of Designs. By JOHN STARFORTH, Architect. 102 Engravings. Second Edition, medium 4to, £2, 17s. 6d.

STATISTICAL ACCOUNT OF SCOTLAND. Complete, with Index, 15 vols, 8vo, £16, 16s.
Each County sold separately, with Title, Index, and Map, neatly bound in cloth, forming a very valuable Manual to the Landowner, the Tenant, the Manufacturer, the Naturalist, the Tourist, &c.

STEPHENS. The Book of the Farm ; detailing the Labours of the Farmer, Farm-Steward, Ploughman, Shepherd, Hedger, Farm-Labourer, Field-Worker, and Cattleman. By HENRY STEPHENS, F.R.S.E. Illustrated with Portraits of Animals painted from the life ; and with 557 Engravings on Wood, representing the principal Field Operations, Implements, and Animals treated of in the Work. A New and Revised Edition, the third, in great part Rewritten. 2 vols. large 8vo, £2, 10s.

—— The Book of Farm Buildings ; their Arrangement and Construction. By HENRY STEPHENS, F.R.S.E., Author of 'The Book of the Farm ;' and ROBERT SCOTT BURN. Illustrated with 1045 Plates and Engravings. Large 8vo, uniform with 'The Book of the Farm,' &c. £1, 11s. 6d.

—— The Book of Farm Implements and Machines. By J. SLIGHT and R. SCOTT BURN, Engineers. Edited by HENRY STEPHENS. Large 8vo, uniform with 'The Book of the Farm,' £2, 2s.

—— Catechism of Practical Agriculture. With Engravings. 1s.

STEWART. Advice to Purchasers of Horses. By JOHN STEWART, V.S., Author of 'Stable Economy.' 2s. 6d.

—— Stable Economy. A Treatise on the Management of Horses in relation to Stabling, Grooming, Feeding, Watering, and Working. Seventh Edition, fcap. 8vo, 6s. 6d.

LIST OF BOOKS PUBLISHED BY

STONE. Hugh Moore: a Novel. By EVELYN STONE. 2 vols. crown 8vo, 17s.

STORMONTH. Etymological and Pronouncing Dictionary of the English Language. Including a very Copious Selection of Scientific Terms. For Use in Schools and Colleges, and as a Book of General Reference. By the Rev. JAMES STORMONTH. The Pronunciation carefully Revised by the Rev. P. H. PHELP, M.A. Cantab. Eighth Edition, Revised throughout, containing many words not to be found in any other Dictionary. Crown 8vo, pp. 800. 7s. 6d.

—— Dictionary of the English Language, Pronouncing, Etymological, and Explanatory. Revised by the Rev. P. H. PHELP. Library Edition. Imperial 8vo, handsomely bound in half morocco, 31s. 6d.

—— The School Etymological Dictionary and Word-Book. Combining the advantages of an ordinary pronouncing School Dictionary and an Etymological Spelling-book. Fcap. 8vo, pp. 254. 2s.

STORY. Graffiti D'Italia. By W. W. STORY, Author of 'Roba di Roma.' Second Edition, fcap. 8vo, 7s. 6d.

—— Nero; A Historical Play. Fcap. 8vo, 6s.

—— Vallombrosa. Post 8vo, 5s.

—— He and She; or, A Poet's Portfolio. Fcap. 8vo, in parchment, 3s. 6d.

STRICKLAND. Lives of the Queens of Scotland, and English Princesses connected with the Regal Succession of Great Britain. By AGNES STRICKLAND. With Portraits and Historical Vignettes. 8 vols. post 8vo, £4, 4s.

STURGIS. John-a-Dreams. A Tale. By JULIAN STURGIS. New Edition, crown 8vo, 3s. 6d.

—— Little Comedies, Old and New. Crown 8vo, 7s. 6d.

SUTHERLAND. Handbook of Hardy Herbaceous and Alpine Flowers, for general Garden Decoration. Containing Descriptions, in Plain Language, of upwards of 1000 Species of Ornamental Hardy Perennial and Alpine Plants, adapted to all classes of Flower-Gardens, Rockwork, and Waters; along with Concise and Plain Instructions for their Propagation and Culture. By WILLIAM SUTHERLAND, Gardener to the Earl of Minto; formerly Manager of the Herbaceous Department at Kew. Crown 8vo, 7s. 6d.

TAYLOR. Destruction and Reconstruction: Personal Experiences of the Late War in the United States. By RICHARD TAYLOR, Lieutenant-General in the Confederate Army. 8vo, 10s. 6d.

TAYLOR. The Story of My Life. By the late Colonel MEADOWS TAYLOR, Author of 'The Confessions of a Thug,' &c. &c. Edited by his Daughter. New and cheaper Edition, being the Fourth. Crown 8vo, 6s.

TEMPLE. Lancelot Ward, M.P. A Love-Story. By GEORGE TEMPLE. Crown 8vo. 7s. 6d.

THOLUCK. Hours of Christian Devotion. Translated from the German of A. Tholuck, D.D., Professor of Theology in the University of Halle. By the Rev. ROBERT MENZIES, D.D. With a Preface written for this Translation by the Author. Second Edition, crown 8vo, 7s. 6d.

THOMSON. Handy Book of the Flower-Garden: being Practical Directions for the Propagation, Culture, and Arrangement of Plants in Flower-Gardens all the year round. Embracing all classes of Gardens, from the largest to the smallest. With Engraved and Coloured Plans, illustrative of the various systems of Grouping in Beds and Borders. By DAVID THOMSON, Gardener to his Grace the Duke of Buccleuch, K.G., at Drumlanrig. Third Edition, crown 8vo, 7s. 6d.

—— The Handy Book of Fruit-Culture under Glass: being a series of Elaborate Practical Treatises on the Cultivation and Forcing of Pines, Vines, Peaches, Figs, Melons, Strawberries, and Cucumbers. With Engravings of Hothouses, &c., most suitable for the Cultivation and Forcing of these Fruits. Second Edition. Crown 8vo, with Engravings, 7s. 6d.

THOMSON. A Practical Treatise on the Cultivation of the Grape-Vine. By WILLIAM THOMSON, Tweed Vineyards. Tenth Edition, 8vo, 5s.
TOM CRINGLE'S LOG. A New Edition, with Illustrations. Crown 8vo, cloth gilt, 5s. Cheap Edition, 2s.
TRAILL. Recaptured Rhymes. Being a Batch of Political and other Fugitives arrested and brought to Book. By H. D. TRAILL. Crown 8vo, 5s.
TRANSACTIONS OF THE HIGHLAND AND AGRICULTURAL SOCIETY OF SCOTLAND. Published annually, price 5s.
TROLLOPE. An Autobiography by Anthony Trollope. Two Volumes, post 8vo, with Portrait. Second Edition. Price 21s.
——— The Fixed Period. 2 vols. fcap. 8vo, 12s.
——— An Old Man's Love. 2 vols. crown 8vo, 12s.
TULLOCH. Rational Theology and Christian Philosophy in England in the Seventeenth Century. By JOHN TULLOCH, D.D., Principal of St Mary's College in the University of St Andrews; and one of her Majesty's Chaplains in Ordinary in Scotland. Second Edition. 2 vols. 8vo, 28s.
——— Modern Theories in Philosophy and Religion. 8vo, 15s.
——— The Christian Doctrine of Sin ; being the Croall Lecture for 1876. Crown 8vo, 6s.
——— Theism. The Witness of Reason and Nature to an All-Wise and Beneficent Creator. 8vo, 10s. 6d.
——— Luther, and other Leaders of the Reformation. Third Edition, enlarged. Crown 8vo, 7s. 6d.
TWO STORIES OF THE SEEN AND THE UNSEEN. 'THE OPEN DOOR,' 'OLD LADY MARY.' Crown 8vo, cloth, 2s. 6d.
VEITCH. Institutes of Logic. By JOHN VEITCH, LL.D., Professor of Logic and Rhetoric in the University of Glasgow. Post 8vo.
[In the press.
VIRGIL. The Æneid of Virgil. Translated in English Blank Verse by G. K. RICKARDS, M.A., and Lord RAVENSWORTH. 2 vols. fcap. 8vo, 10s.
WALFORD. The Novels of L. B. WALFORD. New and Uniform Edition, in Monthly Vols. Crown 8vo, each 5s.
MR SMITH: A PART OF HIS LIFE. Ready.
COUSINS. Ready.
PAULINE.
TROUBLESOME DAUGHTERS.
DICK NETHERBY.
THE BABY'S GRANDMOTHER.
——— Nan, and other Stories. 2 vols. crown 8vo, 12s.
WARDEN. Poems. By FRANCIS HEYWOOD WARDEN. With a Notice by Dr Vanroth. One vol. crown 8vo. [In the press.
WARREN'S (SAMUEL) WORKS. People's Edition, 4 vols. crown 8vo, cloth, 15s. 6d. Or separately:—
Diary of a Late Physician. Cloth, 2s. 6d.; boards, 2s. Illustrated, crown 8vo, 7s. 6d.
Ten Thousand A-Year. Cloth, 3s. 6d.; boards, 2s. 6d.
Now and Then. The Lily and the Bee. Intellectual and Moral Development of the Present Age. 4s. 6d.
Essays: Critical, Imaginative, and Juridical. 5s.
WARREN. The Five Books of the Psalms. With Marginal Notes. By Rev. SAMUEL L. WARREN, Rector of Esher, Surrey; late Fellow, Dean, and Divinity Lecturer, Wadham College, Oxford. Crown 8vo, 5s.
WATSON. Christ's Authority; and other Sermons. By the late ARCHIBALD WATSON, D.D., Minister of the Parish of Dundee, and one of Her Majesty's Chaplains for Scotland. With Introduction by the Very Rev. PRINCIPAL CAIRD, Glasgow. Crown 8vo, 7s. 6d.

WEBSTER. The Angler and the Loop-Rod. By DAVID WEBSTER.
In one vol. crown 8vo, with Illustrations. [*In the press.*

WELLINGTON. Wellington Prize Essays on "the System of Field Manœuvres best adapted for enabling our Troops to meet a Continental Army." Edited by Major-General Sir EDWARD BRUCE HAMLEY, K.C.M.G. 8vo, 12s. 6d.

WESTMINSTER ASSEMBLY. Minutes of the Westminster Assembly, while engaged in preparing their Directory for Church Government, Confession of Faith, and Catechisms (November 1644 to March 1649). Printed from Transcripts of the Originals procured by the General Assembly of the Church of Scotland. Edited by the Rev. ALEX. T. MITCHELL, D.D., Professor of Ecclesiastical History in the University of St Andrews, and the Rev. JOHN STRUTHERS, LL.D., Minister of Prestonpans. With a Historical and Critical Introduction by Professor Mitchell. 8vo, 15s.

WHITE. The Eighteen Christian Centuries. By the Rev. JAMES WHITE, Author of 'The History of France.' Seventh Edition, post 8vo, with Index, 6s.

—— History of France, from the Earliest Times. Sixth Thousand, post 8vo, with Index, 6s.

WHITE. Archæological Sketches in Scotland—Kintyre and Knapdale. By Captain T. P. WHITE, R.E., of the Ordnance Survey. With numerous Illustrations. 2 vols. folio, £4, 4s. Vol. I., Kintyre, sold separately, £2, 2s.

WILLS AND GREENE. Drawing-room Dramas for Children. By W. G. WILLS and the Hon. Mrs GREENE. Crown 8vo, 6s.

WILSON. Works of Professor Wilson. Edited by his Son-in-Law Professor FERRIER. 12 vols. crown 8vo, £2, 8s.

—— Christopher in his Sporting-Jacket. 2 vols., 8s.

—— Isle of Palms, City of the Plague, and other Poems. 4s.

—— Lights and Shadows of Scottish Life, and other Tales. 4s.

—— Essays, Critical and Imaginative. 4 vols., 16s.

—— The Noctes Ambrosianæ. Complete, 4 vols., 14s.

—— The Comedy of the Noctes Ambrosianæ. By CHRISTOPHER NORTH. Edited by JOHN SKELTON, Advocate. With a Portrait of Professor Wilson and of the Ettrick Shepherd, engraved on Steel. Crown 8vo, 7s. 6d.

—— Homer and his Translators, and the Greek Drama. Crown 8vo, 4s.

WINGATE. Annie Weir, and other Poems. By DAVID WINGATE.
Fcap. 8vo, 5s.

—— Lily Neil. A Poem. Crown 8vo, 4s. 6d.

WORDSWORTH. The Historical Plays of Shakspeare. With Introductions and Notes. By CHARLES WORDSWORTH, D.C.L., Bishop of S. Andrews. 3 vols. post 8vo, each price 7s. 6d.

—— A Discourse on Scottish Church History. From the Reformation to the Present Time. With Prefatory Remarks on the St Giles' Lectures, and Appendix of Notes and References. Crown 8vo, cloth, 2s. 6d.

WORSLEY. Poems and Translations. By PHILIP STANHOPE WORSLEY, M.A. Edited by EDWARD WORSLEY. Second Edition, enlarged. Fcap. 8vo, 6s.

YOUNG. Songs of Béranger done into English Verse. By WILLIAM YOUNG. New Edition, revised. Fcap. 8vo, 4s. 6d.

YULE. Fortification: for the Use of Officers in the Army, and Readers of Military History. By Col. YULE, Bengal Engineers. 8vo, with numerous Illustrations, 10s. 6d.

IN ONE VOLUME. THE LIBRARY EDITION OF

STORMONTH'S DICTIONARY

OF THE

ENGLISH LANGUAGE,

PRONOUNCING, ETYMOLOGICAL, AND EXPLANATORY.

Embracing Scientific and other Terms, numerous Familiar Terms, and a Copious Selection of Old English Words. To which are appended Lists of Scripture and other Proper Names, Abbreviations, and Foreign Words and Phrases.

BY THE REV. JAMES STORMONTH.

The PRONUNCIATION carefully revised by the Rev. P. H. PHELP, M.A. CANTAB.

Royal 8vo, handsomely bound in half-morocco, 31s. 6d.

Opinions of the British and American Press.

Times.—"This may serve in great measure the purposes of an English cyclopedia. It gives lucid and succinct definitions of the technical terms in science and art, in law and medicine. We have the explanation of words and phrases that puzzle most people, showing wonderfully comprehensive and out-of-the-way research. . . . We need only add, that the dictionary appears in all its departments to have been brought down to meet the latest demands of the day, and that it is admirably printed."

Pall Mall Gazette.—"The pronunciation of every word is given, the symbols employed for marking the sounds being commendably clear. . . . After the pronunciation comes the etymology. It has, we think, been well managed here. And the matter is, on the whole, as judiciously chosen as it is skilfully compressed and arranged."

Scotsman.—"There can be no question that the work when completed will form one of the best and most serviceable works of reference of its class. . . . It is admirably adapted to meet the requirements of every ordinary reader, and there are few occasions of special reference to which it will not be found adequate. The definitions are necessarily brief, but they are almost always clear and pointed. . . . A word of praise is due to the beauty and clearness of the printing."

STORMONTH'S DICTIONARY—*Continued.*

Opinions of the British and American Press—*Continued.*

Civil Service Gazette.—"We have had occasion to notice the peculiar features and merits of 'Stormonth's Dictionary,' and we need not repeat our commendations both of the judicious plan and the admirable execution. . . . This is a pre-eminently good, comprehensive, and authentic English lexicon, embracing not only all the words to be found in previous dictionaries, but all the modern words—scientific, new coined, and adopted from foreign languages, and now naturalised and legitimised."

Notes and Queries.—"The whole constitutes a work of high utility."

Dublin Irish Times.—"The book has the singular merit of being a dictionary of the highest order in every department and in every arrangement, without being cumbersome; whilst for ease of reference there is no dictionary we know of that equals it. . . . For the library table it is also, we must repeat, precisely the sort of volume required, and indispensable to every large reader or literary worker."

Liverpool Mercury.—"Every page bears the evidence of extensive scholarship and laborious research, nothing necessary to the elucidation of present-day language being omitted. . . . As a book of reference for terms in every department of English speech, this work must be accorded a high place—in fact, it is quite a library in itself. . . . It is a marvel of accuracy."

New York Tribune.—"The work exhibits all the freshness and best results of modern lexicographic scholarship, and is arranged with great care, so as to facilitate reference."

New York Mail and Express.—"It is certainly a monumental work."

Philadelphia Times.—"Its merits will be discovered and commended until the book takes its place among our standard and best English dictionaries."

Christian Intelligencer, New York.—"A trustworthy, truly scholarly dictionary of our English language."

Boston Gazette.—"There can be but little doubt that, when completed, the work will be one of the most serviceable and most accurate that English lexicography has yet produced for general use."

Boston Post.—"The work will be a most valuable addition to the library of the scholar and of the general reader. It can have for the present no possible rival in its own field."

Toronto Globe.—"In every respect this is one of the best works of the kind in the language."

WILLIAM BLACKWOOD & SONS, EDINBURGH AND LONDON.

www.ingramcontent.com/pod-product-compliance
Lightning Source LLC
Chambersburg PA
CBHW051726300426
44115CB00007B/478